FAMOUS PUCCINI OPERAS

*An analytical guide for the opera-goer
and armchair listener*

by

SPIKE HUGHES

WITH 245 MUSICAL ILLUSTRATIONS

SECOND REVISED EDITION

DOVER PUBLICATIONS, INC., NEW YORK

To
MY WIFE

Published in Canada by General Publishing Company, Ltd., 30 Lesmill Road, Don Mills, Toronto, Ontario.
Published in the United Kingdom by Constable and Company, Ltd.,

This Dover edition, first published in 1972, is a revised republication of the work originally published by Robert Hale Limited in London in 1959.

International Standard Book Number: 0-486-22857-6
Library of Congress Catalog Card Number: 77-166534

Manufactured in the United States of America
Dover Publications, Inc.
180 Varick Street
New York, N.Y. 10014

CONTENTS

		Page
PUCCINI AND THE OPERA		9
MANON LESCAUT		17
	ACT I	21
	ACT II	31
	ACT III	42
	ACT IV	46
LA BOHÈME		51
	ACT I	55
	ACT II	63
	ACT III	69
	ACT IV	74
TOSCA		83
	ACT I	87
	ACT II	96
	ACT III	104
MADAM BUTTERFLY		111
	ACT I	115
	ACT II (PART ONE)	124
	ACT II (PART TWO)	132
THE GIRL OF THE GOLDEN WEST		139
	ACT I	143
	ACT II	157
	ACT III	164
IL TRITTICO		173
IL TABARRO		174
SUOR ANGELICA		186
GIANNI SCHICCHI		196
TURANDOT		211
	ACT I	213
	ACT II	225
	ACT III	238
APPENDIX		253
GENERAL INDEX		255
INDEX OF PUCCINI'S ORCHESTRATION		258

GIACOMO PUCCINI

BORN: Lucca, December 22, 1858
DIED: Brussels, November 29, 1924

PUCCINI AND THE OPERA

I F, as I suggested in *Famous Mozart Operas*, the public as a whole has decided that for all practical purposes Opera begins with Mozart, then I think it is equally certain that for perhaps an even greater number of people Opera ends with Puccini. For Puccini was not only the last great figure in Italian opera: he was the last opera composer of any stature who can be said to have had any kind of lasting and truly universal popular appeal. Today, more than 45 years after his death, Puccini's popularity throughout the world seems to be as great as ever it was, his operas still played more often than those of any other composer except Verdi. Which, so far as the public is concerned, is very much how things have been for more than half a century now, except that in addition to the undyingly popular *Bohème*, *Tosca* and *Madam Butterfly*, the less immediately acceptable operas such as *Manon Lescaut*, *Il Tabarro*, *Gianni Schicchi* and *Turandot* are increasingly finding favour with the public.

But while, during his lifetime, Puccini's music was more or less accepted without question by the layman and loved by many thousands more who had never been inside an opera house, it was scarcely more than patronizingly tolerated by critics and musicians. It was considered "sickly", and one heard his long and infectious, soaring tunes described as "cheap" and "empty". All in all, the best his detractors would grudgingly say about Puccini was that he had a great sense of the theatre —a not inconsiderable asset, let us admit, to a composer who hoped to earn a living in the opera house.

Since Puccini's death, however, there have been many second thoughts, and reconsidered opinion has posthumously awarded him a higher rating among composers than he enjoyed in his lifetime. His so-called "weaknesses" are slowly being recognized as his greatest virtues; his gift for melody, his essentially personal style, his superb craftsmanship and, particularly, his handling of the orchestra, have shown only too clearly how lacking in these qualities his successors have been. Whatever anybody may think of Puccini it has to be admitted that since his death no opera composer has arisen who is capable of writing such a genuinely popular tune as, for instance, "One Fine Day". Nor, among the many hundreds of new operas that have been heard since the posthumous première of *Turandot* in 1926, has there been one to take its place in the international repertoire as a genuine world success alongside *Manon Lescaut*, *La Bohème*, *Tosca*, *Madam Butterfly* or *Turandot* itself.

Indeed, so far as the general public is concerned opera seems to have come to a full stop; or at least to a semi-colon. There is no lack of operatic endeavour among modern composers, and the audience for opera has been increased by millions with the development of radio, television and the long-playing record, but little has emerged which has not either been over the head of the man in the street, too dull to interest him, or both. Puccini's greatness lay in his ability to appeal to the man in the street and at the same time, having gained his confidence, to sweep him along so that he was not left behind or perplexed by the composer's natural musical development and exploration of unfamiliar technical fields.

Puccini's musical development, while neither so spectacular nor so prolonged as Verdi's, for instance, nevertheless provides an interesting study of the growth of an artist from youth to maturity. Now that one can review his work in perspective one can see that in spite of a world-wide popularity that might have tempted him to keep on providing the mixture as before, Puccini spent a lifetime experimenting, profiting by experience and learning from his younger contemporaries, so that he never became an "elder statesman". He could, and did, teach his revolutionary juniors a thing or two and he maintained an intense interest in every new trend of music in his time.

Whereas Verdi, with his three distinct operatic phases, changed the whole course of opera in his own lifetime, Puccini, except for his first and last uncharacteristic essay in teutonic mythology with *Le Villi* (1884), and the quaint mystic interlude of *Suor Angelica* (1918), was more or less content to accept and adhere to the basic principles of *verismo* first demonstrated by Bizet in the picaresque realism of *Carmen* and developed wholeheartedly by Mascagni, Leoncavallo and lesser contemporaries of Puccini. He was happy with the *form* of opera as he found it and in consequence the difference in style between Verdi's *Nabucco* (1842) and *Aida* (1871) is incomparably greater than between *Manon Lescaut* (1893) and *Turandot* (1924), even allowing for the suggestions of a completely new style that are to be heard in Puccini's last opera.

For the most part Puccini's adherence to the tenets of *verismo* was a matter of choosing bourgeois as opposed to heroic subjects (always excepting the exceptional *Turandot* which was the exception to so many of his rules). He did not go the whole way with the *verismo* movement, whose presentation of what it considered Real Life on the opera stage was largely a question of presenting Low Life as lived by people who have not learned to keep their tempers and to whom the solution of all life's problems is a knife in the back of the other fellow. Puccini's characters, it must be said, usually rose above the level of social behaviour encountered in *Cavalleria rusticana* and *Pagliacci*. His operas, nevertheless, were always operas of movement, their stories based on subjects that were possible and probable, and in spite of his prodigious fund of melodic invention he never took so long over his moments of lyrical repose that the tempo and intensity of the dramatic action were in any way unbalanced. The underlying tempo of Puccini's operas, indeed, was one of the most constant and important factors of their success. He had an instinctive sense of timing and a gift for the creation of an instantaneously effective dramatic atmosphere in which he was equalled by few opera composers and surpassed by none. He was, in fact, a master of musical "theatre". The musical characterization of his *dramatis personae* was never quite so subtle or detailed as Verdi's, but he still made his characters real enough to move and rouse the sympathies of the audience.

Puccini did not possess the majestic nobility of Verdi, but within his chosen limits he was unequalled in his musical expression of the emotions of everyday people. The death of Mimi in *La Bohème*, Cavaradossi's soliloquy as he awaits death in the last act of *Tosca*, Cho-Cho-San's farewell to her child in *Madam Butterfly* are moments of genuine pathos created by a composer with a great and rare understanding of the lyrical and dramatic power of music to touch the heart where words alone would fail.

For all his tendency towards a nice bit of blood-and-thunder and a melancholy delight in making his heroines suffer physical pain, Puccini was at his happiest with what one can best describe as his Little Girls. His heroines were life-size, but they were not much bigger than Junior Miss. Manon Lescaut, Mimi, Madam Butterfly, and Liù, the slave girl in *Turandot*, were typical Puccini creations: the Little Girls for whom, in spite of their charm and intense likeableness, things always turned out wrong. Only Tosca, the prima donna, was drawn in anything approaching heroic dimensions, and as a result she is perhaps the least sympathetic of all Puccini's women. (Turandot is another matter, of course, for she is deliberately characterized as hard, cruel and cold to contrast with the gentleness and devotion of Liù.)

As an opera composer Puccini took comparatively long to get going, though no longer than Verdi, whose first opera, *Oberto, Conte di Bonifacio* (1839), was written when he was 26—the same age as Puccini was when he wrote his first opera, *Le Villi*, in 1884. But once he had started Verdi's productivity was intense: his first 18 operas were composed in the course of 14 years. With Puccini, on the other hand, it was five years after *Le Villi* before his next work was performed and thereafter his operas came at average intervals of about four years, the final grand total of his life's work for the theatre adding up to 12 operas (including three one-acters and *Turandot*, which was left unfinished) written in a period of 40 working years.

It was not that Puccini was a slow worker. It was just that his preoccupation, not only with his search for the right subject, but with the business of getting his librettists to write exactly what he wanted them to write once he had found it, took up almost more time than the actual composition of the operas. If Puccini had passed the first draft of the final scene of *Turandot* then the opera might have been finished before the composer's death; as it was, he died before he could set the text he finally approved. For the dozen operas he composed in the end there were more than 50 other subjects he gave more than a passing thought to—subjects ranging from King Lear and Buddha to *Trilby* and a triptych of one-act operas based on the three parts of Dante's *Divina Commedia*, Hell, Purgatory and Paradise.

Whether the music he wrote was "cheap" and "empty" or not, in the true tradition of opera it was always the human voice that was Puccini's first and essential medium of expression; and I believe it is because he refused to depart from this tradition and resisted the temptation to make the orchestra anything but a supporting player in the opera cast, that his operas continue to be so well represented in the present day repertoire. Puccini arrived on the scene when the modern orchestra was beginning to get a bit of a handful. Debussy, four years his junior, had already composed several remarkable orchestral pieces, including *L'après-midi d'un faune*, by the time *La Bohème* was first performed; Wagner, Liszt and Rimsky-Korsakov had all made new and astonishing noises, and it would have been understandable if the young Puccini had followed the prevailing contemporary trend of allowing the orchestra to dominate in the opera house. Instead, as a good Italian, he regarded the opera orchestra as his servant, not his master; in his whole career as an opera composer it is hard to think of a single instance when he allowed the orchestra to challenge the authority of the voice as the predominant instrument in the operatic ensemble.

It must not be imagined, however, that anybody interested in the modern orchestra can afford to ignore Puccini merely because he was a popular opera composer who respected the human voice; or because in the standard English work on orchestration his name appears only once—a passing reference to Puccini's use of a gong in *Madam Butterfly*. On the contrary, his respect for the human voice makes the orchestration of his operas an even more fascinating study. Like Mozart's and Verdi's, Puccini's orchestration is something one takes for granted, something one does not notice because it is subservient to the action. But this very unobtrusiveness, which on examination one discovers is a masterly product of superb craftsmanship and an almost unlimited capacity for orchestral invention, is something which makes the detail of his scores an endlessly absorbing subject and his orchestral language as peculiar and personal as Mozart's, Verdi's or Bizet's in its colour and splendid variety. Puccini was no exception to the almost general rule that more orchestral history is made in the opera house than in the concert hall.

As in the case of *Famous Mozart Operas* I have consequently designed this book with the student of orchestration particularly in mind, and I have made an index of Puccini's orchestration on page 272 which I hope will prove a helpful supplement to the vocal scores of Puccini's works and a means of encouraging closer study of all the orchestral scores themselves.

NOTE

I have included as an Appendix what I call an "Index of Contexts". Its purpose is to enable the reader who is listening to an excerpt from a Puccini opera, either as an item in a radio programme or as part of a "recital" on L.P. records, to refer quickly to the dramatic situation in the opera from which it comes. Thus, if the item concerned is "Vecchia zimarra" the reader need do no more than look it up in the Appendix under *La Bohème* to learn that its context is to be found on page 77.

The Author Wishes to Thank

THE Columbia Graphophone Company, the Decca Record Company, the Gramophone Company (HMV) and Rare Records Ltd (Cetra), whose practical assistance and co-operation were invaluable in the preparation of this book;

Messrs G. Ricordi and Co. for permission to quote from their copyright scores of *Manon Lescaut*, *La Bohème*, *Tosca*, *Madam Butterfly*, *The Girl of the Golden West*, *Il Tabarro*, *Suor Angelica*, *Gianni Schicchi* and *Turandot*.

MANON LESCAUT

(Property of G. Ricordi and Co.)

Lyric drama in four acts. First performed at the Teatro Regio, Turin, on 1st February, 1893. First performance in England: Covent Garden, 14th April, 1894. First performance in the United States: Philadelphia, 29th August, 1894.

Puccini's *Manon Lescaut*, the third opera he wrote, was the earliest of his operas to have an international success. It was first performed only a few days before the première of *Falstaff* (9th February, 1893) and if we disregard the understandable talk at the time about "the mantle of Verdi" falling on the shoulders of its composer, there is no doubt that *Manon Lescaut* marked the arrival of a new and important figure on the operatic scene. During 1893, and the years immediately following, *Falstaff* and *Manon Lescaut* were paired together in the schedules of the opera houses up and down Italy almost as inseparably as *Cavalleria rusticana* and *Pagliacci* (though not in the same bill, of course), so that the glorious sunset of Verdi's career was accompanied by the promise of a new dawn which—to mix the clichés thoroughly—would carry on the torch of Italian operatic tradition. And so on.

Now while *Manon Lescaut* was the first to make its way into the international repertoire (it was performed in fifteen different countries within less than three years of its first appearance), and the earliest work of its composer's that we still hear with any regularity or recognize as characteristic of his genius, Puccini's outstanding qualities as a composer had already been acclaimed after the performance in 1884 of *Le Villi*, his very first opera.

Le Villi cannot justifiably qualify as famous enough for inclusion in this study, but it is nevertheless an opera worth a moment's consideration by anybody willing to take advantage of the modern gramophone's increasing tendency to extend the frontiers of the operatic repertoire far beyond those of everyday opera-going experience. Study of the Cetra recording of *Le Villi** shows how early some of Puccini's strongest musical characteristics began to show. An "opera-ballet in two acts" with its story set in the depths of the Black Forest, a heroine who dies of a broken heart (later to reappear as a ghost), and an erring hero whose dalliance in the Big City of Mainz leads him to suffer the legendary fate of all faithless lovers at the hands of the witches (or *villi*) who whirl their victim round in a frenzied dance until he falls lifeless with exhaustion—this is hardly the material of a typical Puccini subject. Yet in the detail of the

---

* Cetra 1251.

music there are many signs of the composer we know today—the very personal, if still over-lush melodic line which in spite of its profusion of grace notes was never quite like that of any of his contemporaries, the strongly individual use of the sudden, unexpected chord, the abrupt change of key to heighten the tension, create a new atmosphere or change the course of the drama in an instant. These are the things which transcend the alien blackness of *Le Villi* and the inevitable influence of Wagner from which no young composer of that time could entirely escape.

The success of *Le Villi* was followed by the indifferent outcome of *Edgar* in 1889, a work with an even sillier libretto than *Le Villi* set to music that had its unmistakably individual moments but did not really show any great advance on that of its predecessor. Certainly, looking at the score of *Edgar* today, it does not prepare one for the tremendous step forward in Puccini's development that is represented by *Manon Lescaut*. Nor, obviously, were his contemporaries prepared for it either. With *Manon Lescaut* Puccini suddenly burst forth as the new and fully armed champion of Italian opera, and if there were chinks in the armour his title was nevertheless not seriously disputed.

Manon Lescaut may be regarded as the first "typical" Puccini opera; and not only for musical and dramatic reasons. It provided the first instance of the wrangling, the quarrelling, the arguments, disputes, indecisions and revisions, tears and turmoil which from then on were to characterize the labour pains attending the birth of nearly all Puccini's operas. The title page of the score of *Manon Lescaut* describes the work as "lyric drama in four acts, music by Giacomo Puccini". The absence of a librettist's name does not mean that there had not been one. On the contrary, no fewer than seven people had a direct or indirect hand in the book of *Manon Lescaut*, including one composer-librettist (Leoncavallo), two dramatists, two poets, Puccini's publisher, Giulio Ricordi, and Puccini himself. But whereas every one of them would have insisted on a credit if he had been contributing to a modern American "musical", not one of them, except the composer, cared to claim a share in the finished opera.

It is obvious now that the libretto of *Manon Lescaut* was going to be a problem all along. Puccini's decision to make an opera out of Abbé Prévost's romance, *The Story of the Chevalier des Grieux and of Manon Lescaut*, no more than six years after Massenet's *Manon* had been launched on a successful career that shows no signs yet of coming to an end, meant that a great deal of everybody's time had to be devoted to the purely negative pursuit of avoiding, as far as possible, the duplication of scenes, situations and incidents found in Massenet's opera. Puccini's famous retort that a woman like Manon should not have only one lover did not necessarily make the task easier.

Exactly how the work was finally apportioned among this anonymous septemvirate is not known for certain, but there resulted from it more than a libretto which, whatever its dramatic inconsistencies and unhomogenous literary style, released a flood of melodic invention of a richness and spontaneity that Puccini never surpassed. From all the confusion and indecision there emerged a composer-dramatist-poet partnership which was to last for the next ten years.

The final intervention in the general dispute was made by Giuseppe Giacosa who, at Giulio Ricordi's request, introduced Luigi Illica to help clear up the mess. Giacosa was already an established playwright who had, in fact, once sketched out an operatic treatment of a Russian story for Puccini, but he had not yet written a libretto of any kind. Illica, on the other hand, had already written the books and lyrics of three operas, including Catalani's *La Wally*.

I do not know whether, in the case of *Manon Lescaut*, Giacosa actually contributed anything material to the opera, but it is evident that something "clicked" on this first professional contact between him and Illica. There began with *Manon Lescaut* a collaboration which produced for Puccini the librettos of *La Bohème*, *Tosca* and *Madam Butterfly*, and which was ended only by the death of Giacosa in 1906.

Even if *Manon Lescaut* had not produced some of Puccini's most exuberantly fresh and youthful music it could still earn our thanks for a patchwork, do-it-yourself libretto which was the direct cause of founding a partnership of a composer and two writers who between them created three of the most popular operas ever written.

CHARACTERS IN ORDER OF APPEARANCE:

EDMONDO, *a student* . . . . . *Tenor*

CHEVALIER RENATO DES GRIEUX, *student* . *Tenor*

LESCAUT, *Sergeant of the King's Guard* . *Baritone*

GERONTE DI RAVOIR, *Treasurer-General* *Basso brillante*

INNKEEPER . . . . . . *Bass*

MANON LESCAUT . . . . . *Soprano*

A MUSICIAN . . . . . *Mezzo-soprano*

A DANCING MASTER . . . . . *Tenor*

A SERGEANT OF ARCHERS . . . . *Bass*

A LAMPLIGHTER . . . . . *Tenor*

A NAVAL COMMANDER . . . . *Bass*

Girls, citizens, townspeople, students, soldiers, musicians, old men and abbés, courtesans, archers, marines, sailors.

Scene: Amiens, Paris, LeHavre, Louisiana. Time: Second half of the 18th century

ACT I

AT AMIENS

Scene: A large square at the Paris Gate. On the right, an avenue. On the left, an inn with a portico under which tables are laid out. A small outside staircase leads to the first floor of the inn.

Puccini had an unusual and highly individual gift for writing immediately arresting opening bars to his operas. To those audiences who heard *Manon Lescaut* for the first time, after hearing *Le Villi* or *Edgar*, the twenty-eight Allegro brillante bars which lead to the rise of the curtain must have had a most startling effect. If the high-spirited youthfulness and exhilaration of this music led the early Puccini audiences to expect a gay, romantic comedy it is understandable, for who on hearing the first brilliant phrases of the Prelude to *Carmen* could honestly imagine that, on musical evidence, they were in for a story which all ends in tears? Puccini was strongly influenced by Bizet's opera, and it is intriguing in its way to see how, apart from the similarity of mood in the opening pages, *Manon Lescaut* resembles *Carmen* in bearing the name of its leading lady although the central character is in fact the upright young man whose infatuation for a worthless and capricious young woman leads to his degradation and downfall.

The introduction to *Manon Lescaut* (in the same A major, incidentally, as the Prelude to *Carmen*) not only sets the mood of the opening scene but also provides it with much of its musical material in the form of little fragments of tunes and rhythmic figures which Puccini develops ingeniously. The most characteristic of these is an orchestral figure based on the first five notes of the phrase:

The whole of that phrase, indeed, plays an important part in the musical construction of the first twelve minutes of the opera when, with the exception of two bars in common time, the music is entirely in triple time. That there is no suggestion of monotony in this long sequence of 3-in-a-bar is due to the quite astonishing profusion of Puccini's melodic ideas. There is also another theme in this introduction which is heard again later. This is the warm and infectiously

singable *dolce* tune which contrasts with the sparkle of the opening
passage:

Tunes pour out unceasingly, and with such rapidity that there is almost
too much to be absorbed in comfort. No sooner has one tune been put
before us than it is whisked away and another is put in its place.

The curtain rises, according to the score, on a scene of "students,
gentry, townspeople, women, girls, soldiers walking leisurely through the
square and along the avenue; others stand chattering in groups, or sit at
the tables drinking and playing cards". Edmondo, who is discovered in
the company of fellow-students, starts singing a nondescript kind of
madrigal in which he hails (in a manner "between the comic and the
sentimental") the gentle evening "with its retinue of zephyrs and stars
so dear to poets and lovers". Edmondo's friends interrupt this rudely with
laughter and cries of "So dear to thieves and drunks!" Edmondo thanks
his fellows for interrupting him as he can see a company of pretty girls
coming along the avenue and the sight inspires him to improvise a
new madrigal to a tune in which students of both sexes (it seems that Amiens
is co-educational) join *con eleganza* with the refrain "Giovinezza è nostro
nome . . ." ("Our name is youth . . ."):

It is the division of the students' chorus into four parts shared by 8
sopranos and 4 tenors that makes these choral passages so particularly
charming in this act, giving them a youthful freshness never suggested by
the gruff heartiness of the all-male chorus of students in Gounod's *Faust*,
for instance. There is nothing complicated about Puccini's writing for his
chorus; it would never qualify as "Fine Choral Writing" in the English
oratorio tradition. But it plays a ravishing part in the creation of what
one might almost describe as the "smell" of this first act and of an atmosphere unlike that of any other scene in Puccini's operas. "Giovinezza è
nostro nome", indeed, might be added as a motto to the sub-heading of
the act, "At Amiens".

The students are joined by the chorus of pretty girls who have been the
subject of all the talk and now enter the square from the avenue. There is
no indication of the time of day in the stage directions of this first scene
of *Manon Lescaut*. Considering how many hands helped in the libretto it
is remarkable that anybody remembered to add any stage directions at
all. References to the text, however, would suggest that the time is about
sundown. Edmondo's interrupted madrigal greeting the "gentle evening"

is followed by the pretty girls singing of the scented breeze, swallows on the wing and the dying sun.

A group of townspeople (tenors and basses only) join in the ensemble with a few bars supporting the students in their admonition "Give your lips, give your hearts to courageous youth" and the Chevalier Des Grieux enters, "simply dressed like the students". Des Grieux greets the company silently and is on his way when Edmondo brings him back to join the rest of his fellows. Why is he so gloomy and silent, he is asked. Is he disappointed in love? Or—as the literal translation of Edmondo's question runs: "Perhaps for some inaccessible lady acute love bites thee?"

Des Grieux retorts that he doesn't know what Edmondo is talking about; he knows nothing of this tragedy—or maybe comedy—called Love. But perhaps, he suggests satirically, the one he dreams of may be found among the pretty girls who surround him, and *con galanteria* and *con grazia* he sings the simple and wonderfully effective tune, the first to stop the show in Puccini's career and which so delighted Bernard Shaw at its first singing at Covent Garden—"Tra voi, belle, brune e bionde" ("Among you, beautiful dark and blonde ones . . .")—

It dawns on the girls that Des Grieux is teasing them, so they turn away from him crossly, shrugging their shoulders, and join Edmondo and the students in a chorus about the joys of evening, dancing and drinking, which builds up to a climax with an exhilarating choral version of the tune in Ex 2.

A postillion's horn (strictly speaking, according to the score, a cornet in A, off-stage) and the sound of horses' bells announce the approach of the diligence from Arras. The crowd collects in the right-hand corner of the square and the coach makes its entrance drawn by at least one real live horse without which no Italian opera audience ever feels it has had its evening's money's worth. The arrival of the coach is accompanied by a reprise of the first few brilliant bars of the introduction to the opera.

The coach comes to a stop at the inn and its passengers get down. Lescaut is first to alight, followed by Geronte who gallantly helps Manon to the ground; the onlookers remark in chorus that the passengers are "galanti" and "eleganti" and make special reference to the beauty of Manon, while Edmondo and the students ask who indeed would not bid so beautiful a *donnina* welcome. Manon makes her first appearance to the accompaniment of a little wood-wind phrase which is associated with her from time to time during the opera:

In its first form, as we hear it at this point in the opera, the phrase brings a new instrumental sound to the music, one we now recognize as having a peculiarly Puccinian flavour and colouring, and which we were to encounter many times in different operas after *Manon Lescaut*.

While Lescaut calls for the landlord, arranges lodgings for the night and enters the inn with Geronte, Des Grieux sees Manon and exclaims in that rapturous aside which young lovers in opera always use on falling in love at first sight and which they have every intention shall be clearly audible to the soul mate, "Heavens, how beautiful!" Manon shows no immediate sign that she has noticed Des Grieux at all. She sits down on a bench near the avenue, the crowd disperses, some of the students return to their tables to drink or gamble; Edmondo stands on one side to watch Manon and Des Grieux, who has never once taken his eyes off her. The young Chevalier walks over to Manon and addresses her; and the strings, muted and divided into six or sometimes seven parts, give us our first melodic hint of an aria for Des Grieux which follows not long afterwards in the scene:

Des Grieux asks Manon her name. She rises to her feet and "with simplicity and modesty" replies, to a phrase which is recognizable as a foreshortened version of Ex 5 to fit the words "Manon Lescaut mi chiamo" ("I am called Manon Lescaut"). In the course of this sequence of conversation with Manon, Des Grieux learns that she is being sent by her father to a convent and that she will be leaving Amiens again at dawn. Musically this scene anticipates the aria based on the opening phrase I have quoted above with such fidelity that the first 21 bars of the one are melodically and harmonically to all intents and purposes identical with the first 21 of the other. The only real differences, in fact, are that the early scene is in G, while the aria is in B flat, that the orchestration as well as the words are quite different, and that where the main tune is broken up to be shared by tenor, soprano and various orchestral instruments the first time, Des Grieux naturally has most of it to himself the second. On a very first hearing of *Manon Lescaut*, however, I do not think we are altogether aware of the connection between the two passages anyway; Puccini was very careful not to make the earlier G major episode stand out as a high spot. By pitching it in a lower key and so keeping Des Grieux on a tight rein, he knew that no tenor can really show off on three or four unimportant G's; indeed, the note is hardly high enough to show off on, and when we come to the full-dress aria we have forgotten that we have heard any of it before.

In consequence the early passage has the effect only of unusually tuneful dialogue accompanied by music which flows along easily and allows us to concentrate on the progress of the action. The orchestration of this scene of the first meeting of Manon and Des Grieux is particularly imaginative and shows how early in his career Puccini established his own peculiar orchestral language. In the space of these few pages there are to be heard some of the first instances of such characteristic touches as the use of three unison flutes in their lowest register, the use of the bass-clarinet to provide the basis of a chord, a long sequence of chords sustained *ppp* by strings divided into nearly a dozen parts across three octaves or more, and the sudden unexpected sound of first and second violins, violas and violoncellos spaced out an octave apart in the unison phrase *pp* *espressivo legato*:

Des Grieux's passionate declaration that she is too beautiful to be imprisoned in a convent touches Manon, and it is obvious that the attraction is rapidly becoming mutual. She asks him his name; his answer, "Renato des Grieux", is the only time in the whole opera that we hear any mention of the Chevalier's Christian name. Even in their most intimate moments Manon never addresses him as anything but Des Grieux. Since he appears to have no Christian name in Massenet's opera or, so far as I can see, in the Abbé Prévost's novel either, I can only assume that the syndicate responsible for the libretto of Puccini's opera must have made it up. At any rate, the name "Renato" is never mentioned again, and any reaction to it on Manon's part is disturbed by the sound of her brother's voice calling her from the inn. Des Grieux tries to prevent her leaving, but she tears herself away though not without promising to come back to meet him later in the evening. Manon joins her brother who has come out on to the balcony of the inn to look for her, and together they go inside.

Des Grieux now sings the aria foreshadowed in his first conversation with Manon, fitting the words "Donna non vidi mai simile a questa" ("I never saw a woman like this one") to the tune of Ex 6 in the key of B flat, which takes him into a more spectacular tonality. The modulation from a chord of D major firmly rooted in the key of G is made in one strangely amateurish stroke by the introduction of a single chord of what is known in the jazz bands of the world as "F-seventh" (in more academic language the dominant-seventh of the key of B flat).

As I have already suggested, the melodic and harmonic structure of the first 21 bars of "Donna non vidi mai" is almost identical with that of the corresponding bars in the sequence beginning with Ex 6. In the aria, however, Manon's phrase, "Manon Lescaut mi chiamo", is quoted by Des Grieux a couple of times in a reflective way, thus maintaining the melodic continuity of the earlier passage and justifying the repetition on dramatic grounds. What might have been a troublesome little problem in fact, is solved very neatly.

The orchestration of the accompaniment of the aria is more involved than in its earlier counterpart, but I do not think it is quite so effective. It is all unmistakably Puccini, nevertheless, showing a typical economy of means as well as an early example of the familiar use of soft syncopated chords in the wood-wind to fill the "middle" of the orchestral texture while the tune is played by the strings, and an ingenious doubling by the harp in octaves of the tune played by a solo horn. The writing for the strings, on the other hand, is unusually fanciful and an accompaniment which begins with the strings divided into nine parts (violins divided into six of them) develops into a cadence with the strings divided into eleven different parts—violins into 4, violas into 2, violoncellos into 4, and the double basses in unison.

To Puccini's credit most of this comes off quite happily, although it doesn't always deserve to. The opening phrase of the aria is carefully written so that the first desk of the first violins and the first desk of the second violins play without mutes while their companions are all muted. These two desks are employed in doubling the tune sung by Des Grieux, the two second violins in the tenor's register, the two first violins two octaves above it. The tune on the missing octave between is supplied by the violas.

The optimistic habit of indicating that two solo violins should play a tune in unison has been widespread for a century or more in the scores of some of the best people, including Verdi. It is an optimistic habit because it is almost impossible to make a tolerable noise with two violins—and only two—playing the same part in unison. One violin, yes; three violins, yes. But two will never sound in tune or like anything but a seriously undermanned string section in a provincial variety theatre. The reason for this is simple and recognized by most experienced orchestral players, one or two conductors, all quartet players, but very very few composers: no matter how closely the intonation of two expert violinists agrees in the playing of a common note, the vibrato used by each player will prove so individual that the result will always sound out of tune. The addition of a third player, with yet another individual vibrato, breaks up the discordance and a neutral sound results.

Why string quartet players know this is explained by a glance at Beethoven's string quartets: where the composer had a unison phrase the second violin was allowed to double the note played by the viola, but never the note played by the first violin. There is no doubt a simple acoustic explanation for this strange fact that violin will not blend with violin, but will blend with an instrument producing a different tone colour, but I have never heard it. To anyone with half an ear, however, it is obvious that what two solo violins must not do in a Beethoven string quartet does not become permissible to two solo violins who happen to be playing in an opera house pit. Few composers of note, apart from Mascagni, have ever had professional experience of orchestral playing, but it is strange that they have not somehow heard tell of this question of two violins failing to sound as one. Or perhaps they do know about it and continue to write for "1st desk only" because they, alone among mortals, like the noise it makes. It is a bewildering blind spot.

Des Grieux's reverie at an end, Edmondo and the students, to the music of the opening of the act, set on him with teasing references to the *bella* and *divina* "cherubina" who has been sent from heaven for his delight. Des Grieux leaves them huffily, an action which proves to the students' satisfaction that he is undoubtedly in love.

A new mood of gaiety comes to the music now with a change of time and tempo to a 3/8 Allegro vivo which has the effervescence of a quick waltz, and a long sequence full of charm, youthfulness and delightful tunes begins with the strangely ominous unison passage for strings:

8

This rather eccentric and agitated cross-rhythmed passage has no dramatic significance, however; it provides a theme which Puccini develops and transforms, in various major and minor key variants, as the high-spirited scherzo-like background to the dialogue and action that follows.

The students return to their drinking and gambling, persuading the pretty girls to sit with them and bring them luck. The girls not only contribute their share of luck but also a new tune which is particularly attractive and infectious, and takes its place as second subject to the themes derived from Ex 8:

9

When the students have settled down, Lescaut and Geronte come down the staircase from the inn and from their conversation it becomes clear that Lescaut is glad his responsibility for Manon's welfare will be over when she enters her convent. Geronte, whose acquaintance with Lescaut dates from their meeting as fellow-passengers in the Arras coach, is rich, elderly and lecherous, and he hints that it would be to everybody's moral and material advantage if Manon were to be saved from the convent and something more congenial arranged. Geronte goes off to discuss his plans with the landlord of the inn and Lescaut wanders slowly over to the table where the students are playing cards. It is now getting dark and lamps and candles are brought out and placed on the tables.

Lescaut insinuates himself into the card game and settles down to drinking and gambling. Geronte reappears with the landlord whom he instructs to have a coach ready and waiting behind the inn for a man and a young girl in an hour's time to drive like the wind to Paris. The landlord accepts a handsome tip and promises to tell nobody of the plan. Geronte and the landlord leave the scene. The game of cards between Lescaut and the students continues uninterruptedly and, according to the score, is "animatissimo".

Edmondo, who has stood apart all this time watching and listening to what has been going on, returns to the scene ruminating in his poetic way on the "ancient, powdered Pluto" who is likely to have trouble with his non-co-operative Proserpine. Des Grieux enters thoughtfully, and the scherzo tempo stops for the first time for 40 pages of score; Edmondo slaps him roughly on the shoulder to bring him back to earth with the information that unless something is done about it Manon will be abducted to Paris by Geronte. Des Grieux is not unnaturally shaken by the news and begs Edmondo to help him. Edmondo promises to see what can be done; leave it to him. He leaves the scene but on his way out he goes over to the table where his friends and Lescaut are playing cards and whispers into the ears of several of the students. The game of cards comes to an end and Lescaut stays drinking with his gaming companions.

The 3/8 of the scherzo dissolves into a broad 9/8 version of "Donna non vidi mai", the tune played richly by cor anglais, bass clarinet and violoncellos in unison, as Manon reappears at the top of the stairs to the terrace. She looks anxiously around and descends when she sees Des Grieux.

"You see?" says Manon *con semplicità*, "I am true to my word. You asked me to come back so fervently that I returned, but I think it would be better not to see you again." Des Grieux pleads with her, praising her beauty and youth, and the naïve 2/4 to which Manon returns is transformed gradually into a slower 6/8 and we hear in the orchestra the first suggestion of the theme which becomes the climax of the scene:

This first statement, by the flute, accompanies a strangely pathetic passage by Manon in which she mourns the gay life she used to lead in a house where there was always the sound of laughter. This 6/8 sequence is marked "Andante amoroso", but while Des Grieux's contributions are *amoroso* enough, Manon's are largely melancholy, and she speaks of herself as a poor girl whose face is not beautiful and whose destiny is "ruled by sorrow", in a mournful variant of the tune quoted in Ex 10:

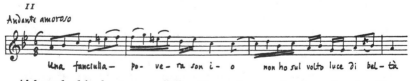

Although this short scene (it hardly ranks as a duet) reaches its climax on the foundation of Ex 10, it is the later tune which somehow makes the deeper impression and which seems to have the stronger melodic personality. Indeed, I have found myself several times turning the later pages of the score in the firm belief that Puccini used the tune with great effect at the end of the opera. He does not appear to have done so, but it is the sort of haunting, wistful tune one feels he ought to have made use of again.

The Andante amoroso finishes with a four-bar cadence in unison for tenor and soprano, Des Grieux proclaiming that Manon's beauty will ensure her a glorious future, and Manon crying that it is not true, it is merely a dream.

The gentle lyrical air of the duet is shattered by Lescaut who rises unsteadily and bangs on the table calling for wine. The students force him to sit down, and they fill his glass again. The sound of Lescaut's voice startles Manon and Des Grieux and the girl turns to go back into the inn; but Des Grieux holds her back, and tells her of Geronte's plan to kidnap her. In the course of the few bars needed for this passage of dialogue (we are back in the earlier scherzo 3/8 again) we hear for the first time a phrase which occurs in a poignant form later in the opera:

We also hear another phrase which plays an important part later on, but not in this Puccini opera. Edmondo arrives on the scene to tell Des Grieux that he has fixed everything and that the carriage is ready; and he does so to the notes:

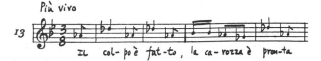

—notes which were to become very familiar in Puccini's next opera, *La Bohème*, whenever the Café Momus music occurred. This is of no great importance in the analysis of *Manon Lescaut*, of course, but it is characteristic of the general profusion of tunes found in the opera that a four-bar phrase thrown away on such an unlyrical pronouncement as Edmondo's "The deed is done, the carriage is ready" should serve the composer as a tune in its own right in *La Bohème*.

Des Grieux pleads with Manon to elope to Paris with him (he is abetted in this by Edmondo who can see the whole plan going awry if the couple hesitate too long). Manon refuses, Des Grieux's pleas become more passionate and urgent with each "No!" until at last Manon gives in and agrees. Edmondo throws his cloak over Des Grieux's head so that his face cannot be seen and all three disappear to find the coach at the back of the inn. Their exeunt is accompanied by a *fortissimo* orchestral reprise of the duet-theme in Ex 10.

Geronte enters, muttering that the hour of seduction has arrived; he notices with satisfaction that Lescaut is still busily occupied at the card table and asks the innkeeper if all is ready. The innkeeper replies "Yes, Excellency."

"Then," says Geronte, "tell the young lady that——"

He is interrupted by Edmondo who has returned and is now enjoying the fun with his friends. "Excellency," says Edmondo, pointing in the direction of the Paris road. "She has gone away with a student!"

Geronte, "in the greatest confusion", runs to Lescaut, who is still playing cards, and shakes him violently. "She's been kidnapped!" he cries.

"Who?" asks Lescaut, without looking up from his cards.

"Your sister!"

Lescaut jumps up, frightening the innkeeper back into his inn, and exclaims: "A thousand thousand bombs!"

Geronte begs Lescaut to do something; they must follow the lovers at once. Lescaut calms him by saying that there is time enough. Manon and Des Grieux, he says, have almost certainly gone to Paris; and knowing his sister's character he is quite sure she will not endure the discomforts of poverty once the student's money has run out—which will not be long. Far better for Geronte to travel with him to Paris the next day where, Lescaut assures him, he can play a parental role to one who already looks on him with affection as a father.

"While I," adds Lescaut, who sees immense economic possibilities in all this, "will complete the family."

Geronte and Lescaut enter the inn to dine together. Lescaut's exposition of his plan to Geronte is accompanied by the students, to the tune of "Tra voi, belle" (Ex 4), mocking the two men with pointed references to old foxes and sour grapes. They crowd round the doorway of the inn when Geronte and Lescaut have gone inside and scatter laughing only when Lescaut returns to threaten them as the curtain falls on one of the longest, but also one of the most profusely tuneful first acts Puccini ever wrote. Not until his last opera, *Turandot*, did he write another first act in which so many ideas poured out so effortlessly or with such genuine vitality and inspiration.

ACT II

IN PARIS

Scene: An elegant room in Geronte's house. At the back, two doors. On the right, luxurious and heavy curtains conceal an alcove. On the left, by the window, a richly appointed dressing table. The furniture includes a sofa, chairs, a table.

In the few bars preceding the rise of the curtain the flute introduces a theme based on a single short phrase originating in what one might term the "middle" of "Tra voi, belle" (Ex 4). Des Grieux sings the words "Palesatemi il destino" ("Tell me the future") to the phrase:

If we do not particularly notice these eight notes when we first hear them in Act I, or again when they occur in the students' chorus at the end of the act, it is hardly surprising. The most interesting parts of Des Grieux's little song are the first and last eight bars so far as the listener is concerned, and Puccini does not "plug" the middle section in any way to suggest that it has any great significance. Consequently any psychological meaning intended by the composer is rather lost on us when Des Grieux's couple of bars are compressed to form part of the flute's little tune in Act II:

It is, in practice, something of a paper transaction, and if Puccini wanted to suggest that we had now reached the *destino* Des Grieux had in mind he should have made far more of a point of it by earlier and stronger emphasis on the importance of the original phrase. As it is, what was obviously clear to the composer is rather lost on the listener who has not consulted the score and noted the connection between the two passages—particularly as the flute theme, and the figures which derive from it and serve as an attractive background to the "business" of the first scene of this act, have so much more musical personality than the episode in the aria.

As the theme is repeated it undergoes many changes in instrumentation,

with the wood-wind predominating and producing many characteristically Puccinian sounds, particularly in the up-and-down unison
arpeggios shared an octave or two apart by flute and clarinet, and in the
doubling of the flute line by the piccolo in the same register which adds a
subtle sheen to the instrumental colour. The student of orchestration,
indeed, who can spare the time to study the wood-wind writing in
general from the beginning of the act to Figure 4 in the score will encounter
a great many practical hints in the art of "voicing" a melodic line shared
by five different instruments.

At the rise of the curtain Manon is discovered sitting at her dressing
table, enveloped in a white dressing gown, while a hairdresser and two
assistants are busy putting the finishing touches to her coiffure. The
dialogue between Manon and the hairdresser is no more than functional
small talk of curls and curlers, combs, scent, powder and cosmetics in
general—trivial lines expertly superimposed on the elegant 6/8 background.

Lescaut comes to visit his sister and in the course of his conversation
with her we learn that things have gone very much according to the
plans and prophecies he was making at the end of the first act. Manon,
as he expected, tired quickly of poverty and accepted the luxury and
comfort offered by life as Geronte's mistress. Lescaut (for the benefit of
the audience) reminds his sister how she lived in a sordid little house with
plenty of kisses but no money. Des Grieux is a good boy, he says, but
(alas) he is not Treasurer-General. It was natural, Lescaut concludes,
that in such circumstances Manon should have left that squalid lodging
for the golden palace she now lives in. The tune to which Lescaut sings
all this is another of those admirable passages in *Manon Lescaut* which
turn up later in a more impressive guise:

Manon's reaction, and an unmistakable look in her eye, lead Lescaut
to ask her if she still longs for "Him"—Des Grieux. She admits she does:
"I left him without a word, without a kiss." Manon looks around the
expensively furnished apartment and her eyes come to rest on the alcove:
"Behind those silken hangings, in that golden alcove is a silence, cold
and deathly, a coldness that turns me to ice. And I, who was accustomed
to the touch of warm lips and passionate arms, now have something quite
different—." These are the sentiments Manon expresses sadly in the first
part of her aria, "In quelle trine morbide . . .":

For the first eight-bar phrase the syncopated chords accompanying the voice are limited to wood-wind only, scored to sound so smoothly *pianissimo* that it comes as something of a surprise to realize that what one would expect from experience to be harsh and unsympathetic is as gentle and lyrical as if it had been given to a mass of *divisi* strings. Puccini had a peculiar genius for this kind of orchestration and not even the introduction in due course of two oboes among the three flutes, two clarinets and two bassoons hardens the orchestral tone of voice.

Manon's broad opening phrase of 16 bars ends with a formal and academic cadence in the dominant key of E flat—namely, B flat. The last two bars of this cadence, sung by Manon and accompanied by a substantially full orchestra, consists of the phrase:

This is another of those instances, in which *Manon Lescaut* seems to abound, of a theme dropped so carelessly at the feet of the listener that he is not to be blamed if he fails to notice it, let alone to pick it up. Studying the music score in hand and at a safe distance of more than 60 years of public experience of the opera, it is easy to believe that this first intimation of a theme that becomes increasingly important as the work proceeds is a subtle anticipation of dramatic things to come. Accordingly, while I am content at this stage to draw attention to the phrase—if only to show that I have noticed it—I will not suggest that its connection with what comes later is even half as convincing as that between Des Grieux's "Palesatemi il destino" and the flute tune which begins Act II. For the benefit of the listener, who will hear the phrase in considerable glory later in the opera, it is enough to remark that when Manon sings it at this stage of the story she does so to the words full of regret: "Now I have something [meaning her unexciting liaison with Geronte] quite different", and leave him to decide how these sentiments can possibly bear even the most subtly subconscious relation to those eventually expressed with such virility, enthusiasm and *tutta la passione* by Des Grieux.

One of the worst by-products of the development of opera in the 19th century was the general public belief that themes and "motifs" were to be found hidden in every nook and cranny of a score. The idea that a composer could use the same phrase twice or three times in different contexts merely because he happened to like the sound of what he had written and had no intention of suggesting any deep psychological connection between the two was something nobody would believe possible. It was forgotten that tunes and fragments of tunes could have a purely *musical* purpose of their own as free of any dramatic association in the scores of Verdi and Puccini as in those of Mozart. The score of *Manon Lescaut* is deceptively rich in fragments that ought to mean something profound but which, bearing a coincidental likeness to other fragments of the same name, do not.

Manon continues her reflections to the same tune as her brother in Ex 16, but in the key of G flat and with the melody scored with remarkable effect for piccolo and oboe *pp dolce* an octave apart. Lescaut, seeing how the land lies, then gives Manon news of Des Grieux. With the tune of "Donna non vidi mai" in the orchestra for the space of a few bars, Lescaut assures his sister that Des Grieux is a great friend of his (as, he adds in an aside, Geronte once was) and he is teaching him to gamble and so make enough money to keep Manon in the state of luxury to which Geronte has accustomed her. Lescaut's report on his pupil's progress is eventually carried on while Manon is soliloquizing passionately about Des Grieux and imploring him to return—an incongruous musical situation, as it turns out, for Lescaut automatically gets swept away by Manon's soaring tune as it rises to her high C climax and we find them singing in unison, Manon about love, and her brother about the advantages of gambling. That, however, is operatic life all over.

This short duet leaves Lescaut laughing with satisfaction, but his sister thoughtful and sad again; then, according to the colourful stage directions in the score, "she looks at herself in the mirror and sees her adorable face; she unconsciously adjusts and smoothes the folds in her dress; then her thoughts change, her lips smile and her eyes sparkle in the triumph of her beauty".

A short reprise of what one might call the "dressing music" of Ex 15 interrupts Manon's reflections and she preens herself, to the expressed admiration of her brother, to receive a group of "powdered personages" who carry sheets of music in their hands, bow before her and then stand to one side.

"Who are these ugly mugs?" asks Lescaut. "Quacks or apothecaries?"

"Musicians!" replies Manon wearily. "Geronte writes madrigals for me", and she leans back on the sofa to listen to the latest composition by H.M.'s Treasurer-General—a much more expert and charming piece of music than Manon's attitude towards it would suggest.

The madrigal, sung by a solo mezzo-soprano assisted by a small chorus of five women's voices, is a characteristic example of Puccini's delight in what one might call the musical counterpart of "reproduction furniture". Even though it began life as the *Agnus Dei* of a youthful Mass, it is in character with the 18th-centuryness of the action, and yet is unmistakably Puccini without, somehow, sounding anachronistic. The simple pizzicato accompaniment by the strings which runs throughout the madrigal is decorated with several masterly little touches of typical woodwind writing, notably a four-bar phrase for two oboes, cor anglais and bassoon in which the highest part is taken by the cor anglais to provide an intriguing instrumental colour:

Apart from the purely sensuous effect of that passage for wood-wind, it is worth noting for an inconsistency in this score which is frequent and puzzling. Again and again one finds the composer—or some anonymous editor—indicating "in the absence of cor anglais the notes are to be played by 2nd oboe"—usually in cases where this is a practicable compromise and a cor anglais would not be missed since its presence would affect the volume rather than the quality of the orchestral sound. But on several occasions—and the madrigal is one of them—the cor anglais has an indispensable part which cannot be cued into the 2nd oboe part (he is already, as in the madrigal, busy in his own right) and which it is not suggested should be taken over by any other instrument. This is perhaps a rather technical digression but to the student of orchestration it is an intriguing and eccentric habit to encounter in the score of one who was usually so magnificently practical and professional in his orchestral writing.

When the madrigal is finished Manon gives Lescaut a purse and tells him sharply to pay the singers. Her brother retorts "What! And insult Art?", and pocketing the money he dismisses the musicians *maestoso* with "You may go, in the name of Glory." The musicians bow and leave without protest; as they go the anteroom through the glass door at the back of the stage is seen to be filling up with the arrival of friends of Geronte, who receives them. Manon draws Lescaut's attention to the anteroom. "Madrigals!" she says. "Dancing! And then music! They are all beautiful things"—and having made the nice distinction between madrigals and music, she yawns ostentatiously as a string quartet come on the scene, take up their position at the back of the stage, and tune their instruments. "Oh, how bored I am!" says Manon.

Geronte enters, followed by the dancing master and others. Lescaut smiles to himself at the obsequious bowing and scraping that goes on as Geronte organizes and prepares the minuet with the dancing master; and he reflects that a woman who is bored is a frightening thing. He decides to fetch Des Grieux, and leaves unobserved.

The string quartet (in practice, the strings of the orchestra, muted) strikes up a minuet and Manon's dancing lesson begins.* Geronte cannot contain his admiration and enthusiastically exclaims, "Oh, exquisite dancer", to be severely reprimanded by the dancing master for talking; The Dance is a serious matter. Geronte is advised *sotto voce* by his friends the gentlemen and abbés (some of whose voices do not seem to have broken yet, for they include four contraltos) to admire in silence as they do.

At this point of the minuet the tempo quickens slightly, the key changes, and the two oboes play a phrase which the composer ought to ask us to take particular notice of, for it plays a dramatic part in the end of the opera, but which we might easily overlook since it is really no more than a musical "prop" introduced while the audience's

---

* This and another minuet heard later in the scene were, in fact, originally two of three minuets for string quartet written by Puccini in the early 1880's. Only two of the set have been published.

attention is focussed on—or perhaps, distracted by—Manon's dancing:

That Puccini should have expected such an undistinguished phrase to register in the listener's mind enough for us to recognize it again in what is meant to be a strong dramatic context is something one can only attribute to the composer's lack of experience. For as anybody knows who remembers Walt Disney's *Fantasia,* visual interest can distract the attention to such an extent that the ear takes in nothing. This was particularly the case with Disney's sequence of Stravinsky's *Sacre du Printemps,* which the cinema-going public took in its stride. But give that same public the *Sacre* in a concert hall or on the radio and it will put its fingers in its ears and scream long words like "cacophony" at it. The weakness of Puccini's minuet theme is that it is never *aurally* impressed on the listener's mind and dramatically it is nothing more than an insignificant sub-incident in an insignificant incident—namely, the incident of Manon's dancing lesson. The eventual use of the bars I have quoted in Ex 19 is something to be discussed in its context later in this study.

The general air of minuettishness continues after Manon has finished dancing, and in a slightly slower tempo she addresses a deliberately flirtatious pastoral song about serene skies and the miracle of love to Geronte. It is a florid and charming little sequence, in which she is supported by the chorus of enthusiastic gentlemen and abbés who call *her* the miracle of love, and which begins with the graceful phrase:

The episode of the madrigals, dancing and music ends with an epilogue by strings playing the full tune of Manon's pastoral in unison to give Geronte and his friends time to leave the stage to Manon, for whom a sedan chair will call so that she can join them all at a fashionable rendezvous elsewhere in Paris.

As soon as she is alone Manon runs to her mirror and looks in it. She is reassured and exclaims happily that she will be the most beautiful woman present at wherever-it-is she is to follow Geronte. She hears sounds coming from outside the room and presumes that a servant has come to

tell her the sedan chair has arrived. She turns to see Des Grieux standing
in the doorway and rushes towards him. With her cries of excitement at
seeing her lover again a long duet begins from which a great deal of
musical material emerges that Puccini makes dramatic use of later in the
opera.

Manon's first excited greeting is met coldly by Des Grieux who is
bitterly resentful of her deserting him. "You don't love me any more
then," replies Manon, and she sets to work to break down her lover's
resistance. She reminds him how much he loved her, of the long blissful
hours they spent together; she apologizes; it was all her fault. Des Grieux
reproaches her for all the loneliness and unhappiness she has caused him.
She begs for forgiveness, and to a theme we hear for the first, but not the
last time—

21

—she tells Des Grieux to look at the richness and luxury around her. She
is rich, she says, and it is all for him. She kneels pleading at his feet as the
music rises to a passionate climax which ends with a short and wonderfully effective unaccompanied passage: "I do not deny it," and Manon
adds *con molta grazia*, "Am I perhaps less pleasing and beautiful than the
Manon of other days?"

This breaks down Des Grieux's defences and he is powerless to resist.
The duet, which had been more of a discussion than anything so far, now
settles down into a more or less regular love scene, but with the man, not
the woman, seduced amid a welter of intervals of the falling seventh, the
lyrical stock-in-trade of love music found long before Wagner's *Tristan*
in the operas of Sir Henry Bishop as well as Mozart.

The tune of "Donna non vidi mai" returns, sung not by Des Grieux
but by Manon as she repeats that she loves him. The Chevalier plays a
subsidiary role in the duet at this point, confessing that he is unable to
continue the struggle any further. He becomes an equal partner once
more when he sings "I am defeated: I love you" to an altered form of the
theme he sang in Act I (Ex 10):

22

The last part of the duet, which at last brings a certain degree of
unanimity to the vocal lines if not to the words of the lovers, introduces
for the first time in full a new theme (already hinted at in Ex 18) which
may be said to become hereafter the most important in the opera. Des
Grieux, *con tutta passione*, tells Manon: "In the depths of your eyes I read

my destiny; all the treasures of the world are in your divine lips" to the
tune of

This has always seemed to me one of the least convincing and congruous
themes in all Puccini's music. Apart from its resemblance to the opening
of Brahms' Third Symphony its whole air is surely too heroic and *maestoso*
for its lyrical context. We know it is to be sung *con tutta passione* and that
it can sound passionate enough—but passionate about what? Its intensity,
its purely musical shape are more appropriate, I feel, to an oath of
allegiance, or revenge, or conspiracy. I am considering solely the musical
aspect of the theme; with the visual aid of a pair of embracing lovers on
the stage its effect will no doubt be in keeping with the general dramatic
excitement and fervour of the scene, but its basic mood is more akin to
the opening of the last act of *Tosca* where a very similar fanfaresque kind
of tune is played by unison horns.

The duet between Manon and Des Grieux reaches its climax with a
top B flat then fades away with a gentle epilogue, an echo of Ex 22 and
the two lovers finally singing the same words as well as the same notes in
the last three *ppp* bars.

The peace and quiet of the scene are now rudely disturbed by the
arrival of Geronte, who appears in the doorway at the back of the stage
to the theme:

Manon and Des Grieux rise hurriedly from the sofa; Des Grieux takes a
step towards Geronte, but Manon stands between them. Geronte,
"ironically but with dignity", remarks that he understands what was
delaying Manon's arrival at his party. He has arrived at an awkward
moment—purely a mistake, and everybody makes mistakes sometimes.
"You, too, I believe," he says to the lovers, "you forgot that you were in
my house. . . ." A grateful gesture, he says to Manon, on her name-day,
and what a way to remind him of the love he has given her.

Manon looks "capricciosamente" at Geronte, then goes over to the
table and picks up a hand mirror. "Love! Love! My dear sir!" she laughs,
holding the glass in front of his face. "Look at yourself! And then look
at us!"

Geronte controls himself magnificently, for Manon, like Carmen, is
surely a natural murderee; he leaves angrily, threatening "arrivederci—
e presto!"

Manon laughs happily. She feels as free as the air and goes to embrace

Des Grieux, but the Chevalier is preoccupied with his thoughts. They must leave at once, he says, Manon must not stay under the wretched old man's roof a moment longer. There is an echo by two flutes of the tune from the minuet (Ex 19) and "almost involuntarily" Manon murmurs: "What a pity—all this splendour, these treasures—and we have to leave."

This wavering is too much for Des Grieux and in an intense and angry passage he upbraids Manon for being always the same—"Ah! Manon mi tradisce il tuo folle pensier. . . ." ("Ah, Manon, your foolish thoughts betray me"):

The scoring of this sequence is wonderfully simple and effective, with the tune doubled in unison for long stretches by flutes, cor anglais, clarinets, bassoons, violas, violoncellos, and from time to time by timpani when the first three notes of the phrase occur as above. Puccini's use of the three flutes in unison in the register I have shown in the musical example above produces a remarkable sound, as penetrating as though three trumpets were playing.

Des Grieux ends in despair, asking Manon into what dark and unpredictable future she is leading him. She replies, holding his hand lovingly, "Once more, once more, please forgive me. I will be faithful and good. I swear it." The notes to which she sings these words, accompanied only by a series of chords on the harp, have virtually nothing about them to distinguish them from any other semi-conversational vocal phrase:

There is certainly nothing to cause one to sit up when one hears them for the first time. But, in fact, like so many of the fragmentary themes in this opera, Puccini inflates it into something much more important later on.

From this point onwards the action of the rest of Act II is of more interest than the music. Except for a breathing space of six bars the 6/8 Allegro con fuoco which now gets under way with a fugato treatment of Ex 24, dominates the drama until the curtain falls. It is a vigorous, brilliant scherzo, with the occasional cross-rhythm reminiscent of the Witches' Dance in *Le Villi*, and considerable use made of the little figure in Ex 12 associated with the flight of Manon and Des Grieux in Act I.

Lescaut enters hurriedly, too out of breath to do more than gesticulate wildly that something is wrong. The lovers are distracted in their efforts to understand what is going on, and it is a full forty frustrating seconds before Lescaut manages to tell them that Geronte is on his way with archers and guards to arrest Manon.

The scene between Lescaut, his sister and Des Grieux now becomes one of growing confusion—with Lescaut advising Des Grieux on means of escape—down the stairs, through the garden—chattering about Manon's chances of being sentenced to transportation, and—supported by Des Grieux—repeatedly imploring Manon to hurry. Manon, however, has decided to take with her as many bits of jewellery and other valuables as she can lay hands on—a diversion which proves her undoing, for when at last she has collected them and wrapped them all in her cloak the archers have surrounded the house; first one way of escape is cut off, then another and Manon is trapped. Geronte stands at one door with soldiers behind him, a sergeant and two archers stand at the other. Manon in her terror and panic drops her cloak, spilling all the stolen jewellery on the floor. When Geronte bursts into ironical laughter at the scene Des Grieux draws his sword, but Lescaut knocks it out of his grasp muttering "If they arrest you, Chevalier, who can save Manon?"

The curtain falls on Des Grieux crying out after Manon in despair, but prevented by Lescaut from following her as she is led away under arrest.

INTERMEZZO

The Prison—The Voyage to Le Havre

The score of this Intermezzo is headed with the following quotation:

DES GRIEUX: ". . . How I love her! My passion is so strong that I feel I am the most unhappy creature alive. What have I not tried in Paris to obtain her release? I have implored the powerful, knocked and petitioned at every door. I have even resorted to violence. All has been in vain. Only one way remained for me: to follow her. And I shall follow her, wherever she may go—even to the ends of the earth."

(*The Story of Manon Lescaut and of the Chevalier Des Grieux* by the Abbé Prévost.)

Puccini's intention in this miniature symphonic poem is to describe the emotions of Manon and Des Grieux in the interlude between the events in Act II and Act III—while Manon is in prison and on her journey to Le Havre to be transported. The composer has taken some half a dozen themes associated with the lovers and developed them ingeniously to form an orchestral interlude of great warmth and appeal. The themes, with one possible exception, will be easily recognized for they have been well "planted" in the earlier parts of the opera. The melancholy introductory bars to this Intermezzo, for instance, are based on slowed-up versions of the tunes in Ex 5 (solo violoncello) and Ex 12 (solo viola). The least familiar theme, which follows this reflective

opening passage for three violas, one violin, one solo violoncello with the
rest of the violoncellos joining him for four bars, is the inflated version of
the one quoted in Ex 26, now given its head in a broad *cantabile*:

27

Puccini extends the original melodic idea and leads us to a gradual
and exciting build-up of sequences we have already heard, such as that
beginning with Manon's tune in Ex 21, her passionate vocal line now
rearranged in an orchestral transcription. After a hint of Ex 10 the music
dies down into a calm and peaceful coda in which the first bar of the
phrase shown in Ex 23 is used as a gradual "dying fall", ending in a
beautifully scored chord of B major for strings divided into 8 parts, two
flutes, piccolo, one oboe and three trumpets, not muted but playing *pppp*.

ACT III

LE HAVRE

Scene: A square near the harbour. The harbour is seen in the background. To the left, the corner of a barracks; on the side facing us a heavily barred window juts out, on the side facing the square is a closed gate with a guard who walks up and down in front of it. The sea takes up the whole of the background in which part of a warship is visible. On the right, a house, then a narrow street with an oil street lamp burning dimly at the corner. It is just before dawn; the sky gradually grows light.

The curtain rises almost at once to the sound of a weary, elegiac theme, marked *misterioso*, given to horns, divided and muted violas, with the bass clarinet supplying a deep pedal note on a low D:

This heavy-hearted, evocative phrase not only introduces a new atmosphere into the opera to contrast vividly with all the gaiety and elegance of what has gone before, but gives us our first clear glimpse of a new Puccini whom we later came to know so well—the Puccini who at his greatest was an unsurpassed master of the expression of pathos. Except in his last opera, *Turandot*, Puccini never achieved, and indeed wisely did not aim at the quality of nobility in his music, but he recognized that the unhappiness of ordinary people could be just as poignant as the unhappiness of those of more heroic stature, that the tragedy of a Mimi, a Butterfly, or a Liù had a dignity of its own which was no less heart-breaking for its affecting a little seamstress instead of a king's mistress, a geisha girl instead of a princess, a slave instead of an empress.

The sadness and anxiety of the first moments of Act III are Des Grieux's. The Chevalier has come from Paris with Manon's brother who has bribed the guard of the barracks, where Manon is imprisoned awaiting transportation at dawn, to free his sister. Lescaut's assurances do little to lessen Des Grieux's torment, until the guard is changed and he points to a new sentry as the man in his pay. Lescaut makes a signal to the soldier to move away; he then goes to the barred window on the ground floor and knocks cautiously on the bars. The window opens and Manon appears, stretching her hands out to Des Grieux who runs excitedly towards her. The gloom goes out of the music at this but there is no passionate excitement to accompany this reunion of lovers; in its place there is a subdued tenderness and echoes, played only by muted and divided strings, of "Donna non vidi mai" (Ex 6), and passages from the Intermezzo and earlier love music. Manon's sighs are interrupted by the appearance of a lamplighter who extinguishes the street light and sings a quaint little song as he does so—"And Kate said to the King: 'Why tempt a poor girl's heart? The Lord made me beautiful for a husband.' And the King smiled and gave her jewels and gold, and a husband who captured her heart."

The lamplighter's song is a typically charming example of the musical *genre* painting that any subject set in France—and only, it seems, in France—always inspired in Puccini. Exactly the same sort of miniature sketch in local colour occurs in *La Bohème* and *Il Tabarro*, but in neither of these operas is it quite so unexpected and effective as in *Manon Lescaut*, because only in this instance has the composer made no attempt to create anything more than the emotional atmosphere of his scene. The wintry Paris dawn of the third act of *La Bohème* and the riverside life of the Seine in *Il Tabarro* are clearly presented in terms of "audible scenery" from the beginning; there is nothing in the music of the opening of Act III of *Manon Lescaut* which suggests either time or place in the same way as they are suggested in Puccini's other two French operas.

The lamplighter episode is most imaginatively orchestrated; flutes, clarinets, bass clarinet, violoncellos divided into three and the harp in its lowest register give it an intriguing flavour of its own.

The lamplighter goes on his way, and dawn begins to break. A clock strikes five and as the lamplighter's voice is heard fading in the distance Manon, with a sudden apprehensive outburst, cries that she has a presentiment of disaster, of some danger which she cannot describe.

Although the tunes do not stumble over each other in their profusion as they did in the first act of the opera, Puccini is no less inventive in this scene; in the course of a mere fifteen bars two new themes are heard which become important to the musical development of the drama. The first, associated with Manon's fear of death, and heard while a patrol of soldiers passes in the background and Des Grieux pleads desperately with Manon not to lose heart, is played by the violas:

29

This tune, one of the most moving in the opera, has its origin in the deep and well-stocked bottom-drawer that Puccini maintained to draw on in his early years as an opera composer; it comes from a string quartet called *Crisantemi* which he wrote in a single night as an elegy on the death of Amedeo of Savoy in 1890. The theme as it occurs in *Manon Lescaut*

differs in one detail from its first form in the quartet, and it provides an interesting glimpse of a composer's second and incomparably better thoughts. In *Crisantemi* the key signature is that of C sharp minor so that the tune is heard as:

—with a D sharp in the third bar instead of the poignant D natural which Puccini uses in his modified version. There is also another passage from the same string quartet that was incorporated in the last act of the opera.

The second theme evolving from the 15-bar sequence referred to is the tune to which Des Grieux finally persuades Manon to discard her fears:

Manon withdraws from the window and to suggest that everything is temporarily all right between the lovers the orchestra plays a short post-lude in which the full statement of the tune of Ex 23 is interrupted roughly by a shot fired off-stage and the sound of voices raising the alarm. Lescaut runs in to say that his plans for Manon's escape have gone wrong; he and Des Grieux must run for their lives. Des Grieux refuses. Manon, reappearing at the window, begs him in God's name to fly if he loves her. Still Des Grieux stands firm.

The square now fills with a crowd of people running from all directions and there is "confusione generale". The uproar is stilled by a drum roll on the stage. The barracks gate opens and the Sergeant appears with a guard escorting a dozen women in chains. The Sergeant forces a way through the crowd as the Commander of the warship comes down the gangway to tell him that the ship is ready and to call the roll.

The calling of the roll of the *filles* who may have brought *joie* to others but scarcely—in their present situation, at least—to themselves, is one of the most effective scenes in the whole opera, an ensemble of great variety and skill in which the crowd reacts with laughter, admiration, sometimes sympathetic, sometimes harshly critical comment to the sight of each of the girls as the Sergeant calls out their names—Rosetta, Madelon, Manon, Ninetta, Caton, Regina, Claretta, Violetta, Nerina, Elisa, Ninon, Giorgetta. The girls for their part react individually as their names are read out—impudently, coquettishly, defiantly, with tears, or with their faces buried in their hands.

The ensemble is built on the melancholy tune of Ex 31 starting with clarinet and bassoon in octaves. When Manon's name is read out, Lescaut makes his way through the crowd in which he had got caught up during the *confusione generale,* and stands with a group of townspeople who are watching Manon; he tries to rouse the bystanders' sympathy for his sister with a harrowing story of the events which have brought her to this final degradation. Soaring above the dialogue and choral comment, the voices of Manon and Des Grieux say a passionate and heart-breaking farewell—she telling him he must return home and forget her, he exclaiming bitterly that his heart is filled with hatred for mankind and God.

The roll call comes to an end; and the Sergeant, forming the prisoners into line, gives the order to march. At this point there is another of the several instances to be found not only in *Manon Lescaut* but in other Puccini operas as well, of the first statement by the orchestra of a tune which later becomes a vocal high spot. As the girls are being marched off bass clarinet, bassoons, violoncellos and double basses play this tune in unison:

The vocal form of this follows not long afterwards. Meanwhile, Manon and Des Grieux cling together; the Sergeant goes over to them and taking Manon roughly by the arm pushes her into line with the other prisoners. Des Grieux wrenches Manon away from the Sergeant, while the crowd, taking his side, go to his assistance by preventing the Sergeant from touching the lovers. The crowd falls back, however, at the sudden appearance of the ship's Commander, and Des Grieux, overcome with emotion, falls at his feet to implore him desperately to take him to America in the ship with Manon. "Guardate, pazzo son"—"Look, I am mad . . ." are the words Des Grieux sings to the tune of Ex 32 which develops, with a strong throbbing accompaniment, into a powerful and virile sequence for the tenor.

Des Grieux finishes his pleading. The Commander, obviously moved by what he has heard, smiles kindly at Des Grieux and says to him ("in the typical rough way of a sailor"): "So you want to populate America do you? Well, off you go!" The Commander claps Des Grieux on the shoulder. "Des Grieux" (run the stage directions) "lets out a yell of joy and kisses the Commander's hand. Manon turns, sees, understands—and her face radiant with supreme joy, from the top of the gangway stretches out her arms to Des Grieux, who runs towards her. Lescaut, standing on one side, looks, shakes his head and walks away." The curtain falls rapidly to a joyous and fully-scored *fortissimo* reprise of Ex 23.

ACT IV

IN AMERICA

Scene: A desert on the borders of New Orleans. The ground is bare and undulating; the horizon "vastissimo"; cloudy sky. Evening is falling.

The curtain rises on four arresting bars scored for full orchestra which create a quite remarkable and instantaneous mood of despair by the simplest means of a couple of minor chords:

Manon and Des Grieux are seen approaching slowly from the background. They are ragged and destitute; Manon is pale and exhausted, and she leans on Des Grieux.

Exactly why Manon and Des Grieux are where they are and in the state they are is not even faintly hinted at in the score or in any programme-synopsis of the opera I have ever seen. Most people, I think, seeing the fourth act of *Manon Lescaut* merely take it for granted that Manon has got into trouble again and as usual the devoted Des Grieux is involved in it, that they are either escaping from one place or trying to reach another for reasons that no longer matter since Manon is obviously dying, and that, in any case, it is the music of a desperate situation that is important not the case history of the situation.

Prévost's novel, however, explains what happened. In the ship which transported them from Le Havre the two lovers reached the settlement of New Orleans where Des Grieux killed the Governor's nephew in a duel in defence of Manon. Des Grieux and Manon had to fly from the scene for their lives, and heading aimlessly across the open countryside lost themselves in the dust and desolation of the plain which is the scene of this last act of Puccini's opera.

The opening passages of dialogue have considerable musical pathos in which a large part is played by a chromatic phrase which appears in various forms and comes from the first bars of the *Crisantemi* quartet:

These early pages, and indeed nearly the whole of this act, abound in examples of Puccini's characteristic orchestration, particularly for woodwind which includes wonderfully effective instances of the use of the bass clarinet as the foundation on which a four-part chord is built (the other three notes being supplied by two clarinets and bassoon), and of the voicing of a chord for two oboes, cor anglais and bassoon in the echo of the opening chord sequence of the act (Ex 33) alternating with strings—

—where once again the highest note of the wood-wind chord is taken by the cor anglais whose possible absence elsewhere in the score is so carefully provided for when the 2nd oboe can take over on its behalf, but whose presence in this particular case is so absolutely essential that the composer (or editor) makes no provision whatever for its replacement.

The instrumentation of this act differs in one respect from the rest of the opera in that Puccini deprives himself of the services of the second of the three flutes in the orchestra pit. The 2nd flute is sent out to play off-stage in Manon's final aria.

What is in effect an extended duet for the lovers proceeds with constant references to themes with which we are familiar—the broad theme from the Intermezzo (Ex 27) and Manon's first theme (Ex 5) which during the whole of this act undergoes some effective variation and alteration of melody, harmonization and orchestration that give it a peculiar and haunting pathos, particularly at the moment when Manon cries that she is tormented by thirst and it is heard pp with the tune played in unison by piccolo, flute and bass clarinet spread over four octaves.

Manon begs Des Grieux to go and look for water to a kind of theme which now makes its first appearance in Puccini's operas and which was to recur frequently in his later works at harrowing moments in the action. Before encountering it in *La Bohème*, *Madam Butterfly* and *Turandot* the characteristic funeral-march figure played pp by strings with long bows drawn across the fingerboard (*sul tasto*) is heard in *Manon Lescaut* in this form:

Des Grieux goes away in search of water. As the horizon darkens Manon is left alone, frightened and cowering, to sing her first and last soliloquy "Sola, perduta, abbandonata" ("Alone, lost, abandoned . . .").

It is a scene of great simplicity built up on a plaintive phrase by the oboe which is echoed by the off-stage flute:

37

Manon reflects on her fate, crying desperately: "I do not want to die!" ("Non voglio morire!") She grows delirious, cursing her fatal beauty and—in one single line—makes a very brief reference to recent events, which hardly puts the audience in the picture, when she exclaims: "They wanted to take me from him!" and in the manner of Lady Macbeth, has visions of blood and bloodstains. The soliloquy ends with one final and heart-rending cry of "Non voglio morire!"

Des Grieux returns to catch Manon in his arms as she is about to faint. The sad tune of Ex 36 returns, played by two flutes in unison in their lowest register, an elegy which accompanies Manon's realization that she is dying, that in spite of Des Grieux's comforting reassurance and encouragement, darkness is falling on her.

To the tune of the *Crisantemi* theme (Ex 29) Manon, in a moving passage, bids her lover not to weep for her; it is the hour of kisses, not of tears, and the time is passing quickly. As the orchestra repeats it, beginning with *tutta forza* and then leaving it to the strings to play quietly, Manon begs Des Grieux to come nearer to her, to kiss her. Des Grieux swears he will follow her into death, but she forbids him to with a sudden solemn imperiousness. Then she smiles: "Was she very loving, your Manon? Do you remember?"

Two flutes and two clarinets play a mournful chromatic version of Manon's first theme again (Ex 5) as she continues: "Do you remember —tell me—how full of light my youth was?—and I shall never see the sun again."

Very quietly and sadly the two flutes echo the phrase from the minuet in Act II, the four bars of Ex 19, and in a faint voice Manon sings: "My faults . . . will be forgotten . . . but my love . . . will not die." Manon dies and Des Grieux falls senseless over her body as the curtain falls to the phrase that raised it at the beginning of the act.

The echo of the minuet as Manon dies is one of the many things that people find puzzling or unsatisfactory in this first successful Puccini opera. Remembering how effectively dramatic the composer made Mimi's death by the unfailing theatrical device summed up in Dante's "There is no greater sorrow than to recall a time of happiness in misery", it is easy to feel disappointed that Manon, in her death-throes, should have remembered one of the least creditable periods of her life instead of her genuine love for Des Grieux. But is it Manon looking back on her life of luxury? I do not think so. When Mimi dies, as we shall see, she herself quotes the things she remembers that she and Rodolfo said; it is not just the orchestra that reminds us of the lovers' meeting. In Manon's case, however, it is the composer who is doing the reminiscing, not the character, and in such a way that, as I have suggested, the idea is in danger of misfiring altogether. When Manon reflects on her faults Puccini reminds the listener by a rather ham-handed musical "illustration" of her life with Geronte.

It is easy at this date to suggest what Puccini ought to have done, that he might have quoted any one of half a dozen themes associated with Manon's love for Des Grieux at this moment in the story. But it obviously just did not occur to him to do anything of the kind until he came to the last act of *La Bohème*. He was not, in short, educated up to that sort of thing when he wrote *Manon Lescaut*. If the minuet quotation means anything it means no more than that Puccini was drawing our attention (unnecessarily, for we could scarcely have forgotten), and with a theme which we might or might not have noticed when it was last played, to the reason for Manon's plight and the source of all her faults. We would still have remembered if Manon had sung the line entirely without accompaniment.

For those who have read Prévost's novel Puccini's *Manon Lescaut* has always and inevitably been an unsatisfactory interpretation of the story. But the average listener is less concerned with what *Manon Lescaut* might have been, or ought to have been, than with what it is. Once we start prodding and poking about in it we can discover numberless flaws in the dramatic fabric—unexplained situations, inconsistent characterization, an incomplete portrait of Des Grieux whose tragedy it really is, and an almost perversely unfavourable presentation of the heroine who is shown —to put it mildly—in a Very Poor Light in the second act. But considering that no fewer than seven hands stirred the pudding that is the libretto of *Manon Lescaut*, it is remarkable how little its weaknesses affect one's enjoyment of the opera. The fact that mistakes were permitted to go uncorrected was clearly Puccini's fault, of course, and I think that can be attributed not to his lack of artistic conscience but to his youthful impetuosity and impatience.

Puccini was so bursting with musical ideas, so lavish with his invention, so impulsive and exultant in his new-found strength that he did not wait to think before breaking into song. He did not have time to notice that Manon, as his librettists had fashioned her in Act II, was a fairly contemptible kind of girl; all he wanted was to get to the love music and forget everything else. To him, Manon and Des Grieux fell in love, and owing to unfortunate occurrences which he almost seemed to regard as none of his concern, were parted, reunited, parted and reunited once more in the unhappiest circumstances and finally tragically parted by death. And wherever these meetings and partings and reunions occurred Puccini created music of great warmth and pathos—in the duets in Act I and Act II, in the fine ensemble in Act III, in Manon's "Sola, perduta . . .", in the final scene of her death—minuet and all.

It may be argued that Manon did not deserve this musical sympathy, but to Puccini, as indeed to the devoted Des Grieux, she was a fascinating creature whose sufferings were no less painful, no less to be pitied because they were largely self-inflicted. There is much in the libretto that is wittier and better written than it is usually given credit for, and though there are many perplexing inconsistencies they are not intolerable, or even unduly disconcerting if, as one has to with the unexplained situation in Act IV, one takes them for granted and gets on with the main business of listening to the music.

After more than 75 years in the repertoire *Manon Lescaut* shows no tendency to lose its appeal; indeed, its popularity seems to be increasing with the years, which is in itself a gratifying thought for it suggests that its unique position among Puccini's operas is being recognized more generally. *Manon Lescaut* has an air and a quality all its own, a youthfulness and vigour, a charm and fire and lyrical exuberance which, once they have taken hold of the affections of the listener, will never let go.

LA BOHÈME

(*Property of G. Ricordi and Co.*)

Opera in four acts by Giuseppe Giacosa and Luigi Illica, based on *Scènes de la Vie de Bohème* by Henri Murger. First performed at the Teatro Regio, Turin, on 1st February, 1896, conducted by Arturo Toscanini. First performance in England: Theatre Royal, Manchester, 22nd April 1897, in English. First performance in the United States: Los Angeles, 14th October, 1897.

La Bohème, it has been said, is an opera for those who are in love, or those who, having grown old, remember what it is like to be in love —which means that it is an opera for almost everybody. It is a simple story, so simple that it scarcely rates as more than an episode. Boy meets girl, boy loses girl, boy and girl are reunited as girl dies of consumption in boy's arms and the curtain falls. There is barely one instance of a genuinely dramatic situation in the four acts. And yet it is one of the most successful and enchanting operas ever written.

Though the curtain falls on a death scene the greater part of the score is devoted to remarkably light-hearted music intended to establish a background of youthful high spirits and young love. It is only in the last scene that we are pulled up with a jerk and we begin to appreciate fully the deliberate gaiety of what has gone before, as Puccini quotes one theme after another, themes which we have heard in happier circumstances and which in their final echoed wistfulness have a heart-breaking poignancy.

In *La Bohème*, perhaps for the very reason that the story is simple and tells itself, Puccini was able to concentrate more fully on the purely musical enjoyment to be had out of the opera than in anything else he ever wrote. He found in it opportunities for humour and horse-play, for charm, for descriptive music, for love songs, quarrels, comedy and wit. His characters are human, his crowds are picturesque, and there is a genuineness in the pathos of the last act which survives all sneers at the composer's sentimentality.

Puccini took only eight months to write the music for *La Bohème*, but it was not until two whole years had been passed in argument, disagreement, pleading, cajoling and wrangling over the construction of the libretto with Giacosa and Illica, who had been called in individually to help out in the last desperate days of *Manon Lescaut* and were now working as a team for the first time.

When it was that Puccini first had the idea of basing an opera on Henri Murger's novel is not known for certain. While he was still at work on *Manon Lescaut*, Ruggiero Leoncavallo, who wrote words as well as music for a living, approached Puccini with a libretto he had written called *La Vita di Bohème*. Puccini declined the offer, either because he was still preoccupied with *Manon Lescaut*, or because he reckoned that if a composer-librettist like Leoncavallo offered another composer a libretto it could not have been very good, otherwise the composer-librettist would obviously have used it himself. Whatever the reason, however, Puccini seems to have forgotten all about it until after the launching of *Manon Lescaut*. Then, meeting Leoncavallo one day in the Galleria in Milan, he chattily observed that he had found a good subject for an opera—one based on Murger's *Vie de Bohème*. Leoncavallo immediately accused Puccini of having stolen the idea from him, revealing at the same time that as Puccini had spurned his original offer of a libretto he had set it to music himself. A first-class row ensued and Leoncavallo, publicly staking his artistic claim in the manner of the time, announced that he had finished his opera called *La Vita di Bohème*. Puccini followed with an announcement in the same day's evening paper that he was just finishing *his* opera on the subject, which would be known as *La Bohème*. The rift that followed between the two composers, who had never been on the most cordial of terms, was further widened when Leoncavallo's opera (now also called simply *La Bohème*) was eventually performed for the first time in Venice in May 1897 on the same night as Puccini's opera, already a success more than a year old, was packing another theatre in the same city.

Whatever the moral rights and wrongs of the *Bohème* affair the quality of Puccini's version told in the end; if the composer did in fact steal the idea from Leoncavallo then the end certainly justified the means, and we can still spare a grateful thought for the man who first saw in it an operatic subject. Without having evidence one way or the other, however, my own belief is that Puccini did not consciously lift the idea from Leoncavallo. If he did then surely he would not have told Leoncavallo about it so blandly and openly. We can take Leoncavallo's word for it that he did offer Puccini the libretto; but we have no proof that Puccini ever noticed what it was that he refused—especially as he was deeply involved not only in the music, but in the confusion of the libretto, of another opera at the time as we know.

It was Stephen Williams, wittiest of broadcasters and gentlest of friends, who before his sadly early death called *La Bohème* "the most instantly captivating and companionable of Puccini's works, and one of the most instantly captivating and companionable operas in the world". But at the time of its first performance *La Bohème* was by no means accepted as instantly captivating or companionable. It was not that it was greeted with any active hostility or even with polite indifference. It was just that the public was puzzled and disappointed by the unfamiliar scale of the whole thing, especially as the novelty immediately preceding it in Toscanini's Turin season had been the first performance in Italian of Wagner's *Götterdämmerung*, and it took time before the opera was appreciated in its proper perspective as an intimate, very human and very true-to-life conception.*

---

* *La Bohème* did not come into complete public favour until after its first performances in Turin and Rome, when at Palermo in April 1896 it was so enthusiastically received that Mimi and Rudolph had to come back and repeat the death scene in their street clothes. The circumstances of the whole occasion are too long to repeat here, but I have set them out in more detail in the Palermo chapter of *Great Opera Houses* (page 244).

Until the appearance of *La Bohème* the public's experience of Love on the opera stage had been of a somewhat lofty emotion of more than life-size dimensions and usually with consequences which (keeping their fingers crossed) the public could reasonably regard as unlikely to apply to them. Tristan and Isolde, Radames and Aida, Otello and Desdemona, even Manon and Des Grieux, belonged to a world far removed from anything the public experienced at home. But with *La Bohème* they were introduced for the first time to a world with which they were familiar, in which they could recognize incidents and situations and emotions they, or somebody they had heard tell of, might have known at first hand. The action of *La Bohème*, however, was more than something that *could* have happened: most of it actually *had* happened, not only in the life of Henri Murger, but a great deal of it also in the life of the composer who set Murger's novel to music thirty years after the author's death.

How far and which characters and incidents of *La Bohème* are based on real life is something best discussed, I think, at the end of this chapter when the story of the opera has been told and the details are familiar to those who may be hearing it for the first time.

CHARACTERS IN ORDER OF APPEARANCE:

MARCEL (Marcello), *a painter*	*Baritone*
RUDOLPH (Rodolfo), *a poet*	*Tenor*
COLLINE, *a philosopher*	*Bass*
SCHAUNARD, *a musician*	*Baritone*
BÉNOIT, *a landlord*	*Bass*
MIMI	*Soprano*
PARPIGNOL, *a toyseller*	*Tenor*
ALCINDORO, *a Councillor of State*	*Bass*
MUSETTA	*Soprano*
CUSTOMS OFFICER	*Bass*
A SERGEANT	*Bass*

Students, soldiers, shopkeepers, midinettes, hawkers, citizens, waiters, children.

Scene: The Latin Quarter of Paris.   Time: About 1830

ACT I

Scene: In the garret. A large window looks out on the roofs of Paris which are covered with snow. On the left there is a stove. The room is furnished with a table, a cupboard, a small bookcase, four chairs, an easel, a bed; there are a few books scattered about, many bundles of paper and two candlesticks. One door centre, another on the left. It is Christmas Eve.

The curtain rises at once on a theme which firmly establishes the inherent gaiety of the opera in the course of a couple of orchestral bars:

This theme, which is associated with the Bohemians throughout the action, was originally the principal subject of a *Capriccio sinfonico*, a work for small orchestra which Puccini wrote as his graduation exercise on leaving the conservatoire at Milan. The *Capriccio* was his first published work and was therefore even lower down in the bottom drawer than the *Crisantemi* string quartet which had provided *Manon Lescaut* with a couple of themes. Whether Puccini deliberately went back to his student days for his theme because it was associated with his own *vie de Bohème*, I do not know, but its first incisive statement is an arresting moment and instantaneously evocative of the atmosphere of youth and high spirits which pervades the opera.

The scene shows Rudolph and Marcel in their garret. Rudolph stands staring thoughtfully out of the window, while Marcel works at his painting of "The Passage of the Red Sea", trying to warm his hands from time to time by blowing on them, and avenging himself, he says, by painting a drowning pharaoh.

Even in these early stages of the opera it is clear that Puccini is concerned with a new operatic technique. Instead of the long flowing phrases which frame the dialogue of the first act of *Manon Lescaut* the conversation in this scene of *La Bohème* is set to music built up on tunes that are scarcely more than fragments; but these fragments are so neatly interlocked, their form so subtly altered and developed in the course of the act, that there is no suggestion of looseness or disjointed musical thinking.

Until very much later in the act there is nothing that faintly resembles a "scene". Rudolph has 16 consecutive bars to himself when, right at the beginning, he reflects poetically on the smoke rising from the chimneys of Paris; but this again is nothing more than the first statement of a theme which plays a considerable part in the construction of the whole —"Nei cieli bigi . . ." ("Into the grey skies . . .") :

This tune is another from Puccini's bottom drawer taken this time, however, not from his student days but rescued from the preliminary sketches he made for the opera he began immediately after *Manon Lescaut*. This was to have been *La Lupa* (The She-Wolf), a blood-and-thunder melodrama with a libretto by Giovanni Verga, author of the play *Cavalleria rusticana*. Puccini changed his mind about it when he realized that Verga's horrors were too much even for him, who was not noticeably squeamish about such things. (His initial enthusiasm for *La Lupa*, which took him to Sicily in search of the right atmosphere, suggests that Leoncavallo's idea of *La Bohème* must have gone in at one of Puccini's ears and out of the other.)

The opening dialogue between Rudolph and Marcel concerns the question of keeping warm. There is no fire in the stove; Marcel offers to burn his "Passage of the Red Sea", but Rudolph maintains that the stink would be unbearable. Instead, says the young poet, better burn the first act of his new play. The manuscript is thrust into the stove and burnt while Rudolph and Marcel draw up their chairs.

The door bursts open noisily and Colline, the philosopher, stamps in—numb with cold, carrying a bundle of books tied together with a handkerchief and which he has been unable to pawn. He throws them angrily on the table and sits down to warm himself at the dying flames of Rudolph's first act. Another act of the drama is put on the stove, and finally the third act goes up in smoke.

There is considerable wit in the libretto of this whole scene, and the authors have drawn the characters of the Bohemians with great care and conviction. Poverty and discomfort are obviously nothing new to these young artists; the wolf has been at the door so frequently that he is almost a co-lodger with whom they are on the most intimate terms. They laugh easily at their own troubles and it is Rudolph, for instance, who remarks on the dramatic virtue of brevity when the manuscript of his first act burns only for a few moments.

As the flames of Rudolph's third act die down (on an effective *ppppp* chord for three muted trumpets which hovers mysteriously over the scene), Marcel and Colline cry "Down with the author!" and there is a sudden commotion. Two errand boys enter the room laden with bundles of wood, cigars, food and bottles of what the Bohemians, who cannot believe their eyes, recognize delightedly as "Bordò!" This unexpected event brings with it a new and understandably elated theme and the general scherzo-like movement of the music is resumed as evening begins to fall:

When the boys have delivered the provisions Schaunard, the musician, makes a triumphant entry and throws a handful of coins on the ground. "Tin!" says Marcel. Schaunard points out the head of Louis-Philippe on the coins and begins to tell his friends how he came by all this sudden wealth.

It seems that Schaunard had met an Englishman ("a lord—or a milord —as the case may be") who was willing to pay handsomely for music lessons. He imitates the Lord's (or Milord's) accent and tells the story in detail. But nobody listens; Schaunard's three companions are too busy laying the table and preparing to eat. Schaunard's story is that on accepting the Englishman's offer he was shown a parrot in a cage and told that his job was to play the piano until the bird died. After three days of incessant playing the bird was still alive, so Schaunard gave it parsley to eat, which killed it "dead as Socrates".

"Who is?" asks Colline, who happens to be passing with a plate.

"Oh, the devil take the lot of you!" exclaims Schaunard with disgust. "Here, what are you doing?"

He goes over to the table where the others are eating and takes the food off the table. "No," he says sternly, "these are the iron rations of the dark and gloomy future. The idea of eating at home on Christmas Eve! And outside, the Latin Quarter beckons with all its delicious food! Have a little respect for religion! Drink at home, by all means, but eat—no!"

At Schaunard's mention of the Latin Quarter there is a quiet first statement of the theme which begins the second act and is associated, both in anticipation and retrospect, with the Bohemians' visit to the Café Momus:

On its first appearance in Act 1 (as well as later) this theme is heard with an appendix in the form of a rhythmic variant of the little phrase I mentioned which occurred in the first act of *Manon Lescaut* (Ex 13). In *La Bohème* it becomes purely an instrumental motif and when first heard at this point is given to piccolo, trumpet and glockenspiel in this form:

Schaunard's hint is taken and the four Bohemians settle down to drink wine when there is a knock on the door and Bénoit, the landlord, is let in. He is at once invited to sit down and is given a glass of wine; he raises the question of the overdue quarter's rent with Marcel. "You promised——" says Bénoit. "And I keep my promise," replies Marcel, pointing, to the horror of Colline and Schaunard, at the pile of money on the table. "You see? Now stay with us and chat for a while." Conversation proceeds mainly to a gentle undulating kind of tune, with much intriguing wood-wind scoring and based on the phrase:

Bénoit gradually begins to get a little drunk and is drawn, by Marcel who does most of the talking, into discussing his amorous conquests; he confesses that he likes plump women and detests the scraggy kind—"like my wife, for instance".

Marcel rises and thumps the table indignantly. How dare Bénoit, a married man, speak like that? How dare this lecherous old philanderer invade the innocent and honest abode of four virtuous, respectable artists? Bénoit is bundled bodily out of the room and the door is locked behind him. "That's paid the quarter's rent," remarks Marcel.

Schaunard again proposes that everybody should adjourn to the Café Momus. The proposal is agreed to. Rudolph announces, with a solo violin and divided strings playing a languid version of "Nei cieli bigi" (Ex 39), that he is going to stay behind to finish an article he is writing, but he will join the others at the porter's lodge downstairs in five minutes.

With a great deal of shouting and noisy falling downstairs, Marcel, Colline and Schaunard leave the scene. As Rudolph settles down to work, a new theme is heard which is obviously associated with Work, for it recurs in a similar situation in the last act:

Or perhaps one should say it is associated with work begun but interrupted, for in both cases it is followed by a cessation of artistic activities. Rudolph lacks inspiration and throws his pen aside; for the first time since the rise of the curtain there is silence in the theatre. But not for long, for the silence is broken by a quiet knock at the door, a woman's voice saying "Excuse me", and the orchestra playing:

This theme is so familiar that few people hearing *La Bohème* for the first time can fail to have heard it somewhere before and to associate it with Mimi, the little seamstress who lives one floor above and has come into the studio because her candle has blown out on her way upstairs.

From this moment onwards until the end of the act the entire character of the music changes. The occasion when boy meets girl for the first time is Puccini's cue to begin a gradual building up to a romantic climax; the boisterous, fun-and-games atmosphere of the Bohemians is forgotten and an unceasing flow of lyrical melody takes its place.

Mimi enters to ask if she can beg a light for her candle, but before Rudolph can light it she collapses coughing in his arms, letting fall her candlestick and her doorkey. Puccini has a particular theme for Mimi's more serious spasms of coughing (for it is clear to us that she is in an advanced stage of consumption). He uses it sparingly and with good effect, and it is heard for the first time at this point in the action played on a clarinet:

Rudolph, perplexed and rather helpless, revives Mimi by splashing cold water on her face (three high rising pizzicato notes from two solo violins illustrate this in the orchestra), and "looking at her with great interest" observes how ill she looks. The little scene which follows, in which Mimi slowly recovers, accepts a glass of wine and, with her candle lighted again, thanks Rudolph and bids him "buona sera", is a wonderfully effective and understated musical sequence consisting of a passage for muted strings playing under their breath, as it were, to punctuate the embarrassed question-and-answer dialogue between the two. It consists of little more than playing five times, with an interlude of four sustained chords, the phrase:

Rudolph sees Mimi to the door, and when she has left, returns quickly to his work; but in a moment—before the "work theme" can even begin —Mimi is back again. She has forgotten her key—"Oh! sventata, sventata!" ("Oh, how stupid of me . . .!"):

It is to this tune, a typically gracious Puccini theme of the kind he often used to accompany the dialogue of lovers and potential lovers, that Mimi and Rudolph get to know each other better. Mimi's candle is blown out by the draught; a moment later Rudolph's goes out and the room is in darkness. Together they grope around on the floor on hands and knees looking for the key; in the course of the search Rudolph discovers himself near the door and locks it. Eventually Rudolph finds the key, but he quickly puts it in his pocket. The "search" continues until, under the table, Rudolph's hand meets Mimi's; and he does not let go.

For the next twelve minutes we have a superbly sustained sequence of lyrical music, perhaps the most faithful and fascinating picture of two young people falling in love to be found in all opera (Verdi's Nanetta and Fenton were already in love before the curtain rose on *Falstaff*). This finale falls naturally into three parts. It begins with Rudolph's "Che gelida manina" ("Your tiny hand is frozen"), which, like so many Puccini "numbers", starts in a monotone:

In the course of his aria Rudolph tells Mimi that he is a poet, and describes the world of his fantasies—"Talor dal mio forziere" ("My hoard of treasure is robbed by two thieves: a pair of beautiful eyes")—which has a faint family resemblance to Ex 43:

This theme, first orchestrated with the violas playing an octave lower than the violoncellos, is developed into the climax of Rudolph's solo, with the strings playing the tune in unison and making the kind of sound, rich and surging, that Puccini knew so well how to make by the most economical means. When he has told his story Rudolph turns to Mimi, asking her to tell him who she is.

For a moment Mimi hesitates and then replies simply: "Mi chiamano Mimì, ma il mio nome è Lucia" ("They call me Mimi, but my name is Lucia"):

Detailed musical analysis and quotation now becomes a little impracticable, for once having started with this tune (first heard on her entry), Mimi proceeds to sing one phrase after another, each of which plays a part in the later musical development of the opera.

Mimi tells Rudolph that she embroiders flowers in silk, and the roses and lilies that she works give her pleasure because they remind her of spring. She lives by herself, she explains, upstairs in a room looking out on the roofs and the sky. When the snow melts and the sun shines, the first kiss of April is hers—and Mimi sings this to her own broad counterpart of Rudolph's broad "Talor dal mio forziere"—"Ma quando vien lo sgelo . . ." ("But when the thaw comes . . ."):

Once again Puccini builds his theme up from *pianissimo* to a moving and intensely singable *fortissimo* phrase. Mimi's little recital comes to an end with a wistful regret that her embroidered flowers have no scent; she can think of no more to say. In a most unusual bar, described by its composer as free of "the rigour of tempo", Mimi sings simply: "I cannot think of anything more to tell you about myself. I am just your neighbour who drops in at awkward moments." (It is interesting to note the similar and typically effective construction of the first two parts of the finale. Both "Che gelida manina" and "Mi chiamano Mimì" begin almost conversationally, then blossom into a warm lyrical sequence to end in a deliberately "thrown-away" and matter-of-fact manner.)

Musically and dramatically the situation now reached is the everyday one of conversation between a young man and a young woman having come to an embarrassing standstill. Neither can think of anything more to say, except perhaps "Well—er——". The tension is broken, however, by raucous voices from the street below.

Marcel, Colline and Schaunard shout to Rudolph to hurry up, asking what on earth he is doing up there all alone. Rudolph replies that he is not alone; there are two of them and they will come on to the Café Momus later.

The fact that Rudolph is not alone does not seem to strike his friends as remarkable; or perhaps they did not hear that bit. At any rate, without making any comment on Rudolph's announcement they disappear in the distance singing.

Rudolph stays by the window to make sure that his friends have left, and the way the Bohemians' little interlude finishes one is quite convinced that the music can now move in an academic manner only into the key of G major. Instead, Puccini takes us unexpectedly; and with characteristic sureness of touch, into the key of A as Mimi moves towards Rudolph and

a shaft of moonlight falls on her face. Rudolph looks at her enraptured—
"O soave fanciulla . . ." ("Lovely maid in the moonlight . . .").

Slowly the orchestra builds up Rudolph's love theme (Ex 50) and for
the first time the lovers sing the same tune in unison—the first musical
suggestion of emotional unanimity so far heard in the duet. Rudolph
kisses Mimi; she does not immediately free herself from his embrace, but
after a moment suggests that he ought to be going. Rudolph's friends are
expecting him.

"So you're sending me away?" asks Rudolph.

"Well, no. That is—couldn't I come with you?" Mimi replies.

Rudolph, who for all his fanciful poetic dreams (and his having already
asked his companions to reserve two places at the Momus) is a simple
young man at heart, is rather taken aback at this unexpected suggestion;
but he quickly recovers and in turn suggests that it would be cosier to
stay in the garret. Mimi turns the idea down, and the two young people
leave the stage arm in arm to an echo of "Che gelida manina". The
curtain falls on a distant and fading high C from the soprano, and
sometimes from the tenor who dares what Puccini did not write and
Caruso would rarely attempt.

Before coming to the second act of *La Bohème* there is one technical
aspect of this duet to be mentioned, and that is Puccini's orchestration.

The orchestral restraint during the course of what we must consider a
"big" scene is quite remarkable. Up to the departure of Marcel, Colline
and Schaunard the orchestra faithfully underlines the stage action and
the personality of the four Bohemians; their music calls for brilliant and
occasionally rowdy treatment by the orchestra. But with the entrance of
Mimi and during the scenes that follow, the moonlit bewilderment of
young love suddenly infects the orchestra pit. There is a new warmth, a
new quality of charm and spring-like freshness to be heard in the score
which is expressed by instrumental understatement rather than exaggeration. The solo flute, the harp, divided and muted strings, introduce an
entirely new atmosphere, and while the singers are making certain that
they shall be heard (an eventuality for which Puccini had already made
ample provision) the strength of the orchestral accompaniment is often
in inverse ratio to the efforts of tenor and soprano. The end of the love
duet, indeed, is accompanied by what is virtually a chamber orchestra—
two flutes, piccolo, two clarinets, harp and muted strings marked *pppp*.
The last scene of Act I is an altogether exquisite score, the work of a man
whose inspiration, whether one regards it as "cheap" and "empty", or
as convincing and moving, was supported by consummate craftmanship.

ACT II

Scene: In the Latin Quarter. A square where several crossroads meet, flanked by shops and stalls of all kinds. At one side, the Café Momus.

The curtain rises immediately* to the sound of trumpets playing the triads of Schaunard's Café Momus theme (Ex 41) in a loud and festive fashion—

which is now followed frequently by an equally loud and more definite version of the phrase originally taken from *Manon Lescaut* (Ex 42).

It is Christmas Eve. The stage is filled with a huge and colourful crowd of citizens, soldiers, servant girls, boys, children, students, urchins, midinettes and gendarmes. The centre of the square is taken up by hawkers who shout their wares at the passers-by. Standing apart from the throng are Rudolph and Mimi on one side; Colline is at a clothes repairing shop, Schaunard stands outside a junk dealer's buying a pipe and a French horn; Marcel is being pushed hither and thither by the movement of the crowd.

The shops are all brilliantly lit by small lanterns, and a large illuminated sign advertises the Café Momus, which is so crowded inside that customers have had to be seated at tables outside. It is evidently fairly mild weather for the time of year, in spite of the snow seen through the garret window in Act I.

The opening of this second act of *La Bohème* has nothing to do with the story. It is pure "atmosphere"—a kaleidoscope of noise and bustle and high spirits, of tiny thumbnail sketches and detailed *genre* painting which music alone can achieve with such conviction in the theatre. The prototype of this Latin Quarter scene is obviously the opening of the last act of *Carmen*, although in that opera, of course, the brilliance of the crowd scene is carefully built up to anticipate the contrast of the final drama. One knows in *Carmen* that something dramatic and startling is likely to happen; in *La Bohème* there is no indication that life will not go on like this for ever. Indeed, it would have been wrong if Puccini had suggested otherwise, for half the charm of the opera lies in the composer's ability to

---

* In everyday practice. In the score the curtain does not rise until after the voices of the crowd are heard—in other words, until some fifteen seconds (or 28 bars) have elapsed.

translate the childlike faith in the permanence of a first love affair into terms of music.

There is not much plot in this act, and what there is is episodic; but there is no lack of incident. In fact, it seems that scarcely a line of dialogue or a bar of music passes that one does not want to quote or draw close attention to. As in the beginning of Act I, the continuity of the music depends on the development of fragments, the most elaborately developed being the trumpet theme which is not only altered and re-formed but seems to breed little phrases having no superficial resemblance to it but which are in some way obviously blood relations.

The individual characterization amid the general uproar of the scene is unusually clear. Puccini's demand for genuine boys' (not female choristers') voices to sing the parts of the street urchins and children gives the music a distinctive colouring and there are numberless delightful touches like the whining child pestering its mother (to the same phrase as the toyseller's cries) for a trumpet and a toy horse, and the sharp disciplinary unison of the *mamme* packing their children off home to bed to the briskly indignant tune of:

The activities of the crowd are accompanied by music which is restless, vigorous and brilliantly scored. The conversation of the Bohemians, on the other hand, is for the most part against a more leisurely background and not even Colline's excited discovery of a rare second-hand volume of runic grammar disturbs the peace of Puccini's deliberately contrasted mood and tempo.

It being in the nature of opera that a number of points of view, comments and incidents can be expressed or depicted in music simultaneously, Puccini is able to present a great deal of what happens on two or three planes at once; so that while Marcel, Colline and Schaunard are occupied with the business of ordering dinner outside the Café Momus, Rudolph and Mimi are elsewhere in the square buying a bonnet or discussing how much they love one another.

In due course Rudolph introduces Mimi to his friends. "This is Mimi, and her presence completes our company, because I am the poet and she is Poetry." He makes his little speech in an expansive phrase which one expects to be developed into an aria but which ends after eight bars to show that Puccini was really only poking fun with:

The company settles itself round the dinner table and studies the menu "with a kind of admiration and profound analysis". The musical interest now shifts back to the crowd of children, the toyseller and the angry mothers. The children are sent off to bed and conversation at the café table is resumed—or rather, the stage directions tell us, Marcel speaks "as though continuing a conversation". The principal topic of table-talk is the pretty bonnet Rudolph has just bought Mimi; this starts a lyrical train of thought not only in Mimi but in everybody in the party. Reflections, philosophical comment, and finally a toast are heard in a sequence which begins with Mimi's tune:

A pleasant time seems to be enjoyed by all—by all, that is, except Marcel whose enjoyment is suddenly ruined by the arrival of Musetta, an old flame.

Musetta is perhaps the best-drawn character in the opera and the composer has lavished more musical care on her than on any of the others. She is a coquette, her behaviour is wild and spontaneous, she dresses in the height of extravagant fashion, she has a quick temper and a shrill voice; but beneath all this, of course, she has a heart of gold.

Her entrance, to a hectic change of tempo (Allegro moderato brillante, con fuoco) and time (9/8), causes a stir among the crowd, to whom she is obviously a familiar and popular figure, and embarrassment to Marcel. Musetta is accompanied by Alcindoro, a Councillor of State and a stock figure of comedy centuries old: the rich old man courting a young woman he cannot control; and he overdresses appallingly to impress her with his wealth and elegance. Musetta, as we might expect, treats him like a dog—but a pet dog, for she calls him "Lulu" and orders him to sit down as though he were an obstreperous puppy.

Seeing Marcel at the next table, Musetta begins to show off in an attempt to catch his eye; Marcel refuses to look, but goes on with his conversation in which he describes to his friends the type of woman Musetta is: her surname is Temptation and she is a bird of prey whose staple diet is the human heart. Marcel's recital is accompanied by the first appearance of the theme most closely associated with Musetta, which, like others we have already heard, is used to great dramatic effect in the last act:

(The orchestration of the whole of this scene from Musetta's entry onwards is worth careful study for the expertness of Puccini's writing for wood-wind and horns, which between them give the music character which is indeed *brillante* and coloured *con fuoco*.)

Suddenly there is a loud crash of breaking china; Musetta, thinking at least that Marcel will look up now, has dashed her plateful of food on the floor, crying that it is nothing but old cooked-up hash. Still Marcel does not look up—which is a pity, for he is missing a great deal of the comedy which delights his companions and mortifies the unfortunate Alcindoro.

Finally, Musetta stands up and sings her favourite Waltz Song: "Quando me'n vo' . . . ." ("As I wander through the streets the people turn to admire my beauty . . . and this makes me happy."):*

58
Tempo di valzer lento

Quan - - do me'n vo',   quando me'n vo' so - let-ta per la via

While Musetta is singing it is obvious that Marcel is having a great struggle to remain indifferent to her. Alcindoro, whose part is by tradition always "doubled" with that of Bénoit in Act I, interrupts her in vain; Musetta is in full cry and nothing can stop her. Rudolph and Mimi carry on with a little love-scene of their own, Schaunard and Colline rise from the table to get a better view, and the scene works up in an ensemble in which only Marcel of the principals takes no part.

Suddenly Musetta screams, pretending that her shoe is pinching her badly. She takes it off, gives it to Alcindoro and sends him away to a shoemaker's to fetch another pair. Reluctantly, and muttering about his public position, Alcindoro trots off.

Almost with Musetta's first feigned cry of pain Marcel (who is greatly perturbed by her shrieks) begins to sing the tune of the Waltz, to suitably modified words: "You are not dead, my youth—if you were to beat at my door my heart would open it." Another ensemble is built up reaching its climax with Alcindoro's departure, which is the signal for the reunion of Marcel and Musetta who embrace "con grande entusiasmo". "And now," remarks Schaunard, "we are at the last scene."

At this moment a waiter appears at the Bohemians' table and presents a bill. It is an awkward situation. Although Schaunard made his appearance in the first act with a windfall from the musical Milord, and (according to custom) the money has been shared equally among the four friends, not a penny now remains between them. Rudolph spent his share on Mimi's bonnet, Schaunard bought a French horn and a pipe, while Colline, in addition to having his overcoat mended, also bought his rare book of runic grammar. Exactly what Marcel did with his share of the money is never explained, for he is not noticed to buy anything at any time; he does not complain that he has been robbed, nor have we seen him give it away, in a fit of seasonal generosity, to the promenading girls

---

* Puccini thought of the tune of the Waltz Song before any words had been written for it. He advised his librettists that he wanted a lyric to fit the rhythm of "cocolico—cocolico—bistecca"—which can be paraphrased as "cockadoodle-doo, a-doodle-doo, and beefsteak".

he dallies with at the start of the act. It is just possible that the librettists forgot Marcel's share of the windfall altogether—a lapse of what is called "continuity" which would not happen in a film studio. But whatever the answer to the mystery, Marcel's assets are also nil and the four Bohemians are faced with a large bill and no means of paying it.

Musetta comes to the rescue, however, by asking for her bill. She looks at it and then tells the waiter to add the Bohemians' bill to it and give the total amount to be dealt with by Alcindoro on his return.

The whole of this scene, from the waiter's presentation of the bill to the fall of the curtain is sung against a background of a military band of fifes (4 piccolos), six trumpets, and six side drums (tuned in B flat), which is heard approaching from the distance. This music and its dramatic treatment is a direct descendant of the famous fife-and-drum sequence in the first act of *Carmen*. As in the earlier opera the sound of the band attracts a crowd of small boys, together with every other kind of person within earshot. In the 19th century the small military band seems to have had the drawing power with the public that a good street accident has in our own time. The crowd gets excited from the first moment it hears:

59

The Bohemians and their two girl friends are also unable to resist the call of this music, and join the crowd. Musetta, having only one shoe, is carried on the shoulders of Marcel and Colline—a sight which causes the crowd to cheer their popular favourite. Rudolph and Mimi follow arm-in-arm, while Schaunard plays an inaudible accompaniment to the band on his horn.

As the crowd marches behind the band, which has crossed the stage and is now receding in the distance, the voices of all four Bohemians (Schaunard has given up the unequal struggle) are singing the praises of Musetta, "the pride and glory of the Latin Quarter".

The curtain falls when Alcindoro returns to find Musetta and her companions gone and the waiter presenting an enormous bill. Alcindoro, "stupefied and astounded", collapses speechless into a chair.*

Strictly speaking the entire second act of *La Bohème* might be omitted altogether without affecting the course of the plot in any way. It serves dramatically to give us a further glimpse of Rudolph and Mimi in love (though without a hint of Mimi's consumption), to introduce us to Musetta, and let us know that Mimi has been bought a bonnet and that

* I was myself not a little stupefied and astounded to see a performance of *La Bohème* by an English company in which Alcindoro's embarrassment on his return was witnessed by the four Bohemians and the girls who came back to watch the effect of their ruse from a safe distance out of his sight on the stage. The stage instructions in the score state quite clearly what should happen at the end of the second act. However, this production was one of those "breaks with tradition" of which English operatic producers are so fond. It made utter nonsense of the curtain.

Colline has had an old coat mended—two articles of clothing which play a touching part in the last act, but whose existence and sentimental importance we could take for granted without having to trace them back so far. Similarly, the progress of the Mimi-Rudolph love affair (now less than an hour old) might be left to our imagination, while Musetta, who admittedly plays an important part later in the story, could surely have been shown to the audience without raising production costs by the introduction of stage bands, a huge chorus and an army of supernumeraries.

Thank heaven, however, the composer and his librettists resisted all temptation to get on with the story for a full 20 minutes, and by doing so they gave us 20 minutes of unadulterated gaiety and colour and delightful irrelevance which have no equal in the operatic repertoire. Even the gaiety of the first act of *Carmen* is not sustained to the same extent, for sex rears its ugly head before long and Bizet is forced to get on with the plot.

There is not a single expendable bar in the second act of *La Bohème*. It is a perfect example of fun for fun's sake; and that is not anything you come across every day of the week in the opera house.

ACT III

Scene: The Toll-Gate (La Barrière d'Enfer). Beyond the toll-gate, the outer boulevard; in the background, the main road to Orleans which is half hidden by tall houses and the mists and fogs of February. On the left is a small tavern ("Cabaret") with a small open space in front of the toll-gate. On the right, the Boulevard d'Enfer; on the left, the Boulevard St Jacques. Also on the right, the entrance of the Rue d'Enfer leading to the Latin Quarter.

Outside the tavern, as an inn-sign, hangs Marcel's picture, "The Passage of the Red Sea", but underneath it, in large letters, are the words "Au Port de Marseille." On either side of the door are frescoes of a Turk and a Zouave with a huge laurel wreath round his fez. Light shines from the ground floor of the tavern, which faces the toll-gate.

Tall grey and gaunt plane-trees flank the open space in front of the gate and lead diagonally towards the two boulevards. Between each pair of trees is a marble bench. It is the end of February and the ground is covered with snow.

The curtain rises at once on two rapid *ff* notes from the full orchestra to show the scene in the dim light of the earliest dawn. Seated in front of a brazier is a group of drowsing customs officers. From the tavern at intervals come laughter, shouts and the clinking of glasses. A customs officer comes out of the tavern with wine. The toll-gate is closed.

Though the curtain rises on the first notes from the orchestra the first three minutes or so of the scene may well be regarded as a vocal and instrumental prelude to Act III. The scene is set in terms of music, and the only real difference between Puccini's preliminary scene-setting and that of most other composers is that the curtain is raised and we can see as well as hear what it is all about.

And what a brilliant and tremendously effective passage of scene-setting it is! All the coldness of a Paris winter's dawn is suggested in the course of a few bars for flutes and harp:

This icicle-like sound then gives way to a simple little tune on the harp, in which Puccini makes most telling use of the triangle:

A band of scavengers appears behind the toll-gate, stamping their feet, blowing on their frost-bitten hands and shouting for the customs officers to open the gate. The *douaniers* do not move; the shouts are repeated, and eventually one sleepy officer gets up and unlocks the gate. The scavengers come in and disappear into the Rue d'Enfer; the gate is closed once more.

Next, from the tavern, we hear the sound of women's voices (with a percussion accompaniment of glasses) singing the tune first played on the solo harp (Ex 61). This phrase leads to fourteen bars from Musetta, who sings a snatch of her Waltz Song, a performance rounded off by a few bars from the men and general joyous laughter. (Like the title of Marcel's picture, the words of Musetta's song have been altered and now run: "If there is pleasure to be found in the glass, there is love in young lips.")

The orchestral contribution to the whole of this "prelude" is one of remarkable simplicity—a flute, a harp, a stroke on the triangle, a high sustained note on the piccolo and the unchanging tremolo of the violoncellos; it is a little masterpiece of restraint and imaginative certainty of touch. A sudden *fortissimo* brings a modulation, the violoncellos continue their tremolo (marked *pppp*) and a return to the "icicle music" of the beginning introduces a further set of characters at the toll-gate.

A sergeant comes out of the tavern and orders the gate to be opened to let in milk-sellers, carters and peasant women bringing their goods to market. They pay duty at the customs and, after arranging when they will meet again, disappear towards the city by various routes.

This effective and "atmospheric" prelude, with its neat, subdued cross-section of Parisian types and the characteristic thumbnail *genre* sketch which Puccini always included in those operas of his set in France, comes to an end when we hear the strings play the opening phrase of "Mi chiamano Mimì" (Ex 51). The whole mood changes at once as Mimi enters from the Rue d'Enfer. She looks around anxiously as if she did not know where she was, and when she reaches the first plane tree she is seized by a violent fit of coughing. She recovers herself, and seeing the sergeant asks him if the tavern is the one where a painter is working. The sergeant replies that it is. A servant girl comes out of the tavern and Mimi asks her to take a message to Marcel, telling him that she is waiting outside for him.

It is now daylight, a sad, foggy winter's day. More people pass through the toll-gate and one or two couples leave the tavern. The bells of the Hospice Marie Thérèse are heard sounding the matins. Marcel comes out of the tavern, surprised to find Mimi outside waiting for him.

Mimi is greatly relieved to have found Marcel again. It seems that he and Musetta have been living at the "Port de Marseille" for a month; he paints murals while Musetta teaches singing to any and everybody who visits the tavern. Marcel suggests that Mimi should come indoors, out of the cold, but she refuses when he tells her that Rudolph is there. "Why not?" asks Marcel, who is understandably puzzled.

Mimi explains, and she does so to the first really passionate—as distinct from sentimental—music we have heard so far in *La Bohème*. Mimi's passion is a mixture of love and despair, which she expresses in the kind of phrase which we now hear for the first time:

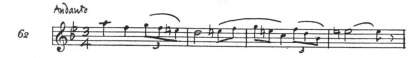

She tells Marcel that Rudolph loves her but that he is insanely jealous. What is she to do? Marcel advises her that the best thing to do is to give up living with Rudolph and to leave him for good.

Mimi agrees, whereon Marcel says that he will go and wake Rudolph and tell him.

"Wake him?" asks Mimi.

"He fell asleep an hour before dawn," replies Marcel, and he motions Mimi to look through the window of the tavern. Mimi is now coughing unceasingly and she remarks to Marcel that Rudolph's behaviour on top of it all is almost too much too bear; he had left her that very night saying that all was over between them.

Rudolph is now seen by Marcel to be stirring. Marcel begs Mimi to go home and not to make a scene.* He gently pushes her to the corner of the tavern, which she peers round at once as Rudolph comes out.

Having heard one side of the question, Marcel now hears the other as Rudolph tells his version of the story—of how heartless and flirtatious Mimi can be. Marcel does not believe him, and Rudolph admits that he doesn't honestly know what to think. He loves Mimi, but he is afraid.

Mimi, overhearing all this, comes closer under cover of the trees and then hears Rudolph say: "Mimi is seriously ill, and grows worse every day. The poor child is dying." He sings this in a monotone against a figure which is very typical of Puccini—

—a musical characteristic we heard first in *Manon Lescaut* (Ex 36) and which we hear again frequently in moments of sorrow in later Puccini operas.

Rudolph goes on to describe the symptoms of Mimi's illness to a

* The actual words in the libretto are "Now go home, Mimi, for charity's sake. Don't make scenes here." In his recorded version Toscanini—or somebody—has modified this to the gentler: "Return home and I'll speak to him. Later I will tell you everything", which is more in keeping with Marcel's kindliness than the gruff and unmannerly impatience of the original words in the score.

broad, sobbing and not very distinguished tune, marked to be played *con stanchezza* ("with tiredness"), which can deteriorate very easily into caricature if it is dawdled over too long:

Every detail of Rudolph's description is heard by Mimi from her hiding place; he finally blames himself, his poverty and his squalid lodgings for the turn her illness has taken. "Love alone is not enough to bring her back to life," he sings.

Mimi's coughs and sobs as she listens to Rudolph give her presence away; Rudolph turns round and rushing towards her he takes her in his arms. Marcel leaves the scene at this point as he hears Musetta laughing loudly inside the tavern in a manner which suggests she is up to some mischief or other. Mimi and Rudolph are left alone.

There now follows what is customarily called "Mimi's Farewell". To music consisting mainly of fragments and tunes already heard in earlier scenes, she frees herself from Rudolph's embrace and develops the familiar theme of "These Foolish Things"—would he please wrap up her belongings and leave them with the porter—the gold bracelet, the prayer book he gave her. And the bonnet he bought her on Christmas Eve; it is under the pillow; perhaps he would like to keep it to remind him of their love affair? It must be a parting without bitterness, says Mimi—"Addio senza rancor"—and she starts to sing a farewell to the things that have meant so much in their lives: "Addio, dolce svegliare alla mattina . . ." ("Farewell to that sweet awakening in the morning . . ."):*

In this duet, which is not a love duet or even a duet of reconciliation, but a farewell duet, we are back in the tender vein of the first act; there is indeed no bitterness, but a great deal of sadness. We hear the Mimi and Rudolph we first knew, still young and romantically endearing; but they are now a wiser couple and the whole scene has a strangely moving quality of melancholy and nostalgic regret that such things cannot go on for ever.

The duet becomes a quartet suddenly when Marcel and Musetta appear on the scene and continue a quarrel which obviously began inside the tavern. Mimi and Rudolph continue in their own sweetly oblivious way while the other two, in some admirably characterized music, snap

* This tune was originally a "mattinata" called *Sole e amore* which Puccini wrote for a Genoese musical journal in 1888.

angrily at each other. It is an ingenious and happy musical blending of romance and comedy.

The quartet becomes a duet again when Musetta shouts a couple of final insults from the steps of the tavern and Marcel chases her as she runs inside.

The final phrases before the curtain falls are quite exquisitely scored. As at the end of Act I the orchestra is reduced to almost chamber-music dimensions—a solo violin, a solo violoncello, the rest of the strings limited to a single player from each desk, an oboe echoing wistfully and remotely the little phrase of four notes with which the opera begins, and the harp with an important and telling solo part of considerable variety—it is a magical accompaniment for Mimi and Rudolph who, with that incomprehensible lack of logic peculiar to the young in love, disappear into the distance, arm-in-arm, vowing eternal fidelity and saying farewell in the same breath.

The puzzling end to this scene may, on first encountering it, seem a typically operatic inconsistency: in fact, it is a characteristic comment on Real Life made with a touch of genius which makes the end of this third act of *La Bohème* one of the most unashamedly sentimental and irresistibly captivating moments in all opera. To anybody who has ever been in love Puccini has set the whole perplexing business to music in the last few pages of this third act.

ACT IV

Scene: The same as Act I.

The curtain rises at once on a slightly louder and more fully-scored version of the "Bohemians' theme" than that which began Act I (Ex 38). Marcel and Rudolph are discovered at work—Marcel in front of his easel, Rudolph at his writing table. Each is trying to pretend to the other that he is working hard, whereas, in fact, they are both distracted and gossiping, for Marcel is thinking of Musetta and Rudolph longs for Mimi.

The scene, which takes place some months after the action of Act III, opens with two neatly symmetrical sequences. In the first Marcel learns that Rudolph has seen Musetta riding around in a carriage and pair. The forced laughter and feigned indifference of his reaction to this news is entirely unconvincing and Rudolph notices as much in an aside. It is then Marcel's turn to tell Rudolph that he has seen Mimi driving around, dressed like a queen. Rudolph's protest that he is glad to hear it is as unconvincing as his friend's had been and is greeted with the same kind of aside by Marcel. They both return feverishly to work for a few moments, to the tune of the "work theme" in Act I (Ex 44).

But this sudden industry does not last long. Rudolph cries that his pen won't write; Marcel complains that his brush is awful and without Rudolph noticing it, takes a silk ribbon from his pocket and kisses it. Rudolph is lost in his own thoughts and soliloquizes: "O Mimì, tu più non torni . . ." ("You do not return, Mimi, nor those lovely days . . ."):

The tune is taken up by Marcel and the result is a charming duet in which the two men sing reflectively of their respective loves. Marcel puts away the silk ribbon and stares at his canvas; Rudolph takes Mimi's bonnet from the drawer of his table and presses it to his heart. (Rudolph didn't leave the bonnet with the concièrge, after all.) The scene is rounded off by a wistful little orchestral epilogue in which a solo violin and a solo violoncello echo the opening tune of the duet two octaves apart against a characteristically-scored background of harp and four wood-wind instruments in which the bass part is supplied by bass clarinet. There is an odd absence of any great suggestion of grief in the music, and the general effect is one of it'll-all-come-right-in-the-end.

From this point onwards Puccini carefully builds up a non-serious atmosphere in the music—a deliberate device to contrast as strikingly as possible with the final tragic ending to the story. Schaunard and Colline, with a return of Schaunard's tune (Ex 40), arrive with the "dinner"—a handful of rolls and a paper bag which contains one salt herring. The four Bohemians sit down to a mock banquet; a carafe of water is placed in Colline's hat which they pretend is an ice bucket. A glass is filled (the only glass they possess) and passed round with great ceremony. It is a scene full of charm and fun in which the wit and gaiety of the libretto is given every chance by the lightness and brilliance of Puccini's orchestration.

In the course of this sequence there is another instance comparable to that in *Manon Lescaut* (Ex 13) of a single phrase making its first appearance to be used with effect on a larger scale in a later work. In this case it is a rapid passage consisting of a melodic and harmonic sequence which became, without alteration, the sinister theme associated with Scarpia and dominating the whole of *Tosca*:

I do not suggest that there is any profound significance in these transformations of fragments into themes, though no doubt the new school of musical psychologists will produce some theory to explain the connection between the four notes played as Schaunard solemnly stands on a chair and raises a glass of water in a mock toast, and the same four notes as used to characterize (and with tremendous effect) a lecherous and sadistic figure in a blood-and-thunder melodrama. I draw attention to them only because they are interesting cases of Puccini's habit of thinking second-thoughts on musical ideas which one cannot honestly say one would ever have noticed but for their eventual application to entirely different circumstances. Whether this process was conscious or unconscious on the part of the composer one cannot possibly tell, of course; but either way it offers an intriguing glimpse of the workings of Puccini's mind even though we shall never know what it was that made him choose precisely those particular and seemingly unpromising fragments of *Manon Lescaut* and *La Bohème* to work on.

After the "banquet" there is dancing—a gavotte, a fandango (ending in Toscanini's recording with an effective but unauthorized "Olé!" from the singers) and a quadrille in which Rudolph, who is in the best of undepressed spirits in this entire Bohemian episode, partners the equally cheerful Marcel, who dances the part of the "lady". An argument about correct procedure in the quadrille interrupts the dance and leads to a duel between Schaunard and Colline to satisfy their honour.

Puccini exploits all his genius for what one may call thumbnail comedy;

he recreates the mood of the first act by deft and brilliant touches and makes his comic effects in the space of a few bars. The gavotte lasts seven bars, the fandango is over and done with in four. Nothing is exaggerated and every point is made with a minimum of effort and a maximum of effect.

The horse-play and the fun are at their height when Musetta appears at the door. The smile goes from the music at once as Musetta says that Mimi is ill and barely able to climb the stairs. Rudolph and Marcel rush to the door to support Mimi as she enters; they lead her towards the bed while Musetta brings her a glass of water. Musetta turns to Marcel and explains that Mimi has left the rich viscount with whom she had been living and asked to be brought back to the attic, to die in the surroundings where she had been so happy with Rudolph.

The music accompanying the greater part of the action from this point onwards is the most poignant in the whole opera, for it consists of echoes of the love-scene in the first act. We hear short phrases associated with Mimi's first timid appearance at the door and the duet which followed, but the phrases are altered and broadened and in some way transformed to take on an almost unbearable quality of pathos. This is the full sadness of Dante's "times of happiness recalled in misery" expressed as only music can express it.

Mimi lies down on the bed and Rudolph draws the coverlet over her. The others discuss what can be done for her; there is no coffee and no wine. She will be dead in half an hour, whispers Schaunard. Mimi says she is feeling cold; if only she had a muff to warm her hands. Rudolph takes her hands in his to warm them, telling her not to talk as it makes her tired. Mimi replies that she has a bit of a cough, that's all; and in a touchingly simple phrase she turns to greet Marcel, Schaunard and Colline, "all here to smile at Mimi" (Mimi has a quaint tendency to talk of herself in the third person):

68

Buon gior- no, Mar- cel - lo, Schaunard, Col- li - ne buon gior-no

The simple effect of this passage is matched by the equally effective simplicity of the orchestral accompaniment—a harp, muted strings in seven parts, a sustained "G" in octaves by piccolo and flute *pppp*, one of the characteristically sure and original Puccini touches in which this last scene is unusually rich.

Musetta takes Marcel on one side and gives him her ear-rings, asking him to go out and sell them in order to buy some medicine and bring back a doctor. Mimi gradually grows drowsy; Rudolph takes a chair and sits beside her. Marcel is about to go out when Musetta stops him. "Listen," she says, "perhaps this is the last time that she'll ever ask for anything. I will come with you and get the muff." Musetta and Marcel leave.

While they have been talking Colline has taken off his overcoat, the one we first heard about on Christmas Eve. He sings a solemn farewell to the rusty old garment in whose pockets he carried about his books of philosophy and poetry:

69

Colline's "Song to the Coat", with its sparing and melancholy accompaniment, has a musical pathos of its own and gives the bass a chance to sing an effective little aria, as a change from the comic part he has had to play so far. But it can be a disturbing element in the drama of *La Bohème*; it depends on how it is sung, on whether the singer treats it as a genuinely sad moment, or whether he introduces a note of mock sorrow into the scene. Puccini himself, although he confessed frankly that he did not regard the aria as more than an expedient to give the bass a chance, makes no suggestion that it should be treated as anything but a serious matter, for he ends this moving little sequence with the phrase which forms—in the same key, with one minor alteration of the ryhthm—the very last bars of the opera:

70

Colline folds up the coat, puts it under his arm and turns to leave; but seeing Schaunard he says quietly: "Let us both do something. I'm going to pawn my coat; you just come with me and leave these two alone." Schaunard, who has been unable to contribute anything useful, understands; to justify his exit he picks up the water bottle and goes out after Colline, closing the door behind him.

Schaunard and Colline leave to a subdued and melancholy version of the theme associated with Schaunard's first boisterous and prosperous entrance in Act 1 (Ex 40).

Mimi opens her eyes, and seeing that everybody has gone, holds out her hand to Rudolph who kisses it. This little bit of action is accompanied by the orchestra playing the "big" tune from the final duet in the first act—Rudolph's "Talor dal mio forziere" (Ex 50).

"Have they gone?" asks Mimi. "I was only pretending to be asleep, so that I could be alone with you."—"Sono andati?"

71

This is the first new theme associated with Mimi to be heard in this act. Like the funeral-march motif in Act III (Ex 63), it is an unmistakable Puccini fingerprint—a fingerprint found in one after another of his operas whose heroines die to the same kind of melodic cadence and the same kind of sad, heart-rending harmony.

A few moments later there is a short reprise of that very same elegiac theme from the third act, as though the composer meant us to associate the two passages. "You are as beautiful as the dawn," says Rudolph. "No," replies Mimi, "you mean beautiful as a sunset."

As she lies in Rudolph's arms, Mimi echoes the words and music of their first meeting—"Mi chiamano Mimì". Rudolph takes the bonnet he had hidden in his breast and places it on Mimi's head. Then with a sudden gaiety, she remembers more details of that meeting, how it was dark so that Rudolph could not see that she blushed as he held her hand under the table when they were looking for the key ("You'd already found the key long before that", she says), and she echoes, like a faint, weak memory, Rudolph's words: "Che gelida manina."

Suddenly Mimi is seized by a spasm of coughing. Schaunard enters, but Mimi assures him that the coughing is nothing; she feels better already. Musetta and Marcel return; Musetta is carrying a muff and Marcel a phial of medicine. Mimi lies back on the bed, but sits up excitedly when Musetta approaches her and she takes the muff with "an almost infantile joy".

Since Mimi's spasm of coughing the music has dropped virtually to a whisper. The echoes of the tunes from the first act are barely audible; two flutes and the harp take us back to "Che gelida manina" with *pppp* quotations:

Two solo muted violins repeat the phrase as Mimi puts her hands in her muff, lies back and rests her cheek against it. She appears to be asleep. Rudolph moves away, motioning the others not to make any noise. He turns to Marcel: "What did the doctor say?" "He will come," replies Marcel.

The air of *silence* created by Puccini in this closing scene, comparable to the silence at the beginning of the last act of *La Traviata*, is now almost uncanny. Rudolph, Marcel, Musetta and Schaunard move about quietly, heating the medicine on a spirit stove, looking occasionally at Mimi. Schaunard goes to the bedside; he returns and whispers hoarsely to Marcel: "She is dead."

Colline enters quietly and puts some money on the table near Musetta. Rudolph, who has been trying to shade Mimi's face from a sudden shaft of sunlight with Musetta's cloak, turns to see Musetta making a sign that the medicine is now ready. As he goes towards her he notices the strange expression on the faces of Schaunard and Marcel. "What does it all mean?" he cries in a speaking voice. "All this coming and going? Why do you look at me like that?" He glances from one to the other. Marcel puts his arm round his shoulder and murmurs "Courage! . . ."

The curtain falls on Rudolph flinging himself grief-stricken beside Mimi's bed as the orchestra ("con tutta forza") plays the theme Mimi sang earlier—"Sono andati?" The music comes to an end with a ff return to the coda of Colline's song (Ex 70) and dies away to a fading ppp.

La Bohème is perhaps Puccini's most nearly perfect opera. It lacks many qualities found elsewhere in his work, but in none of his operas do we find such a concentration of his gifts; his unfailing sense of theatre, his sense of comedy and great musical versatility, his genius for the creation of an instantaneously effective atmosphere and mood, his warm lyrical invention, his unobtrusively original and translucent orchestration—all these are combined so neatly and inevitably that there is not a single bar that can be cut or a note that is false. It is a work of consummate operatic craftmanship applied with a sureness of touch and exhilarating vigour, "coming off" in the theatre in a way equalled by few works in the whole repertoire and surpassed by none.

Above all things, however, there is about *La Bohème*, its charm and warmth, gaiety and genuine pathos, a unique quality deriving from a peculiar authenticity, and the infectious youthfulness of music by a man who remained so happily young in heart, written for an opera about young people. The authenticity of *La Bohème*, in short, is the authenticity of experience for, as I have said, much of it was based on incidents not only in the life of the author of the original novel, but in that of the composer also.

Henri Murger's novel, *Scènes de la Vie de Bohème*, which was first published as a serial in 1848, is so closely based on facts and real characters that in some cases the author barely takes the trouble to change the names. Schaunard, for instance, was modelled on a figure called Schanne. In Murger's original manuscript he was called "Schannard", but a misprint turned him into "Schaunard" in the first instalment so Murger decided to stick to it.

Marcel is a combination of two real characters, both painters, who lived in the Latin Quarter of Paris where Murger spent the first working years of a short life which was ended when he was thirty-eight by a disease aggravated by—of all things—a surfeit of coffee-drinking. One of the models for Marcel was called Tabar, who set out to paint a picture of the Passage of the Red Sea, but had to give up because the cost of models and costumes was beyond his means. Tabar's Red Sea underwent an even stranger transformation than Marcel's. Marcel sold his Red Sea as "Au port de Marseille". Tabar showed his in the Salon of 1842 as "Niobe and her children slain by the arrows of Apollo and Diana".

The character of Rudolph is pure self-portraiture by Murger—even to the un-Bohemian prosperity which Rudolph and Marcel came to share a year after the death of Mimi. Murger's novel was made into a play and was so successful that he was able to leave the Left Bank of the Seine and live in splendour in a smarter part of Paris with a country retreat as well, where he did a lot of shooting. Unlike Puccini he was a very poor shot.

Of the two girls, Mimi and Musetta, who played such a part in the lives of Rudolph and Marcel, Mimi occurred at least three times in Murger's real life, and the name became a kind of generic term for all his young ladies. After the first one, who was really called Mimi, Murger nicknamed the others Mimi in her memory—without, one trusts, letting them know that. What was astonishing, however, was the coincidence that all three of Murger's Mimis should have died of consumption.

According to the aria "They call me Mimi, but my name is Lucia". In the original Murger her name was in fact Lucile, which is near enough; but examined a little more closely we find that Mimi isn't Mimi or Lucile either in the episode used by Puccini. Her name is Francine and the young man is not a poet called Rudolph but a sculptor called Jacques, and the situation and the sad story it leads to—Francine dies of consumption and keeps her hands warm in a muff—is virtually no more than an irrelevant anecdote among Murger's scenes of Bohemian life. Jacques, we are told, knows Rudolph, but we never hear either of him or Francine before or after their moving chapter (they are both dead by the end of it). But many of the chapters in the book are rather like that; they have neat tag-lines worthy of O. Henry and P. G. Wodehouse—not unnaturally, since so much of the action is taken up with the ingenious schemes of the four Bohemians and their friends to make an easy living, and it was only the genius of Puccini, his two librettists and the ever-helpful publisher, Giulio Ricordi, that somehow made a remarkable operatic entity of what is really a rather disjointed prose narrative (the first draft by Giacosa and Illica was in 20 scenes). Above all it was Puccini's music—in a way peculiar to music—which gave the series of episodes the continuity of a formal structure.

Musetta, on the other hand, was always more or less Musetta, leading in real life what was described as an irregular existence in a regular fashion, careful with her money and in the end amassing a vast sum which enabled her to set out from Paris for Algiers to live there with her married sister, taking all her considerable wealth with her in a single trunk. She left Marseilles on the packet-boat Atlas in 1863 and was never heard of again. The Atlas, Musetta, and two hundred other passengers sank without trace in the Mediterranean.

Schaunard, or Alexandre Schanne, was in real life perhaps the most fantastic of the original four Bohemians. He could never make up his mind whether he was a painter or a composer; he played, as he said, "on the hunting horn without being a hunter", and as a result of painting from the top of Notre Dame and seeing so much blue sky became so obsessed with blue in his picture that he composed a work called "Symphony on the Importance of Blue in Art".

Colline, the philosopher, was based on two real people, both authors of books on theology, and one of them the owner of an almost legendary great coat with four pockets always so crammed full of books that they were each called after one of the four public libraries of Paris.

Puccini's own experience of Bohemianism was thorough and first-hand, and in fact also included an episode of having to sell a coat—not quite in the same tragic circumstances as Colline, perhaps, but with physically inconvenient consequences, nevertheless; he sold his coat in the depths of a Milan winter in order to be able to take a young ballerina with an unreasonable appetite out to dinner. That was in his student days when he shared lodgings with Mascagni and learnt at first-hand all the tricks of evasive action against creditors, the burning of manuscripts to keep warm and a dozen other things which he recognized as only-too-familiar experiences when he came to read Murger's novel. At the time he wrote his opera—when he was 38—we know Puccini cultivated a deliberate Bohemianism with his friends in a hut on the lakeside at his home at Torre del Lago—the Club Bohème, which had once been a café whose owner had emigrated to Brazil when Puccini and his other non-paying guests had reduced him to near-bankruptcy. Puccini wrote the greater part of his opera in the noisy club room, where the neo-Bohemians had a set of characteristically boyish rules and regulations like "Silence is strictly forbidden", "The treasurer is empowered to abscond with the funds", and "It is strictly forbidden to play fair".

But the inspiration of the gaiety which emphasizes the tragedy of *La Bohème* was something Puccini drew from his own youth, from experiences which led him to keep what he called a diary of "Bohemian Life" where he entered such items as "Supper for four people: one herring", an incident which went straight into the mock-banquet scene in the last act of the opera. The composer's Bohemian youth is echoed in all the poverty and hand-to-mouth fun and high spirits of the opera's setting, and in the uniquely youthful quality of the music; all that his own experience lacked was a Mimi. But as Verdi said of Shakespeare, to copy reality was good, to invent it was even better. And that is surely what Puccini did with the heroine of *La Bohème*.

TOSCA

(Property of G. Ricordi and Co.)

Melodrama in three acts by Giuseppe Giacosa and Luigi Illica, after the play *La Tosca* by Victorien Sardou. First performed at the Teatro Costanzi, Rome, on 14th January, 1900. First performance in England: Covent Garden, 12th July, 1900. First performance in the United States: New York, 4th February, 1901.

T wo factors originally contributed to Puccini's choice of Sardou's *La Tosca* as an operatic subject—the third opera in a row to be based on a French "original". Shortly after finishing *Edgar* (1889) the composer saw a performance of the play by Sarah Bernhardt in Milan, and though he understood not a word of French he sensed that here was a highly dramatic subject which would translate effectively into the operatic medium. A little later, Puccini heard that Verdi had had an idea to use Sardou's play as an opera but had felt that he was too old to set about it.

The combination of these two circumstances fired Puccini with enthusiasm for the subject; but he hesitated to begin work on the opera and the idea was forgotten until after the launching of *La Bohème*. Even then the matter might not have been revived in Puccini's mind had he not suddenly come to hear of a *Tosca* actually being composed by a composer called Alberto Franchetti to a libretto by Luigi Illica.

From then on Puccini's whole energy was concentrated on making certain that he and nobody else should have *Tosca*. This time, however, there were no acrimonious scenes between composers, as there had been over *La Bohème*. Illica and Giulio Ricordi, who was not only Puccini's publisher but also Franchetti's, went about things in a much more subtle way. They *talked* Franchetti out of *Tosca* by telling him what an unsuitable subject it was, how the libretto was "too political", and that the whole idea could end in nothing but artistic and financial catastrophe.

Franchetti, by the time this blatant piece of sharp practice had been performed, was almost pleased to be rid of *Tosca* and inclined to consider that he had had a narrow escape from disaster. The day after Franchetti (who, ironically, had been a pupil of Puccini's father) renounced his claim Puccini signed a contract with Ricordi for a three act opera to be called *Tosca*.

But the completion of the *Tosca* we know today took a considerable time. As he had done in the case of *Manon Lescaut* and *La Bohème* Puccini again worried his librettists as a terrier worries a rat; he cut, he added, he altered, he rewrote until the final text was barely recognizable as having any connection with the first draft of the same name. Puccini found, above all, that his collaborators had to be watched with the greatest possible care or they would introduce quite ridiculous operatic conventions at the

least appropriate moments. Thus Giacosa and Illica proposed that a
formal quartet should be sung while Cavaradossi is being tortured.
Perhaps the young Verdi could have made something of the idea, but
Puccini was a *verista* and his conception of effective dramatic realism was
utterly irreconcilable with the use of any music or musical form which did
not have a direct bearing on the action.

It is impossible not to speculate on .what kind of a *Tosca* Verdi would
have produced if he had ever come to consider the idea more closely.
Personally, I believe he would have changed his mind and dropped the
subject when he really began to think about it, for not even Verdi, I feel
sure, could ever have breathed musical life into the puppet-like characters
of the story. Puccini's description of *Tosca* as a "melodrama in three
acts" is a much more apt description of the opera than at first appears,
for of all Puccini's operas *Tosca* is the only one in which the music seems
to *accompany*, instead of spring from, the action.

The listener hearing *Tosca* for the first time, therefore, must not expect
to find an opera with the captivating and companionable appeal of *La
Bohème*. There are many fine moments in *Tosca*, both lyrical and dramatic,
and it is a work put together with all the skill of a master-craftsman of the
musical theatre; but the characters very rarely excite our sympathy as
they do in *La Bohème*. Scarpia, Tosca and Cavaradossi are stock types,
representing respectively cruelty and lust, love and jealousy, youth and
enthusiasm; we never really care what happens to them because however
realistically they are portrayed we never quite believe in them.

And yet *Tosca* is a fascinating opera, having the fascination perhaps of
a murder trial which holds our attention from beginning to end for the
very reason that it is so far removed from our own lives and experience.
But as in a murder trial there are moments in *Tosca* when we do feel a
little sympathy for the leading characters of the drama; and it is significant that these moments are the occasion for the only popular arias
in the opera: Tosca's "Vissi d'arte" and Cavaradossi's "E lucevan le
stelle".

In these two passages Puccini interests us in his characters and for a
period they become human beings whose feelings we can understand
when we see them in situations (from which heaven preserve the rest of
us) that are none the less real for being unusual.

Like *La Bohème* before it, *Tosca* was not immediately successful with the
public. But whereas *La Bohème* took two months to make its indelible
mark, *Tosca* took only two performances. The first performance, however,
was as nearly disastrous as can be imagined, but what was later proved to
have been more comedy than tragedy was also shown to have had
nothing to do with the quality of the music or the public's appreciation
of it. The farcical situation which led to the curtain being rung down when
it had scarcely been rung up on Act I, the panic created in the mind of
the unhappy conductor (again Mugnone, who had been concerned with
the famous Palermo *Bohème* referred to on page 52), by the mysterious
police warning of bombs that were to be thrown in the theatre—it was a

hilarious and typical combination of those familiar natural hazards to which the most fascinating of all forms of entertainment is constantly subjected.*

* The detailed story of the notorious *Tosca* première in Rome is unfortunately too long to repeat here. The incident is reported at greater length, however, in the chapter on the Teatro dell'Opera in *Great Opera Houses*, pp. 171-3.

CHARACTERS IN ORDER OF APPEARANCE:

CESARE ANGELOTTI, *an escaped political prisoner*   *Bass*

THE SACRISTAN .   .   .   .   . *Baritone*

MARIO CAVARADOSSI, *a painter* .   .   . *Tenor*

FLORIA. TOSCA, *a celebrated singer* .   .   . *Soprano*

BARON SCARPIA, *Chief of Police* .   .   . *Baritone*

SCIARRONE, *a gendarme* .   .   .   . *Bass*

SPOLETTA, *a police agent* .   .   .   . *Tenor*

A SHEPHERD BOY .   .   .   .   . *Boy's voice*

A GAOLER .   .   .   .   .   . *Bass*

A cardinal, a judge, Roberti (an executioner), a scribe, an officer, a sergeant, soldiers, police agents, ladies, noblemen, citizens.

Scene: Rome.   Time: June, 1800

ACT I

Scene.: The church of Sant'Andrea della Valle. The Attavanti Chapel is on the right. To the left, a scaffolding, a dais, an easel supporting a large picture covered by a cloth. Beside the easel are various painter's materials and a basket of food.

The curtain rises after these bars from the orchestra:

The *fff* statement of this theme, which will be recognized as having its origin in the last act of *La Bohème* (Ex 67), is one of the most superbly arresting beginnings to an opera to be found in the entire repertoire. It is a theme which characterizes the evil genius of Scarpia and in one form or another dominates the opera as the figure of Scarpia dominates the story even after his death in Act II.

Angelotti enters the empty church hurriedly. He has escaped from a prison in the Castel Sant'Angelo; he is harassed and dishevelled, he is wearing prison clothes and almost breathless with fear. He looks anxiously around him and catches sight of a pillar-shrine containing an image of the Virgin. " 'At the feet of the Madonna' is what my sister wrote", Angelotti says to himself. He searches feverishly beneath the feet of the image but finds nothing. He looks again and after a moment's despair discovers the key and takes it to open the gates of the Attavanti Chapel (his sister is the Marchesa Attavanti) and disappears inside it, closing the gates behind him.

This opening sequence is largely built round an urgent, syncopated theme on which the curtain rises and which is associated in this act with Angelotti:

As there is more "business" than singing in this first scene the musical interest is almost entirely orchestral; and as usual, it is rich in details of typical Puccini orchestration, especially in the writing for wood-wind which is well worth the student's careful study, for the composer's characteristic use of the bass clarinet first encountered in *Manon Lescaut*.

The stage remains empty for a few moments after Angelotti's disappearance into the Chapel until the Sacristan enters. The Sacristan is a small, ridiculous figure given to muttering to himself—a curious (perhaps occupational?) habit I have noticed among sacristans—and he suffers from a nervous tic that causes him to twitch at moments which, like the pinches of snuff he takes, are carefully indicated in the score. The Sacristan also has his own theme, a sprightly, fussy little tune very much in keeping with his character:

Although neither of the themes quoted immediately above has the dramatic significance of the sinister Scarpia phrase, it is by the neat interweaving and development of fragmentary tunes such as these that Puccini keeps the musical continuity of his melodramatic commentary going. Perhaps because *Tosca* is fundamentally an artificial drama in which the chief characters are types instead of convincing human beings as they are in *La Bohème*, Puccini seems to have been far more preoccupied with the formal mechanics of the music in this score than in any other he ever wrote. The composer, as though despairing of finding the inspiration of genuine human emotion in the creatures of his libretto, resorts to endless intriguing manipulations of his themes. He contracts and extends, inverts and contorts them, adds piquant harmonic and orchestral colouring, varies their tempi and rhythms; he makes effective use, in short, of the stock-in-trade of symphonic writing, but without for a moment being side-tracked by what he is doing to lose sight of his dramatic objective. On the contrary, Puccini's ingenious treatment of his themes is one of the elements which gives this opera its peculiar dramatic tensity and excitement.

The Sacristan makes his entrance holding a bundle of paint brushes and moaning that however often he washes them they are still as filthy as a choirboy's collar. He is surprised to see that there is nobody on the dais; he looks inside the basket and sees that the food has not been touched. The Angelus rings and the Sacristan kneels and prays out loud in a monotone to a rather undistinguished Andante religioso for three flutes, harp and string quartet in F—a key Puccini often associated with religious music, for it plays a great part in the hymn and prayer sequences of *Suor Angelica*.* The Sacristan is discovered on his knees by Cavaradossi, who enters a few moments later.

* There is in the Museum of La Scala in Milan the manuscript of the beginning of a Requiem by Puccini which is also in F, written in 1905 in memory of Verdi.

Cavaradossi mounts the dais and uncovers the picture, and as he does so we have one of those characteristic first hints of themes heard later in a fuller form which abounded in *Manon Lescaut*. In this case the listener already familiar with *Tosca* will recognize a brief anticipation of the theme in Ex 81. Whether one is familiar with *Tosca* or not, however, it is never quite clear what that later tune, which is associated—one would have thought exclusively—with the love of Tosca and Cavaradossi, is doing in the present context, for the picture the painter uncovers is an unfinished painting of Mary Magdalene with wide blue eyes and a mass of golden hair. The Sacristan has evidently not seen the picture properly before, for he remarks with surprise that, by all the holy ampullas, it is "her" portrait.

"Whose?" asks Cavaradossi.

"Why, that unknown lady who has been here praying so often recently."

The painter explains that while the unknown woman had been praying he had painted her portrait—a confession which scandalizes the Sacristan into a sudden fever of brush-washing and embarrassed, but helpful, activity.

Cavaradossi starts to work on his picture, comparing the portrait now and then with a miniature which he takes from his pocket. As he works he sings one of those arias which Puccini, like Verdi, delighted in introducing so early in their operas that the late-comer who is only five minutes late can miss them altogether. "Questa o quella" and "Celeste Aida" are never referred to again, and neither is this first song by Cavaradossi, "Recondita armonia . . ." ("Strange harmony of contrasts . . .").

In this aria, of which the harmony is anything but recondite, Cavaradossi compares the beauty of his unknown Mary Magdalene and Tosca —the one with blue eyes, the other with black; but in a phrase leading to a high and stimulating B flat, he tells us that his only thoughts are of Tosca. Like so many Puccini arias this begins almost in a monotone before it blossoms out into a characteristic lyrical tune:

76
Andante lento

The Sacristan mutters a great deal through this aria, but confines his comments mostly (though not entirely) to those moments when the tenor is not singing. When, as often happens, "Recondita armonia" is encored in the theatre, it may be noticed that the Sacristan keeps his mouth shut during the repeat and lets the tenor have the field to himself.

At the end of the aria the Sacristan mumbles and crosses himself. He is a pessimistic character, like most sacristans one encounters, and his life-long motto has obviously always been, "No good will come of this, mark my words." He informs Cavaradossi that he is going to leave the church, that the basket of food has not been touched, and asks the painter please to lock up when he goes.

The Sacristan shuffles off with his little tune tripping after him.

Angelotti, thinking the church is empty, unlocks the gates of the Chapel, but, seeing the painter, is about to take refuge again when he recognizes him. "Cavaradossi! Don't you recognize me? Has prison changed me so much?"

"Angelotti!" cries Cavaradossi. "The Consul of the short-lived Roman republic!" (This ham-handed phrase is the first indication of the identity of Angelotti and it is very helpful if we are to understand the political background of the story.) Angelotti, overjoyed at finding Cavaradossi, tells him how he escaped from the Castel Sant'Angelo and we hear the first suggestion of another theme associated with the fugitive which comes to play an important part in the pattern of the music a little later in the scene:

Angelotti's conversation with Cavaradossi is interrupted by a woman's voice heard outside calling "Mario!" It is Tosca come to see Cavaradossi. The painter explains that she is a very jealous woman and suggests that Angelotti should hide in the Chapel again, taking the basket of food with him until Tosca has left, which (Cavaradossi expects) will not be very long. Angelotti, who is exhausted and very hungry, takes the basket and goes back into the Chapel.

Cavaradossi opens the church door and Tosca enters to a solo flute and a solo violoncello playing this tune two octaves apart with a pizzicato arpeggio accompaniment:

Tosca looks around suspiciously. She refuses Cavaradossi's embrace, wants to know why the church was shut, whom he was speaking to and the name of the woman whose swishing skirts she had heard clearly from outside. Cavaradossi has answers to all these questions, though they do not convince Tosca. He tries again to kiss her, but she will not let him; instead she decorates a statue of the Madonna with flowers. As she does so she suggests that she and Cavaradossi should spend the night at their country cottage. Tosca has to sing in the evening, but it is a short performance; they could leave early.

Cavaradossi, his mind clearly on other things, is very off-hand with his answers and Tosca reproves him, telling him to pay attention. She then sings of the joys of their life together: does not Mario long for the peace and quiet of the hideaway, of—the word is actually in the Italian libretto —the "nest" which is sacred to them?

Tosca's recital is not passionate. It is rather matter-of-fact and set to what one may call Puccini's special "lovers' conversational" music, which was first encountered when Mimi lost her door key in the first act of *La Bohème*:

Cavaradossi finally succumbs to the attraction of Tosca's suggestion. She rests her head on his shoulder sentimentally while he looks anxiously towards the Attavanti Chapel.

"And now let me work," he says. Tosca is a little surprised by her lover's peremptoriness but prepares to leave in a fairly good humour. As she goes, however, she turns to look at Cavaradossi and sees his painting. She returns hurriedly and in great agitation.

"Who is that blonde woman?" she demands angrily.

"The Magdalene. Do you like it?"

After a moment's thought Tosca recognizes the face of the Marchesa Attavanti. She grows suspicious at once and accuses Cavaradossi of being in love with his model. Cavaradossi begins by teasing Tosca, but on seeing that she is desperately serious, tries to explain that he has never even met the Marchesa. Tosca calms down after a while but still cannot take her eyes off the picture; she continues to stare at it even when Cavaradossi takes her hands and swears that no eyes in the world are so beautiful as hers—"Qual occhio al mondo . . .?":

This tune begins a love duet in which Tosca begs her lover's forgiveness for tormenting him. Cavaradossi reproves her good-humouredly and the incident is forgotten in a typical surging passage of Puccini love music which plays a big part later in the opera:

For the sake of reference this tune may be called simply the Love Theme.

The duet ends with Tosca leaving the church with a final kittenish remark about the picture, followed by the cadence of the Love Theme, played by strings *sul ponticello* to sound, as the composer indicates in the score, "like the rustle of a skirt". Cavaradossi stands thinking for a few moments; then, remembering Angelotti, he goes over to the Chapel and tells him the coast is clear. Angelotti explains that his sister, the Marchesa Attavanti, has left him some women's clothes with which to disguise himself; it is a complete outfit, including a veil and a fan, and he proposes to make use of it after dark.

Cavaradossi, however, suggests a better plan. He gives Angelotti a key to his villa and tells him to go there at once; he can get there easily by going through a door leading out of the Chapel and following a rough path across some fields. Once at the villa Angelotti can hide in a well in a garden and be quite safe. The orchestral accompaniment to this sequence includes a remarkable passage of *pp* scoring for oboe, three flutes, bassoon, celeste, harp, timpani and double bass which gives the familiar progression of Scarpia chords, played three times, a new and uncannily sinister quality. It is quite astonishing, indeed, how strongly conscious of Scarpia's character Puccini has made us from the very outset of the opera by the use of this simple and uncannily evil motif. Long before we meet him in person we have developed an almost physical loathing and terror of this sinister figure.

Cavaradossi's instructions are interrupted by the sound of a cannon shot from the Castel Sant'Angelo signalling that Angelotti's escape has been discovered. Angelotti bids a hasty farewell, but Cavaradossi says he will go with him, and they leave hurriedly together.

As soon as they are gone, the Sacristan rushes in, full of breathless excitement to a loud and elated version of his little tune; but his excited cry of "Glorious news, your Excellency!" falls rather flat when he finds the church deserted.

It is not deserted for long, however, for the Sacristan is followed by a noisy crowd of acolytes and choristers whom he tries in vain to drive into the sacristy to prepare for a special celebration. The crowd is far too excited at the prospect of a double fee for singing a Te Deum and a Gloria in honour of victory over Napoleon to take any notice of the Sacristan.

When the noise is at its height (created by a spirited 6/8 chorus anticipating the joys of a gala performance that night in addition to the Te Deum) Scarpia appears unexpectedly at the doorway of the church. A sudden, frightened silence falls as the orchestra cuts in dramatically with Scarpia's theme. Puccini had a great gift of being able to change the entire mood and atmosphere of a scene within the course of a single bar, and by no more complicated a device than the introduction of an unexpected chord. This harmonic "quick cutting" was encountered in the last act of *La Bohème*, at the entry of Musetta when the mock duel was in progress; it happens again now in *Tosca* with the same lightning and unfailing effect, and it can be as unnerving for the audience as it is intended to be for the crowd on the stage.*

Scarpia's appearance, and his sudden authoritative reproof of the crowd's behaviour in church, is one of the great dramatic entries of opera. In a moment the crowd of choirboys and acolytes has slunk away and Scarpia and his henchman, Spoletta, and a bodyguard of police agents are left in command of the scene. The Sacristan, having tried to creep away with the rest, is recalled sharply by Scarpia.

While Spoletta and the agents search the church, Scarpia tells the Sacristan of the escape of a political prisoner believed to be taking refuge in Sant'Andrea della Valle.

"Where is the Chapel of the Attavanti?" asks Scarpia.

The Sacristan shows him, but finds the gates of the Chapel open and a different key in the lock. Scarpia, who has something of the detective in him, is intrigued by this discovery; he goes into the Chapel, but comes out again, having found nothing of any importance except a woman's fan.

"It was obviously a mistake to fire that cannon," he reflects, "it gave him a chance to escape."

Scarpia plays absent-mindedly with the fan, but as he does so he notices that it is decorated with a coat of arms, the arms of the Attavanti family. He looks around the Church once more, as a matter of police routine, and catches sight of Cavaradossi's painting. He recognizes it as a portrait of the Marchesa Attavanti and asks the Sacristan who painted it. The Sacristan tells him: Il cavalier Cavaradossi.

"Cavaradossi?" says Scarpia to himself. "Tosca's lover. A suspect! *Un volterrian!*"†

Meanwhile one of Scarpia's agents has come out of the Chapel with the basket; it is empty, and the Sacristan is so surprised that Scarpia asks him what is the matter. The Sacristan explains that he left the basket by the easel, full of food for the painter.

"Then he's eaten it," says Scarpia.

"Not in the Chapel," replies the Sacristan. "The Chapel was closed and he didn't have a key."

"Then it was eaten by Angelotti," says Scarpia to himself.

At this moment Tosca enters nervously; she goes to the scaffolding, but

* Those whose acquaintance with *La Bohème* and *Tosca* has been limited to recent television productions of these operas in England will, I fear, have been denied the dramatic impact of the two moments I have mentioned. In the last act of *La Bohème* the viewer was shown Mimi and Musetta climbing the stairs while the mock duel was "out of shot", and in *Tosca* Scarpia was preceded by so many flunkeys and outriders that even the cavorting choirboys would have guessed that something unusual was going to happen, instead of being stopped dead in their tracks by the sudden appearance of Scarpia as Puccini intended. Incredibly, television succeeded in killing two of the most arresting moments in opera absolutely stone dead.

† It is interesting to note that any liberal-minded person opposed to the idea of Scarpia's secret-police government was branded as *un volterriano*—a Voltairian. The phrase does not mean, as the author of a recent American study of Puccini seemed to believe, that Cavaradossi was literally a disciple of Voltaire in addition to being a painter.

failing to find Cavaradossi she searches for him in the church. Scarpia, at the first sight of Tosca, hides behind the pillar on which is the holy water font, motioning the Sacristan to stay where he is. Tosca continues her search and calls "Mario!" The Sacristan tells her that if she means the painter Cavaradossi, then nobody knows where he is; he has vanished as if by magic.

Tosca goes to the holy water stoup to find Scarpia standing beside it holding out his fingers to her after dipping them in holy water. Tosca touches his fingers and crosses herself. Scarpia now sets to work to arouse Tosca's jealousy; he flatters her by saying what a noble example she sets by coming to church to pray. Not like some women, continues Scarpia, pointing to Cavaradossi's picture, who come to meet their lovers in church. Scarpia's insinuation is not lost on Tosca and she demands proof. He shows her the fan, with the Attavanti arms on it, and Scarpia's calculatedly Iago-like trick begins to work. Tosca's jealousy is awakened.

The greater part of this scene in which the thoughts of neither can be considered in any way religious, is played against a *quasi religioso* orchestral background based on a phrase played by bells back stage:

As Tosca's jealousy grows Puccini makes an unexpectedly macabre sound of a whole-tone version of Ex 77 by scoring the phrase for double basses, violoncellos, bass clarinet, oboe and piccolo *ppp* in unison across four octaves. It is a remarkably effective passage full of that sinister quality peculiar to the orchestral colouring of *Tosca*.

With a final and violent oath addressed to the picture—"You shall not have him tonight! I swear it!"—Tosca scandalizes Scarpia (at least, he acts that way) and leaves in tears, hoping to surprise her lover in the arms of another woman. Scarpia accompanies her to the door of the church, pretending to reassure and comfort her.

As soon as Tosca has left the church begins to fill with people coming for the service. Scarpia returns to his favourite pillar and makes a sign which brings Spoletta, the Police Chief's head agent, on to the scene from some hiding place. Spoletta is told to take three agents and a carriage and follow Tosca wherever she goes.

Distant bells ring; the congregation, which is rapidly growing, prepares for the arrival of the Cardinal, and the great final scene of the first act of *Tosca* is under way—a scene which is actually labelled in the score "Finale primo" in the traditional 19th-century manner, the only instance I know of this uncharacteristic formality in Puccini's work. The tolling of the bells forms a kind of ground bass:

On this *ostinato* Puccini builds up a tremendous musical and dramatic climax, beginning with a simple, dignified theme which develops broadly throughout the scene until the last seventeen bars of the score:

The dramatic and musical action is now purely religious. The bells ring, the organ plays, the victorious firing of cannon in the distance punctuates the steady pace of the music, the Cardinal makes his ceremonial entrance accompanied by the Swiss Guard; only Scarpia remains as in a dream, reflecting on the beauty of Tosca and the subtle irony of his plan to possess her and send her lover to his death. The scene builds up in an effortless and relentless manner, the broad pendulating theme dominating the whole sequence, growing in strength at each repetition (with some particularly fine scoring for trumpets and trombones throughout), while Scarpia, realizing that Tosca has made him forget the existence of God, joins in with the choir, four off-stage horns and four off-stage trombones in the last tremendous unison phrase of the Te Deum.

The curtain falls as the orchestra plays Scarpia's own theme.

This final scene of the first act of *Tosca* must rank as one of Puccini's finest achievements; not because we are in any way sentimentally affected by it, but because it is a superb passage of musical drama which reaches its climax at exactly the right moment. Puccini was a master of that unteachable theatrical quality—timing. There is not a single note too many in these final minutes of the act. It would have been difficult to misfire with this sequence, anyway, for the dramatic juxtaposition of sacred and profane love, Scarpia's soliloquized "Go! Tosca!" uttered ironically at the moment he kneels for the entrance of the Cardinal, are among the most effective elements of a drama which, whatever its shortcomings, is one of the most exciting, purely theatrical stories ever set to music. *Tosca*, with all its faults and its lack of genuine human qualities to touch the heart, is first-rate Theatre; and as such, Puccini was perhaps the ideal composer to have set it to music.

ACT II

Scene: The Palazzo Farnese. Scarpia's apartment on the top floor. A table is laid for supper for one. A large window overlooks the courtyard of the Palace. It is night. *

The curtain rises almost at once to disclose Scarpia alone, seated at supper. He interrupts his meal from time to time to reflect; he is agitated and uneasy and frequently looks at his watch. Scarpia's reflections are on the success—so far—of his plan; his agents should have arrested Angelotti and Cavaradossi by now, both of whom will be hanged at dawn, and he is confident that he will win Tosca. The musical background to this opening soliloquy is composed of echoes of three already familiar themes (Exx 77, 80, 81) together with the three-bar orchestral phrase which begins the act—a phrase seemingly associated only with Scarpia's supper and which is never developed in any way, being heard every time it occurs in the act in identically the same time, tempo and harmonic form. Only the orchestration and dynamics vary at all.

Scarpia rings a bell to summon Sciarrone, one of his gendarmes, and asks whether Tosca has arrived at the Palace yet—for the gala performance announced by the Sacristan in Act I. A page has been sent for her; she should be there shortly. On Scarpia's instructions Sciarrone opens the window and the sound of a gavotte (for flute, viola and harp off-stage) is heard coming from the courtyard below where, as only close examination of the stage directions in the score will ever tell us, the Queen is giving an entertainment in honour of General Melas' victory over Napoleon. Sciarrone leaves with a note from Scarpia to be given to Tosca as soon as she arrives.

Alone once more, Scarpia soliloquizes on his peculiarities as a lover, on how he has no time for moonlight and serenades but must get straight to the point. It is an undistinguished kind of Credo to the typically undistinguished kind of music Puccini seemed to reserve for Scarpia in this opera. No villain of an opera surely ever had less memorable music to sing than Scarpia; on the other hand, no villain ever had such an effectively simple and dominating theme for us to remember him by.

Scarpia's reverie is interrupted by the return of Sciarrone bringing Spoletta with him. Spoletta has followed Tosca as instructed; the chase led him to Cavaradossi's villa where he found no signs of Angelotti, but as

---

* The score does not specifically state that the time of the action in Act II is a few hours later than that of Act I, but it is clear from the stage situation that the dramatic construction of *Tosca* keeps very strictly to the Aristotelian unities of time, action and place. The entire action of *Tosca* takes place in considerably less than twenty-four hours.

Cavaradossi's manner was highly suspicious Spoletta had arrested him and brought him to the Palazzo Farnese.

Scarpia walks about the room thoughtfully. Through the open window comes the sound of a cantata with Tosca taking the solo part. While the off-stage singing continues Cavaradossi, accompanied by three guards, the Judge, a Scribe, and Roberti, the executioner, is brought in for interrogation; from the orchestra comes a new and sinister theme played first by flutes in unison:

Like Bizet, Puccini understood the dramatic versatility of the flute and he exploited the lower register of the instrument in a masterly way all through *Tosca* as a means of creating a sinister atmosphere.

Scarpia cross-examines Cavaradossi, but the painter refuses to talk, denying all knowledge of the whereabouts of Angelotti. The sound of the cantata ceases abruptly when Scarpia, irritated by the music, closes the window violently. The ironic juxtaposition of Scarpia's relentless questioning with the gentle elegance of the cantata is now forgotten, and the musical commentary is concentrated entirely on the drama we see before us. A ferocious new theme is heard which makes its effect by the simplest means: by the introduction of the unfailingly sinister interval of the bare augmented fourth:

The interrogation of Cavaradossi continues against the insistent repetition of this phrase until, for the last time, Scarpia demands to know the hiding place of Angelotti.

Tosca now enters, surprised to find Cavaradossi, who whispers a warning not to answer Scarpia's questions. Scarpia turns to Cavaradossi and tells him that the Judge is waiting to take his deposition; Sciarrone opens the door of the torture chamber and Roberti is instructed to "begin with the usual pressure". The Judge goes into the torture chamber; the others follow, leaving Tosca and Scarpia alone on the stage.

From this point on, the second act of *Tosca* develops along the lines of frank but superbly effective grand guignol. With characteristic smoothness Scarpia starts a rather matter-of-fact conversation with Tosca. "We two," he says, "we'll sit down and talk like old friends, shall we?" They sit down together while Scarpia, in a social and conversational way, cross-examines Tosca on what she found at Cavaradossi's villa.

"He was alone," she says.

"Are you sure?" asks Scarpia. "The Marchesa Attavanti wasn't there?"

"No."

Scarpia goes to the door of the torture chamber and calls out to Sciarrone: "What does he say?"

"Nothing," replies Sciarrone.

"In that case," says Scarpia, "we had better press the question."

Tosca tells Scarpia that it is useless to question Cavaradossi—unless, of course, Scarpia wants to hear a lot of lies, if that gives him any pleasure.

"The truth, madam," says Scarpia, "the truth will spare him a most unpleasant hour."

It now dawns on Tosca that something is going on behind the closed doors of the torture chamber. And she learns from Scarpia that her lover is bound hand and foot and that on his brow there is a spiked steel hoop which draws blood every time she refuses to answer.

Scarpia's first intimation that Cavaradossi is being tortured brings another sinister theme from the orchestra, a theme which bears an oddly close resemblance to one associated, twenty-four years later, with torture in *Turandot*:

This menacing theme forms the background of Scarpia's two-way torture—his physical torture of Cavaradossi and his equally effective emotional torture of Tosca. Cavaradossi cries out in agony from the torture chamber; Tosca offers to speak if her lover's suffering is spared. For a brief moment, on Scarpia's orders Cavaradossi is allowed a respite. But he warns Tosca to be silent, and she refuses to answer Scarpia's questions.

Scarpia orders the doors of the torture chamber to be opened so that the cries of the victim can be heard. Tosca's resistance gradually breaks down and she begs Scarpia to stop the torture, with a phrase which occurs with poignant effect in the last act:

As Tosca begins to weaken Scarpia motions Spoletta to open the door of the torture chamber so that she can see inside. She leans against the doorway and pleads with Cavaradossi to let her speak. Her lover refuses angrily: "Stupid! What do you know? What can you say?" Scarpia, the stage instructions tell us, is "highly irritated by Cavaradossi's words, and fearing that they will encourage Tosca to keep silent" shouts to Spoletta to silence the prisoner. There is a terrifying cry from Cavaradossi as the torture is renewed and Tosca finally breaks down: she tells Scarpia that Angelotti is hidden in the well in the garden of Cavaradossi's villa.

Cavaradossi is carried in from the torture chamber and Tosca embraces him, reassuring him that she has not given away any secrets. The music to this little scene is unexpectedly affecting, its softness, and effective orchestral echo of Cavaradossi's "Qual occhio al mondo" (Ex 80) coming like a gentle, moving sigh of relief after the horrors of what has just occurred. For the first time in the opera the listener is confronted with a situation which is genuinely sympathetic.

No sooner has Tosca promised her lover that she has said nothing than Cavaradossi hears Scarpia saying pointedly and clearly to Spoletta: "In the well in the garden—go, Spoletta!"

Cavaradossi turns on Tosca. "You betrayed me!" he cries; but before he can say any more Sciarrone enters bringing the news that General Melas has been defeated. Napoleon has won the battle of Marengo.

Cavaradossi rises to his feet in triumph, crying "Vittoria!" and singing an exultant hymn of praise to liberty:

The sudden introduction of this virile tune into the melodramatic mood of this second act has a startling effect, and for the first time in the opera Cavaradossi becomes a character with personality. It is not a long tune; it certainly is not a good tune; but it has an unexpected excitement about it which suddenly "lifts" the scene in a sensational manner.

Cavaradossi's triumph is short-lived, however. Tosca implores him to be silent; but he ignores her, and Scarpia orders him to be led away to execution. Once more Scarpia and Tosca are alone together; the Chief of Police returns to his table to resume his "poor, interrupted supper" (the "supper theme" that opened the act is heard again in the orchestra) and bids Tosca be seated. He offers her a glass of "wine of Spain" (sherry? malaga? tarragona? the libretto does not commit itself), which she refuses.

There is a moment's silence.

"How much?" asks Tosca.

Scarpia laughs, saying he does not sell himself to women for money, a

declaration which is accompanied by the first statement of a theme closely
associated with Scarpia's insatiable passion for Tosca:

His price, continues Scarpia, is the complete possession of Tosca and he
states his case to one of the worst tunes Puccini ever wrote:

It is a tune without style or character, and typical, I feel, of Puccini's
lack of *musical* interest in the characters of *Tosca*. One has only to consider
how full-blooded and passionate Puccini's only other baritone villains
were—Jack Rance in *The Girl of the Golden West* and Michele in *Il Tabarro*
—to recognize the melodic poverty and insipidness of what should have
been a stirring outburst by Scarpia.

There is frankly not much music in the scene which follows, though
there is a great deal of action provided by Scarpia's chasing of Tosca
around the room. Tosca shrieks for help, but nobody hears. Scarpia, now
past the stage when he sings, shouts in a frenzy of sexual excitement which
Puccini does not bother to set to music. Tosca's fate is postponed by the
sudden and dramatic sound of drums being played off stage. As they
grow louder Scarpia explains that the drums are leading the escort of
men on their way to the scaffold. He points out of a window to where a
gallows has been erected and reminds Tosca that, thanks to her, Mario
Cavaradossi has only an hour to live.

The sound of drums dies. Broken down by grief Tosca falls back on the
sofa while Scarpia, leaning calmly against the table, pours himself out
some coffee and watches her intently. The stage is now set for Tosca's
famous "Vissi d'arte, vissi d'amore" ("I have lived by art and love . . ."):

This aria is so well known, it is usually forgotten that it was once known
as "Tosca's Prayer", for it is not, as it sometimes seems, an appeal to
Scarpia but an appeal to God for mercy. "Vissi d'arte" is the first moment
in *Tosca* that the heroine really has our sympathy. Up to now she has been

a rather stupid and jealous opera singer; in "Vissi d'arte" she becomes a woman—not a typical Puccini "Little Girl", perhaps, but at least a woman whose suffering can move us.

After the opening phrase shown above, the music of the aria is based on a theme already familiar from the first act (Ex 78), played by the orchestra as a background against which the voice part provides a kind of descant. ('l'he tune of Ex 78 is never sung note-for-note in its entirety, only played by the orchestra.) The theme for Tosca's variations is beautifully scored, first for flute and solo muted violoncello (*dolcissimo con grande sentimento*), then ingeniously for violins with all the violoncellos an octave lower and the violas yet an octave below the violoncellos.

Puccini himself considered this aria held up the action of the opera, and when, during rehearsals for a performance of the work at the Vienna Opera in 1914, Maria Jeritza slipped in her struggles with Scarpia and sang "Vissi d'arte" lying flat on the ground on her stomach, the composer was so delighted by the effect that he asked the singer always to do it that way—which she did. It gave the aria life, said Puccini.

But it also gave the impression, frequently given by other non-prostrate sopranos, that Tosca is grovelling before Scarpia. It is not until after her prayer that she turns to him and entreats him to spare her lover's life. There is, incidentally, an effective two-and-a-half bar coda to "Vissi d'arte" which is rarely heard in the theatre or in recordings of the opera. Following Tosca's final note of the aria there is a *pianissimo* cadence formed by the Scarpia theme in the lower register of the strings as Scarpia says to Tosca: "Have you made up your mind?" and she replies: "Do you want me to kneel at your feet?" It is clear from this line that Tosca is still on her feet, or at least on the sofa where she collapsed. That the coda is usually omitted, however, is not really surprising: not only would it invariably be drowned by applause following the end of the aria, but it would be redundant since the great majority of Toscas are on their knees by then anyway.

Scarpia returns *appassionato* to the attack, but he is interrupted by a knock at the door. Spoletta enters to say that Angelotti has committed suicide.

"And the other?" asks Scarpia.

"Everything is ready," replies Spoletta.

"Wait," says Scarpia. There is a wonderfully effective moment of *pp* scoring for wood-wind and double bass at this point, which is particularly a typical instance of the peculiar orchestral language of *Tosca*. It consists simply of a unison E spread over five octaves ranging from the bottom note of the double bass, bass clarinet, two clarinets, and two flutes *a due* to a piccolo.

Scarpia turns to Tosca and says "Well?"

Tosca nods her consent. As Scarpia begins to give Spoletta instructions Tosca interrupts, insisting that Cavaradossi must be set free at once. Scarpia explains that it is not as simple as all that: Cavaradossi must be thought to have been executed. The subject of the mock execution is discussed to the accompaniment of a new and arresting theme which is given an ironic twist in the last act:

To reassure Tosca, who does not trust him, Scarpia gives the order to Spoletta: Cavaradossi will not be hanged, but will be shot. The execution will be a mock affair—"as in the case of Palmieri", adds Scarpia significantly. Tosca says she wants to tell Cavaradossi herself of the plan; Scarpia replies that he will give her a pass. Spoletta, repeating "con intenzione" that it shall be as it was with Palmieri, leaves the room, and Scarpia turns to Tosca saying that he has fulfilled his promise.

Tosca says there is one thing more: she must have a safe-conduct pass for herself and Cavaradossi which will enable them to leave the country without let or hindrance. Scarpia sits down to write and the action which follows is accompanied by this tune played by violins, on their G strings, in unison with the violas:

Tosca, drinking the glass of wine Scarpia poured out for her earlier, catches sight of a sharp-pointed knife lying on the table; without Scarpia seeing her, she takes it stealthily and hides it behind her back. Scarpia fixes his seal on the passport and goes to embrace Tosca. As he opens his arms she stabs him in the breast.

With Tosca gloating over him, shouting "Die! Die! Your blood is suffocating you, isn't it?" Scarpia dies. Tosca stands over him a moment and when she is sure he is dead, says: "Now I forgive him." The theme of Ex 94 is now played ff and is once again an accompaniment to silent action. Without taking her eyes off Scarpia's body Tosca goes to the table, dips a napkin in the water jug, and washes her hands. She suddenly remembers the passport, but cannot find it on the table. She looks around the room for it and finally finds it clutched in Scarpia's hand. She takes it and hides it away in the bosom of her dress.

As she looks at Scarpia lying on the floor Tosca reflects quietly: "And before him, all Rome trembled." These words, too often spoken melodramatically instead of sung in the monotone carefully written by the composer, were one of Puccini's two important personal contributions to the letter of the libretto. Sardou's original line at this point of the play was

"Et c'est devant ça que tremblait toute une ville." Although *Tosca* was Sardou's own story, the contemptuous "And before *that* a whole city trembled" does not make half the dramatic effect of Puccini's amendment. Sardou's Scarpia is made to sound almost as if the whole city had been wrong to have trembled before such an insignificant figure that "ça" suggests. Puccini's "E avanti a lui tremava tutta Roma" conjures up the whole horror of Scarpia's reign of terror, and in a subtle way justifies Tosca's killing of him not as the act of a woman defending her honour but as a blow struck in the cause of liberty and justice against a man who had terrorized not just vaguely "a whole city" but the Eternal City itself. Puccini's dramatic instinct was never surer than in such details as these.

Tosca turns to go but seeing two candles on a bracket she takes them, lights them at the candelabra on Scarpia's table and places one on either side of his head. Looking round again she sees a crucifix hanging on the wall; she takes it down and places it reverently on Scarpia's breast. Then, with a final glance around the room she leaves, closing the door cautiously behind her. The curtain falls.

The music leading from Tosca's last words, "E avanti a lui . . ." to the fall of the curtain of this second act is some of the most dramatic and unerringly effective its composer ever put into an opera. And once more it is achieved by the simplest means—the simplest means, that is, of a genius with grease-paint in his veins. Puccini creates an eerie air of silence and stealth by the distortion or variation of familiar themes— distorting the theme of Scarpia's burning lust for Tosca (Ex 90) and colouring it with the dark tones of a clarinet in its lowest register and the tremolo of the violas, varying the harmony of Scarpia's theme (Ex 73) by the introduction for the first time of a minor chord in what had always been a sequence of major chords. In its *ppp* echo—*il più p possibile*— played three times by violas, divided violoncellos and double basses in their lowest registers, the harmonic sequence of the three chords that began the opera ends with the chord of E minor instead of E major, scored for clarinet and three flutes and given a barely audible emphasis by the faint beat of a gong, bass drum and the low notes of the harp each time.

On the sudden *forte* of a more harshly orchestrated chord of E minor (with the cor anglais playing the highest note of a chord shared with two oboes, bassoon, violas and muted horns) the distant sound of a roll on side drums is heard off-stage—a sinister detail which adds a final ominous touch to the atmosphere of the music as the curtain falls.

ACT III

Scene: The platform of the Castel Sant'Angelo. There is a casemate on the left, also a table, bench and stool. On the table are a lantern, a large register book and writing materials. Hung on one of the walls is a crucifix with a votive lamp in front of it. On the right, the opening to a small staircase leading up to the platform. The Vatican and St Peter's are visible in the distance.

Before the curtain rises there is a lengthy flourish for horns, *ff* and in unison, which begins:

95

As the passage dies away the curtain rises. It is just before dawn and the stars are shining brightly in a clear sky. Once the curtain is up, Puccini begins his prelude proper. As with the prelude to the third act of *La Bohème*, and like Verdi with the prelude to the last act of *La Traviata*, Puccini does his musical scene-setting with the scene in full view of the audience; and once again his long introduction is vocal as well as instrumental.

The opening to the last act of *Tosca* is one of Puccini's most imaginative conceptions; with characteristic economy of means he gives us the sound of Rome as the dawn approaches—the sound of the shepherd boy (too often sung by a buxom soprano) singing in the distance below, the tinkle of sheep bells and the growing symphony of church bells. It is a remarkably effective sound-picture which almost smells of a warm June morning in Rome. But it is an idyllic scene constantly disturbed by echoes of Scarpia's theme; they occur in an unfamiliar form at unexpected moments, but with the inescapable, persistent pricking of a bad conscience.

The gaoler enters with a lantern and goes to light the lamp in front of the crucifix; he then lights the lantern on the table. He goes to the back of the platform and looks down into the courtyard below to see if the escort bringing the prisoner has yet arrived; he exchanges a few words with a sentry guarding the platform and returns to the casemate to sit down and wait. One by one the church bells stop ringing, and a picket commanded by a sergeant of the guard arrives on the scene with Cavaradossi.

The entrance of Cavaradossi is accompanied by another of these tunes in the orchestra with which Puccini liked to anticipate a later aria. In this case it is the first hint of "E lucevan le stelle":

The sergeant takes Cavaradossi to the casemate and hands a piece of paper to the gaoler, who begins to write in the register, and leaves with his picket.

Cavaradossi is told by the gaoler that he has an hour to wait before his execution; a priest is available, if required. Cavaradossi refuses the services of the priest and asks instead to be allowed to write a final letter; the gaoler, in return for a ring which the prisoner gives him, grants his request.

As Cavaradossi sits and writes, the love theme of the first act (Ex 81) is heard in a slow, calm version played by four solo violoncellos. It is a rich sound, with much of the poignancy of those echoes of the love music in the last act of *La Bohème* as further fragments (such as Ex 88) are added to form links in a long melodic chain of great warmth and emotional effect.

The mood and heavy-hearted tempo that has persisted since his entrance are maintained when, after writing a few lines, Cavaradossi puts down his pen and reflects on the woman and the life he has loved so much and which he is now about to lose for ever—"E lucevan le stelle ..." ("The stars were shining ...").

The aria keeps to the familiar Puccini pattern, beginning in a monotone for the singer while a solo clarinet plays the tune of Ex 96 in the background until the voice is ready to take it over and bring it to a climax. "E lucevan le stelle" succeeds, as "Vissi d'arte" succeeds, because it has a quality of genuine pathos which is particularly strong when it is heard in its dramatic context. No man with only an hour to live can fail to capture some of our sympathy, if only because we automatically put ourselves in his position. In the case of Cavaradossi, Puccini makes us experience the condemned man's thoughts so vividly that his agony becomes our agony and we are deeply moved by his desperately sad reflections.

Despair, indeed, is the principal feeling underlying this aria and it was the composer himself who introduced the words of Cavaradossi's hopeless, reiterated cry of "muoio disperato!"—"I die despairing" —Puccini's other contribution to the letter of the drama. Melodically "E lucevan le stelle" is a model of simplicity and in its construction and the way it blossoms when the voice takes over the tune it is one of Puccini's most successful and inspired arias.

As Cavaradossi ends his aria in tears and buries his head in his hands, the tempo quickens for the first time when Spoletta enters with Tosca. He indicates where Cavaradossi is to be found, and beckoning the gaoler to follow him leaves by the staircase again, having first warned the sentry to keep an eye on the prisoner. Tosca, meanwhile, rushes to her lover; she is too moved to speak, but lifts his head and shows him the safe-conduct.

Cavaradossi, scarcely able to believe his eyes, reads the document and remarks that this must have been Scarpia's first gracious act. "It was his last," says Tosca, and she goes on to tell her lover how she killed Scarpia.

It is a story told at great speed, and since its substance is already familiar to the audience Puccini accompanies it with easily recogniz-able themes associated with the situation to make doubly certain that the recital is immediately clear. Tosca's narrative includes one ingenious orchestral touch. When she refers to the sound of drums she had heard in the Palazzo Farnese Puccini does not use real drums to remind us. Tosca is not hearing drums, but merely remembering the sound of them, so the composer imitates the beating of drums by divided violas and violoncellos—the violas bowing a rhythmical *staccato* beat, the violoncellos playing pizzicato a cluster of three semitones, E flat, E natural and F.

During Tosca's recital the tune of Ex 94, hitherto heard only as an instrumental accompaniment to the stage action immediately before and after Scarpia's murder, acquires words for the first time, and she sings the tune—at a faster tempo than in Act II—to recall how she took the knife while Scarpia was writing the safe-conduct. I must confess I have never really understood the exact significance of this tune. It seems in every context to be associated with the death of Scarpia from Tosca's point of view—it is her actions that it accompanies in Act II, and her narrative that is based on it now. Then why should it be such an intensely melancholy lyrical theme, as though we were expected to be sorry for Scarpia's fate? I may have missed the point of this particular theme, but it strikes me very much as though it was a case where Puccini had invented a tune he was very fond of and was determined we should hear.

Cavaradossi is greatly touched by Tosca's devotion and courage. "My hands were covered with blood," she tells him. He takes her hands and kisses them tenderly—"O dolci mani . . ." (" O sweet hands . . ."):

This phrase, which worried Giulio Ricordi so much by what he considered was its inappropriate gentleness and fragmentary, unheroic character when he first saw Puccini's manuscript, was salvaged from the demolition of Act IV of *Edgar* when that opera was revised soon after its performance in 1889. The composer's determination to keep the tune in *Tosca* was fully justified by results: it is the lyrical gentleness and frag-mentary quality of this and the other scenes between Cavaradossi and

Tosca which, in this third act, at last give a touch of conviction to the opera.*

Tosca brings an air of matter-of-factness back into the music with her instructions to Cavaradossi about his mock execution; before they can leave for the port of Civitavecchia and freedom he is to be "shot" with blank cartridges. "When the soldiers fire you must fall down, and when they have gone—we are saved and free!"

A charming lyrical scene follows this in which the lovers discuss their plans for the future, not in a formal duet but in a duologue free of any suggestion of passionate unisons or the like. Against a gently swaying accompaniment for harp and wood-wind Cavaradossi begins with the phrase later taken over by Tosca:

Before Tosca comes to her statement of the tune there is a quite remarkably incongruous couple of bars from the orchestra which seem to have strayed in from an extremely foreign musical world:

The *chinoiserie* of this pentatonic phrase is not only emphasized by the tinkling scoring (celeste, pizzicato violins, triangle, etc.), but also by the realization that the tune of the first bar was later used note-for-note in *Turandot*. Where, one must admit, it more properly belongs.†

Once more Tosca returns to reality, and in the same matter-of-fact tones as before briefs Cavaradossi again on the details of his "execution"; he must take care not to hurt himself when he falls. Cavaradossi interrupts her and taking her in his arms they join together (*con grande entusiasmo*) in an unaccompanied and unison declaration—in very poetic language— of their hopes, to the tune of the solemn flourish with which the horns began the act (Ex 95). This is another sequence with a fetching coda, in which Tosca promises her lover "I will close your eyes with a thousand kisses and tell you a thousand names for love." For the first time in the opera Tosca has a genuinely captivating unselfconscious charm.

A clock strikes four and the gaoler appears to tell Cavaradossi to prepare for his execution. Tosca gives a few last-minute words of instruction and encouragement: not to move when he falls until she

* It is interesting to note Puccini's fondness in his early days for tunes which began on the rising notes of the tonic chord. The first few bars of the tune from *La Lupa* in *La Bohème* (Ex 39), of "Tra voi belle" in *Manon Lescaut* (Ex 4), and this passage by *Edgar* out of *Tosca* can be played in a common key simultaneously without much difficulty or discord.

† It occurs three times at the end of the children's chorus immediately before the funeral march (Fig. 21) in Act I of *Turandot*. (See page 218.)

calls him, to fall convincingly ("like Tosca on the stage", says Cavaradossi with a smile); and *not* to smile.

The firing party, headed by an officer, enters to the last sinister theme of the opera—the funeral march rhythm of

100

Spoletta follows the firing party and gives the necessary instructions. Cavaradossi embraces Tosca, who remains in the casemate, and takes up his position against the wall on the right of the stage. He refuses the bandage which the sergeant offers for his eyes. These preliminary formalities try Tosca's patience, even though she knows the whole business is make-believe. The funeral-march theme builds slowly to its climax, merging at its height into the relentless repetition of the "execution" theme of Ex 93. At last the soldiers load their muskets; Tosca puts her fingers in her ears and gives a final reassuring nod to Cavaradossi. The officer raises his sword, a volley is fired and Cavaradossi falls to the ground with a realism that delights Tosca—"What an artist!" she cries.

The funeral march rings out *fortissimo*. The sergeant inspects the body carefully while Spoletta restrains him from giving the customary *coup de grâce*. The firing squad forms into marching order and the officer, Spoletta, the sergeant, the gaoler and the sentry all leave the scene as the music dies away to silence.

Tosca waits until the stage is empty before she goes over to Cavaradossi. She tells him that everything is safe now; he can get up and they can leave at once. Cavaradossi does not reply. Tosca then realizes that he really is dead. Scarpia has tricked her. This is what he had meant by an execution "as in the case of Palmieri".

From below the battlement come the excited shouts of Spoletta, Sciarrone and the soldiers. Scarpia's murder has been discovered. Spoletta and his company arrive on the platform to find Tosca prostrate across Cavaradossi's body. To the sound of some oddly unmusical "hurry music", which includes one last rapid but not clearly pointed reference to Scarpia's theme, Tosca rises quickly, pushing Spoletta away from her so violently that he falls over, and rushes to the parapet. With a final cry of "Scarpia! avanti a Dio!" ("Scarpia! We shall meet before God!") she throws herself into space, and the curtain falls to the sound of a powerful orchestral *tutti* playing the opening bars of "E lucevan le stelle".

As a matter of purely personal opinion it seems to me that Puccini missed one great dramatic opportunity: when the final curtain falls and Tosca calls Scarpia's name, why isn't Scarpia's theme heard again? Those three unforgettable, sinister chords have been heard throughout the opera, invading the prelude and even more of the last act; and yet when they most demand to be heard, which is when the dead Scarpia has the last superbly ironic word, there is no suggestion of them. Perhaps Puccini considered the quotation would have been too obvious. It is possible; but it would have been logical and, I believe, it would have been a fitting theatrical climax to one of the most thoroughly theatrical operas ever written.

There is one respect in which *Tosca* differs noticeably from most of Puccini's other operas, and that is in the profusion of detailed stage directions found in the pages of its score. Most of these are concerned with the mechanics of the stage action, of course, and therefore have a functional purpose; but there are a few which are quite ludicrously beside the point, such as the direction in Act II that Tosca "suddenly has the idea of taking refuge with the Queen and runs to the door", whereon Scarpia "guesses her thoughts and pulls her back"—all this, let it be noted, to be "registered" by the singers and conveyed to the audience (who have never heard a word about the Queen anyway) in the space of one and a half beats at a tempo of 69 beats to the minute.

It is a significant difference and symptomatic, I feel, of the whole nature of the opera: it is what the characters do, not what they feel, that is the principal dramatic factor in *Tosca*. This, I believe, explains why most of the best music in the opera comes from the underlining of a dramatic situation, rather than from the expression of personal emotion. Scarpia's music at the end of Act I is magnificent, for he is a figure in a situation of great dramatic irony; his music in the attempted rape scene is abysmally undistinguished, for he is engaged in the "registering" of type-cast emotion. *Tosca* being the kind of opera it is, the dramatic and not the lyrical side of Puccini's musical nature inevitably received greater stimulus, and although we are told that what attracted him most to the subject was the character of Tosca herself, the quality of the lyrical outcome of the composer's enthusiasm for her hardly suggests this.

So it is that, for me at any rate, the musical high spots of *Tosca* are found in the dramatic moments—in moments like the entrance of Scarpia in Act I, and the great finale to the act; in the impact of the arresting chords that begin the opera and the juxtaposition of the off-stage cantata and the interrogation of Cavaradossi; in the mounting tension of the torture scene and the sudden sound of the drums that interrupts the struggles of Tosca and Scarpia; in the wonderful sense of stealth and silence in the music that brings down the curtain of the second act; in the crescendo of the funeral march in the final scene leading with almost unbearable suspense to the firing of the muskets, and its diminuendo as the soldiers march away to leave Tosca to discover that Cavaradossi is dead.

How Puccini created these moments of drama has been described in the course of this chapter, and their effect in the theatre is as strong today as ever it was, even though in some cases some of the dissonances employed in their making may have dated. On paper: but not in practice, for the fact is that while composers have invented and worn to death a great many nastier chords since he wrote *Tosca* Puccini's use of dissonance still comes off because of its dramatic context and its application as a contrast.

The lyrical element of *Tosca* can hardly be called inspired. Much of the melodic invention is commonplace and Tosca's music in particular suffers from what one can only regard as lack of breeding. She is a slightly tarted-up Musetta, but without Musetta's genuineness and heart of gold. It is not until "Vissi d'arte" that she makes any real impression as a personality or awakens our sympathy. In the last act, however, she is an entirely different person—thanks to the only sustained lyrical scene of any quality in the opera, which significantly was the result of the composer's flat refusal to accept what his librettists first offered him and of his own determined alternative proposal.

In the form it reached Puccini, after its removal from the grasp of the unfortunate Franchetti, the libretto provided for a "Latin Hymn" to be sung by Cavaradossi as he waited for his execution. It was designed as a solemn peroration on Art and Life. Puccini, with his instinct for such things, rejected the whole project. A condemned man who was in love with a woman he was never to see again would have neither time nor inclination for any cultural or philosophical reflections. What the librettists were made to contribute instead, with its final "muoio disperato" supplied as the motto for the whole aria by Puccini himself, was the framework of "E lucevan le stelle", the first really authentic and up-to-standard scene of lyrical music in the opera. Puccini's revision did not affect only Cavaradossi's solo scene; it influenced the quality and substance of all the music from the beginning of the passage for four solo violoncellos to the coda of the last unison declaration of hope by the two lovers.

But in spite of this last-minute return to form *Tosca* is still basically the melodrama that Puccini described on the title page, a melodrama differing from what we understand by the English use of the word only in that the dialogue is sung to a musical accompaniment instead of spoken. As a work of art it is a *tour de force*, a tremendous and fascinating one, just as Sarah Bernhardt's performance of the play Sardou wrote for her was a *tour de force*. As a play *Tosca* was kept alive so long as Bernhardt was there to act in it, and no longer. As an opera *Tosca* has been more fortunate; it has not had to depend for its survival on the virtuoso performance of one individual. It has been sustained by the music of one of the most universally loved composers who ever lived.

MADAM BUTTERFLY

(Property of G. Ricordi and Co.)

A Japanese tragedy in two acts (three scenes) by Giuseppe Giacosa and Luigi Illica, based on David Belasco's dramatization of a short story by John Luther Long. First performed at La Scala, Milan, on 17th February, 1904. Revised version performed at the Teatro Grande, Brescia, on 28th May, 1904. First performance in England: Covent Garden, 10th July, 1905. First Performance in the United States: Belasco Theatre, Washington, D.C., 15th October, 1906 (in English).

OF the three classic instances of a popular masterpiece that was a catastrophic failure at its first performance, *Madam Butterfly* is the only one for which the music itself can be held in any way responsible. In the case of *The Barber of Seville* disaster was due entirely to non-musical factors: the management of the theatre was unpopular with the public, Don Basilio fell through a trap door, the theatre cat came on to the stage, the tenor had constant difficulty with the tuning of his guitar in the first act, and there was in any case the presence in the theatre of Paisiello's supporters who turned up in force to ruin the performance of an opera that threatened to be a rival to their man's *Barber*. The fiasco of *La Traviata*, on its first production in 1853 in Venice, was caused by elements beyond the composer's control—the tenor who lost his voice, the baritone who sulked because he considered his part unworthy, the soprano whose figure the Venetians euphemistically described as "troppo prosperosa" for a woman dying of consumption.

But whereas, without a note being altered, the second night of Rossini's opera was as great a success as the first had been a failure, and *La Traviata* was note-for-note the same opera at its second and successful production in Venice that it had been at its unfortunate first, the second performance which redeemed the fortunes of *Madam Butterfly* was of an opera that had undergone considerable revision after its disastrous première.

The first performance of *Madam Butterfly* at La Scala might well have been the last, for the public was in an ugly mood by the end of the first act. Its temper was worse by the end of the second act, which in the original *Butterfly* lasted more than an hour and a half. It was annoyed, too, because the tenor did not appear again after the first act until the end of the opera and then not for long. But these are things which, after all, a first night audience (even allowing for those members of it who had studied the libretto and vocal score before the performance) could not have foreseen during the first quarter of an hour or so of an unknown opera, which is when the trouble seems to have started. The silent indifference which had greeted the rise of the curtain developed into vociferous disapproval when a phrase in the music of Butterfly's entry led to cries of "*Bohème!* That's from *Bohème!*" From this point onwards the audience settled down to enjoy itself. It was not only able to shout rude remarks about the music, but about the familiar natural hazards of opera production as well. The idea of dressing tenor and baritone in contemporary costume, for instance, began to strike the audience of La Scala as extremely comical, and the evening passed in a crescendo of jeers and noisy interruption; the artificial bird noises coming from hidden points in the auditorium, which were added for effect in the dawn sequence, set the audience barking, braying and mewing, obscene remarks were yelled at Rosina Storchio, the leading lady, and "One Fine Day" was shouted down into inaudibility. There was not a single curtain call at the end.*

The following morning Puccini refunded the 20,000 lire (then about £800) which he had received from the management, withdrew the opera and set to work to revise it. As in the case of La Bohème, Puccini had enormous faith in the eventual success of his work; he had one or two bitter things to say about the attitude of the Press, but he was so convinced of the merit of Madam Butterfly that he believed it was only a matter of months before it would become a world-wide favourite like its two predecessors. He was proved right when the opera was performed in its present form in the little theatre at Brescia in May 1904 and was a stupendous success.

Puccini's revisions consisted of shortening the wedding ceremony in Act I, cutting the long scene in the same act in which Butterfly's uncle got drunk (Yakusidé can still be observed in the score to be anxiously asking for wine, but a great deal of that is frequently cut in performance and what remains is virtually lost in the general ensemble), dividing the long second act into two distinct parts with an interval in between, and giving the tenor something in the nature of an aria before he leaves the stage for good in the last scene. He changed, too, the scene of Kate Pinkerton's meeting with Butterfly. In the first version she was made to ask Butterfly for the baby at the very same instant as the little Japanese girl realizes that Pinkerton has deserted her—a sadistic little touch in unusually poor taste devised by Puccini and his librettists between them.

It will be seen from the nature of these revisions that Puccini could not be entirely absolved from blame for the opera's poor reception at the première. Much of the uproar may have been organized by anti-Puccini factions in the audience and it may well have influenced the behaviour of those who, while they were clearly disappointed by the music, might not otherwise have been led to make such spectacular vocal demonstrations of disapproval.

Certainly his librettists had done their best to dissuade him from the idea of a second act all in one piece, but Puccini had been obstinate and his obstinacy led to what must have been the only theatrical miscalculation of his career. It is possible that he was influenced in this by the form

* Yet another factor, which I have not seen put forward before, but which undoubtedly contributed to the general air of hostility was the unpopularity of Toscanini with the Scala audience. He had walked out in a spectacular rage during the previous season and Rosina Storchio was not only his mistress, but was noticeably bearing his child—an obvious sight which did not escape the notice of the gallery, as Filippo Sacchi has described vividly in his book on Toscanini, The Magic Baton.

of David Belasco's play which had given Puccini the idea for his opera in the first place. When he was in London in 1900 for the rehearsals of *Tosca* at Covent Garden, Puccini went to the Duke of York's Theatre to see Belasco's stage version of John Luther Long's short story, *Madame Butterfly*. The play seems to have been in one act of two scenes linked by a long sequence of mime depicting Butterfly's preparations for Pinkerton's return and her vigil with her child through the night. Puccini saw the play. His knowledge of the English language was limited to the numbers up to ten and a few addresses he could go to by cab; even if it had been more extensive it is likely that he would still have been a little perplexed by dialogue which included such gems of pidgin-American as "An' if they got a nize bebby yaet—don' they—all, don' *aevery*body lig that?" As it was, *Madame Butterfly*, like Sarah Bernhardt's *Tosca* before it, made an impact on Puccini the power and speed of which was unaffected by any question of language.

It is obvious, I think, that the hostile atmosphere created during the early stages of *Madam Butterfly* at its première affected the judgment of both public and Press. Otherwise, even allowing that the sequence of Butterfly's uncle was superfluous and second-rate, it is difficult to understand how the audience failed to recognize that there was so much excellent music in the act, so many new and original touches of colour (to say nothing of the lovely duet which brought the act to a close), that the virtues of the music in the end easily outweighed the dramatic weaknesses.

Though Puccini in effect divided *Madam Butterfly* into three acts (which is the way it is commonly described in the programme), he persisted obstinately in the orchestral score that there were still only two acts: Act II is divided carefully into "Part One" and "Part Two". A recent move to dispense with the interval altogether in Act II and, keeping the curtain up, to revert to something like the original uninterrupted form of the first version has been made at Covent Garden, with what success or to what purpose I have not tried to discover. It strikes me as an even more pointless departure from accepted practice than the same theatre's reversion to Dumas' original names for the characters in *La Traviata*—as though Verdi had originally meant to set Dumas' play to music but had set Piave's libretto by mistake instead. The abolition of the dividing interval between Parts One and Two of the second act of *Butterfly* is not only unfair on the orchestral musician, but can hardly be received joyfully by the unfortunate soprano who sings Cho-Cho-San and, once she appears on the stage in the first act, never leaves it except for a short period of less than nine minutes all told in the last scene.

Like *Manon Lescaut*, *La Bohème* and *Tosca*, *Madam Butterfly* has its own peculiar colour and atmosphere. In this case, of course, the atmosphere is deliberately exotic; in the orchestral writing, particularly, we hear sounds we have not heard from Puccini before, but which show how wide open he kept his ears when listening to the music of his contemporaries. The score makes frequent and original use of muted trumpets, of oriental gongs and the rest, but the local colour comes naturally out of the action and is never oppressive or obviously used for its own sake.

With characteristic thoroughness Puccini went to a great deal of trouble to assimilate the musical background of Japan, a study in which he was greatly helped by the wife of the Japanese Ambassador to Rome who gave him some important advice on Japanese customs generally, some of which he took and some of which he did not. He ignored the warning, for instance, that Yamadori was not a suitable name for a man. It is certain that Puccini used one or two of the Japanese themes he heard as themes for his opera, but without chapter and verse it is extremely difficult to pin them down. He had his own way of dealing with musical contributions from outside and it is difficult to know where these end and Puccini begins. He absorbed the atmosphere of operatic subjects such as *Madam Butterfly* and *Turandot* like a chameleon, so that the quoted folk-songs have a Puccinian twist while the genuine Puccini tunes are given a twist appropriate to the setting. As a rule, however, the "big" moments of Puccini remain unmistakably the composer's own and this was never more the case than in *Madam Butterfly*, an opera centred around Puccini's most enchanting and sympathetic character and the one which he loved above all others.

CHARACTERS IN ORDER OF APPEARANCE:

LIEUT. B. F. PINKERTON, *U.S. Navy** . .	*Tenor*
GORO, *a marriage broker*	*Tenor*
SUZUKI, *servant to Madam Butterfly* . .	*Mezzo-soprano*
SHARPLESS, *U.S. Consul in Nagasaki* . .	*Baritone*
MADAM BUTTERFLY (Cho-Cho-San) . .	*Soprano*
THE BONZE, *a Japanese priest and Butterfly's uncle*	Bass
PRINCE YAMADORI . *Tenor (often sung by baritone)*
KATE PINKERTON	*Mezzo-soprano*

Butterfly's mother, aunt, cousins and other relatives; her friends, her child; the Imperial Commissioner; the Official Registrar; servants.

Scene: Nagasaki.   Time: The Present (i.e. 1904)

* Pinkerton's initials and surname are a constant source of confusion. His full name is "Benjamin Franklin Pinkerton", but in the list of characters in Puccini's score he is referred to as "F. B. Pinkerton", and again addressed in this manner by Butterfly in the course of the dialogue. Only when his full name is mentioned is everything straightened out. The only explanation I can offer for this quaint practice is that it is a survival of the Italian habit in the 19th century and even later of reversing Christian and surnames, so that one encountered the billing, for instance, of "Toscanini Arturo" on the programmes without comma or comment. In Germany, and in the German version found under the Italian words in the small orchestral score published by Ricordi in 1920, "Pinkerton" becomes "Linkerton"—not, as has been naïvely suggested by a Viennese biographer, Richard Specht, to avoid confusion with the famous American firm of detectives, but because "Pinkerton" has a slightly obscene schoolboyish connotation in German—which ought surely to have struck an Austrian writer.

ACT I

Scene: A Japanese house, terrace and garden on a hill overlooking the bay, harbour and town of Nagasaki.

There is a short orchestral prelude before the curtain rises. The main theme of the introduction is treated fugally when it is first heard, but it is later used—in the composer's familiar manner—as a motif during the opera, sometimes at length, sometimes in a contracted form confined to the first easily recognizable couple of bars of the phrase or even less:

The curtain rises to reveal Goro, the marriage broker, showing Pinkerton over the house the American has taken and which he is about to occupy with the Japanese wife he is to marry. The marriage, of course, has been arranged by Goro.

This opening scene, in which the theme of the prelude plays a considerable part, consists largely of expressions of surprise by Pinkerton at the ingenuity of Japanese domestic architecture with its sliding doors and hidden panels. As a final demonstration of efficiency Goro claps his hands to summon the three servants who go with the house, among them Butterfly's maid, Suzuki.

Pinkerton makes appropriate remarks but quickly tires of Suzuki's over-elaborate compliments; Goro claps his hands once more to dismiss the parade.

Goro, one of the busiest and most obsequious of all operatic characters, informs Pinkerton of the company to be expected at the wedding. There will be this official and that, Butterfly's widowed mother, her aunt, grandmother, cousins and other blood relations—"a round two dozen"—who are characterized by what we can call the fussy "family theme" first played quasi-comically by the bassoon:

The recital is cut short by the arrival of Mr Sharpless, the American

Consul, who is out of breath after climbing up the hill. The Consul's appearance adds another theme to the prevailing 2/4 movement of this opening scene, a theme which Puccini uses with good effect in the next act:

Pinkerton sends Goro away to fetch a tray of drinks which is brought out on to the terrace and placed before the two Americans.

To those to whom *Madam Butterfly* is a novelty it may come as a surprise at this point to hear the strains of "The Star Spangled Banner" rising from the orchestra. This is Puccini's rather ham-handed way of introducing the first purely lyrical passage we have heard so far, in which Pinkerton sings of the wandering, adventurous habits of "lo Yankee vagabondo".

The interpolation of their national anthem into an Italian opera caused some Americans considerable concern when *Madam Butterfly* was first heard in the United States. The late Mr Kobbé, in his *Complete Opera Book*, wrote: "The use of the 'Star Spangled Banner' . . . should be objected to by all Americans . . . [it] is highly objectionable and might, in time, become offensive."

Mr Kobbé's fears were unfounded; in any case, if the quotation was ever going to be offensive surely it would be so on a first hearing, not "in time". Time, however, has healed any American susceptibilities that may ever have been wounded and the objectionable has been universally accepted without further comment.

The first four bars of the American anthem lead to a vocal passage which makes a welcome change from the busy, "conversational" music which has dominated the scene until now. This passage, sung by Pinkerton, introduces two themes:

The first of these phrases is the more important for it is developed during the scene which follows between Pinkerton and the Consul. The Lieutenant interrupts his eulogy of the *Yankee vagabondo* to offer his guest a choice of "Milk-Punch" or "wisky". Later evidence in the libretto indicates that, being no fool, Sharpless chooses "wisky", but for some reason when the offer is first made Puccini forgot to add the Consul's reply, so that in some performances Pinkerton's question is received in silence while in others the baritone improvises the answer.

Sharpless learns from his friend about the proposed marriage to Butterfly and he is shocked by Pinkerton's casual approach to the whole affair, for it appears that the bride, like the house, is on a 999 years' lease which is terminable at a month's notice. (These are the very words of the libretto.)

Sharpless confines his disapproval at first to a muttered "Well, that's an easy-going philosophy!" and he echoes Pinkerton's completely irrelevant toast of "America for ever!" (the words are sung in English). It is an irrelevant toast because there is nothing in the dialogue to suggest why it should suddenly be proposed—unless it is that the Americans happen to have glasses in their hands and the librettists needed empty glasses to be refilled as an excuse to interrupt the melodic flow of the scene which follows, when Pinkerton asks if the Consul would like another "wisky".

After the toast to America, Sharpless asks Pinkerton whether his bride is beautiful. The question is answered by Goro, who appears out of nowhere, having overheard everything. She is very beautiful, he says, and if the Consul would like a Japanese girl for himself—only 100 yen? Sharpless declines the offer graciously, then turning to Pinkerton asks what on earth impelled him to start this affair with Butterfly.

Pinkerton rises impatiently and delivers a brief address in praise of Butterfly's charms. This is a sequence set to the most matter-of-fact music; there is nothing even remotely romantic about it. But then, frankly, Pinkerton is not a romantic character. He is a first-class bounder, a grandson of the Duke in *Rigoletto*, but without the first suggestion of the Duke's charm. Puccini evidently thought so too, for the tune accompanying Pinkerton's description of Butterfly to Sharpless (although it includes one beautifully scored passage for three flutes in unison in their low register) is most unattractively prosaic:

Sharpless introduces a sympathetic note into the duet for a brief moment, but Pinkerton characteristically destroys it. The scene, becoming as full of toasts as a Russian banquet, ends with another. Sharpless drinks to Pinkerton's family in America, while the gallant Lieutenant drinks with unbelievable cynicism to the day when he will marry a real American wife. Not a bad ending to a scene which began by the hero justifying his marriage to the heroine. . . . (It has never struck me as a valid point of criticism that the "hero" of *Madam Butterfly* should be such an entirely unsympathetic figure. The less likeable he is then surely the greater the sympathy one feels for Butterfly who is, after all, the central figure of this Japanese tragedy.)

Goro reappears breathlessly to announce that Butterfly and her attendant Geisha girl companions are coming up the hill. Sharpless and Pinkerton retire to the back of the garden, watching the path on the hillside.

We now come to one of the most effective and lovely scenes Puccini ever created: the entrance of Butterfly. As only he knew how, the composer conjures up an entirely new atmosphere in the course of a single bar. From backstage come girls' voices; Butterfly's voice soars above them while a solo violin, solo viola and solo violoncello (all unmuted where the rest of the strings are muted and divided into 9 parts) playing against a beautifully scored orchestral background, introduces us to this theme:

According to Father Dante del Fiorentino's enchanting reminiscences of Puccini, *The Immortal Bohemian*, it was this phrase, when it was sung to Butterfly's words of "spira sul mare e sulla terra", which started the disturbances at the Scala première and led to shouts of *"Bohème!"* Whoever it was who detected any similarity between this and the music of the earlier opera was certainly extremely quick-eared. Basically it is a tune which resembles, in its general melodic shape, at least two themes in *La Bohème*; the opening of Schaunard's theme in Ex 40 (page 57), and of Musetta's waltz (Ex 58, page 66) can both be sung simultaneously with the phrase from *Butterfly* without much trouble or essential divergence. Since the melodic progression common to these three tunes is one of the most frequently encountered in the everyday vocabulary of music, it only seems odd that the vociferous demonstrator at La Scala should have picked on *La Bohème* to make his point instead of, for instance, the first movement of Sibelius' First Symphony.*

The really disgruntled agitator at La Scala on 17th February, 1904, might have pointed out with far more justification that Butterfly's entrance had been modelled on an effective operatic prototype—the lengthy off-stage, first-entrance approach of another Oriental heroine who was the victim of a white man's whim in Delibes' *Lakmé*, an opera written in 1883 which also provided Puccini with the precedent of a Flower Duet.

Whatever the sources of Puccini's inspiration or precedents for the musical and dramatic situation at this point, the orchestral and choral colouring, the immediate sympathy Puccini creates for his heroine, and the beautifully built up climax of Butterfly's final phrase, combine to make this scene one of the highlights in the operatic repertoire.

---

* I was recently consulted in an action for plagiarism on the question of a song based on precisely this melodic progression. I discovered no fewer than forty-three themes (including three of my own) which began in the same way. I advised all concerned to drop the matter, if possible; there seemed to me that once embarked upon there would have been no end to the litigation.

There is heard in the course of this sequence another theme—

—which occurs in various altered and modified forms throughout the opera, sometimes as I have shown it above, and sometimes so that it is little more than an elaboration of Ex 107 from which it is partly derived.

The music dies away as Butterfly and her friends, carrying brightly coloured sunshades, recognize Pinkerton (whom Butterfly introduces as "F. B. Pinkerton") and make their obeisances to a theme which plays a considerable part in the first act from this point onwards:

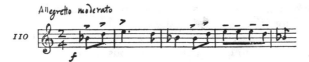

Commonplaces are exchanged all round and Pinkerton is characteristically sarcastic in replying to Butterfly's ingenuous compliments. Sharpless tactfully interrupts and learns from Butterfly something of her history—of how her family fortunes had failed and she had had to earn her living as a Geisha girl. One new theme emerges from this conversation, an important one which is later associated with the worst of Butterfly's sufferings. It occurs now when she recites her family history and says that "even the strongest oaks will fall before a whirl-wind":

The unpredictable Pinkerton now shows signs of something approaching a tender feeling for his bride and says how delighted he is in an aside to Sharpless. The Consul either does not hear him or ignores the aside, and continues his cross-examination of Butterfly. We learn that she has no sisters, that her mother is very poor—and her father? "Dead," replies Butterfly, simply. At the mention of her father's death we hear for the first time a dark and sombre theme of which Puccini makes varied and effective use during the opera, scored at this point for clarinets, bass clarinet and bassoons in their lowest registers and punctuated by pp chords from trombones:

It is a change of orchestral colour which introduces, for the first time, an ominous note into the opera. The mood is dispelled quickly, however, as Sharpless resumes his questions, and we hear that Butterfly is fifteen years old.

Butterfly's relations arrive—her mother, her aunt, a catty cousin who is constantly telling us that Goro had offered the plain and unprepossessing Pinkerton to *her* without success, thirsty uncle Yakusidé whose sole contribution to the conversation is to ask if there is any wine. They stare curiously at the two Americans while the unspeakable Pinkerton, who has led Sharpless to one side, laughingly draws the Consul's attention to the bizarre collection of in-laws he is to acquire. The Imperial Commissioner and the Registrar, who arrived at the same time as the relations, go into the house and wait there.

A noisy general ensemble develops with the relations chattering at the top of their voices; Goro quietens things down and we are able to hear Pinkerton and Sharpless carrying on a conversation about Butterfly in a corner. The Consul agrees that Butterfly is enchanting but warns Pinkerton that she trusts him and that he must not treat his marriage to her lightly.

Butterfly calls for silence and in a coy, childish voice (*con voce infantile*) orders her relations to kneel ("One-two-three—all down!") before the Americans.*

There is a pause, and with his peculiar, sometimes almost Mozartian gift of directness and simplicity, Puccini changes the whole musical topic of conversation with an academic but oddly unexpected change of key—from F major to a *pianissimo* repetition, in C major (hardly an unconventional modulation), of the tune of Butterfly's entrance (Ex 107). The company rises and scatters around the garden or helps itself to sweetmeats which have been laid out on a table for the guests (thirsty Uncle Yakusidé is not catered for in the stage directions).

Pinkerton takes Butterfly by the hand and is about to lead her into the house when she begs to look at the possessions she has brought with her tucked away in her sleeves.

She brings out handkerchiefs, a pipe, a silver buckle, a looking-glass, a fan and other odds and ends in a sequence of music with a peculiar wistfulness which it is difficult to analyse, for it is created by no more complicated means than the varied instrumentation—wood-wind and glockenspiel—of the phrase:

Lastly, Butterfly shows Pinkerton a sheath, but she will not show him its contents in public. She runs into the house with it. While she is out of earshot the helpful, ubiquitous Goro leans over and explains to Pinkerton

---

* The orchestration of this is notable for a passage for bassoon and harp in unison which is an unusual and wonderfully effective instrumental touch.

that the sheath was a present sent by the Mikado to Butterfly's father with a message. "And the father?" asks Pinkerton. "He obeyed," replies Goro, with a sinister pretence of stabbing himself.

Butterfly returns and shows Pinkerton several images which she explains are the souls of her ancestors. She takes him on one side and tells him that on the previous evening she went to the Mission and adopted a new religion. Her uncle, the priest, does not know this, but she wishes to worship the God of her lover Pinkerton and is happy to forget her own people so long as she is with him.

Butterfly makes this moving declaration of faith in a broadened version of Ex 109 played by strings in unison. When she has finished she throws herself into Pinkerton's arms and looks round fearfully lest her relations should have heard her.

Goro now takes the centre of the stage and assumes the role of master of ceremonies. Punctuated by the beating of Japanese gongs on the stage, the wedding ceremony takes place. Bride and bridegroom sign the register, and when her friends kneel before her congratulating "Madam Butterfly", Cho-Cho-San rebukes them sternly with "Madam F. B. Pinkerton". Sharpless leaves with a final word of warning to Pinkerton to be careful. The bridegroom returns to his guests, raises his glass to them with the words "Hip! Hip!", which were apparently in vogue in America at the time as a preliminary to drinking, and the assembled company drinks a toast to the happy pair in saké which servants have just brought in.

The scene is violently disturbed by the sudden arrival of Butterfly's uncle, the Bonze; and he appears to a sharp, dramatic theme in which the trill is given an extra edge by horns and trumpets added to wood-wind and violins:

The Bonze, whose appearance terrifies everybody but Pinkerton, wants to know what Butterfly was doing at the Mission. The relations, who a moment previously had been drinking her health, support the Bonze's accusation against Butterfly and finally join in renouncing her for being unfaithful to the religion of her race. Pinkerton loses his temper and turns everybody out of his property, crying that he will have no "bonzeria" in his house.

At Pinkerton's words the Japanese turn and flee hurriedly down the hill; Butterfly's mother tries to approach her daughter, but she is dragged away by the rest. Still shrieking and shouting the crowd disappears, while Butterfly, who is in tears, puts her hands to her ears to shut out their threats and curses. In a superbly effective orchestral sequence the din gradually subsides and Pinkerton tries to comfort her; she dries her tears to a moving repetition of the theme of Ex 111, now harmonized for the first time and played *dolce e legato* by divided strings.

The rest of the act is taken up by the Love Duet. The sun has now set, and except for a little business from Suzuki and the servants who help Butterfly out of her wedding dress and then retire, there is a sudden and most welcome calm settles on the scene. The Love Duet which ends this first act of *Madam Butterfly* is long (it lasts nearly 13 minutes), but it is most expertly constructed and filled with lovely music.

It begins quietly as Pinkerton reassures Butterfly that she has nothing to fear:

From this theme we come to a more urgent figure leading to an echo of the Bonze's sinister phrase (Ex 113):

Once more the dynamics subside. It is now night; there are stars in the sky and a solo violin plays, answered in an exquisite *pp* by a piccolo and a harp harmonic:

This melody—much admired, the score of *Dearly Beloved* suggests, by the late Mr Jerome Kern—builds up powerfully and brings us to a reprise of the "urgent" tune of Ex 115. Still the expected climax is delayed until, with the tune to which Butterfly entered earlier in the act (Ex 107) the duet gets into its final stride and works up to soprano and tenor singing a high C against an orchestral *fortissimo*.

Butterfly and Pinkerton walk slowly towards the house, the music dies away quietly with the same melody that rounded off Butterfly's entrance (Ex 109) and the curtain falls.

One can only conclude that there was so much barracking and chattering at the Scala première that the audience just did not hear the duet, otherwise it must surely have recognized it as vintage music by the composer of *Manon Lescaut* and *La Bohème*. It differs from the duet at the end of the first act of *La Bohème* in that it is a rapturous experience for only one of the two characters. To Butterfly this duet is the moment she has been waiting for, and Puccini never surpassed it as the musical expression of a woman in love. Even Pinkerton, whose concern is patently only with the immediate consummation of this extremely convenient marriage, is infected by Butterfly's genuineness and warmth enough to suggest occasional charm and gentleness. As music, as distinct from its telling of a dramatic story and its delineation of character, this duet is one of Puccini's most inspired movements. The treatment of the orchestra is wonderfully imaginative, full of exquisite detail and an object lesson in economy of means. The student who wishes to learn, or the sceptic who needs to be convinced, will find this score of Puccini's worth endless study and rich in those little touches which entrance the ear as much the fiftieth time they are heard as the first—touches like the dew-drop effect of the piccolo and harp in Ex 116, and the unexpected *pp* scoring for two solo violins, a solo viola, a solo double bass, flute, bass clarinet and harp at Fig. 121 in the score when Butterfly sings "Somiglio la Dea della luna . . ." It is a moment lasting barely ten seconds, but like so many moments in this loveable duet, it is unforgettable and heart-warming.

ACT II

PART ONE

Scene: Inside Butterfly's house. Late afternoon, three years later.

A graceful little theme played first by two flutes in unison and then subjected to a miniature fugato precedes the rise of the curtain. Since this tune has no thematic value (it is never heard again after this) it does not need quoting. As the curtain rises, however, we have the first hint of a theme which plays an increasingly dramatic part as the action progresses:

The shutters of the room are closed and the place is in semi-darkness. Suzuki, to a gently swaying and beautifully scored accompaniment of muted horn, clarinet, bass clarinet, harp, muted violins and violas, and timpani, is praying before an image of the Buddha; she rings a prayer bell from time to time to attract the attention of the gods. Butterfly lies motionless on the floor, resting her head in her hands.

Suzuki's prayers are for the return of Pinkerton, who, she is convinced, has deserted Butterfly and will never be seen again. Butterfly, with that naïve and touching faith which Puccini translates so surely into music, believes that her husband will return.

Pinkerton had been recalled to America only a few days after the wedding; he left money but it has now almost gone, and unless he comes back immediately, says Suzuki, they will be penniless.

"He will come back," says Butterfly confidently, and we recognize that the theme in Ex 117 is associated with Pinkerton's return.

This opening scene between Butterfly and her maid introduces a short phrase which is used extensively as a motif to represent Butterfly's patient waiting for her lover:

Butterfly's faith is unshakeable, for did not Pinkerton promise to return when the robins build their nests (a subject which Puccini reminds us of with very ingenuous but rather charming robin-noises in the orchestra)? She is irritated by Suzuki's sceptical attitude and angrily makes her repeat the words: "He will come back!" Suzuki bursts into tears, a reaction which Butterfly cannot understand, for she believes blindly that one day a ship will glide into the bay bringing Pinkerton back to her—"Un bel dì, vedremo levarsi un fil di fumo . . ." ("One fine day, we shall see a wisp of smoke rising . . ."):

This aria is perhaps the most popular Puccini ever wrote, but its very familiarity tends to obscure the remarkable effectiveness and originality of its orchestration. It is an accompaniment full of simple, telling effects beginning with the opening phrase, so superbly unprepared by the composer that the aria always takes one by surprise, in which the tune is shared by a solo unmuted violin (the rest are muted), a clarinet and the harp playing harmonics. The accompaniment, indeed, has an almost chamber-music quality in which the characteristic use of wood-wind that colours every Puccini score is particularly prominent, sometimes as the sole harmonic background to the vocal part as well as in the unison support across three octaves given by flute, clarinet and bass clarinet to Butterfly's cadence as she sings the words "s'avvia per la collina" ("he will climb the hill") to a broadened version of Ex 117.

In the passage which follows this there is a typical instance of Puccini's understanding of the nature of muted trumpets, which so many composers in the early 20th century regarded as fit only for grotesque effects. Instead of screaming at us, the trumpets have an ethereal quality created by their overtones. This sensitive, restrained handling of the orchestra affects even the climax of Butterfly's aria, the *ff con molta passione* reprise of the whole tune after the section I have just mentioned. At this climax (Fig. 15 in the score) the harmony is supplied by two muted trumpets who are replaced, as the dynamic intensity drops, by a pair of oboes followed by a pair of horns. The rest of the instruments play the tune in unison with Butterfly in her register, or an octave below, without any hint of harmonic bareness or orchestral thinness (the double basses are *tacit*, incidentally, until the last three beats of the phrase).

It is not part of the purpose of this study to comment on the interpretation of Puccini's operas but there is a detail in the singing of this aria of Butterfly's which I think is worth commenting on for it is a detail of performance which the composer himself authorized and, indeed, asked for. It is found in the vocal phrase accompanied by the muted trumpets to which I have already referred:

Margaret Sheridan, who died only a few days before I wrote this, and was one of the loveliest of all the Cho-Cho-Sans of the years between the two German Wars, told me that when she first rehearsed the part in Italy she did so under the supervision of the composer (Puccini could never keep away from new productions of his operas). It was Puccini who told her to sound breathless and excited as she asked the question: who will it be, coming up the hill, and what will he say? Anybody who ever heard Margaret Sheridan sing this as Puccini suggested will remember how right and human this interpretation sounded—even though it made nonsense of the composer's original notation of the phrase and introduced a noticeable quickening of the tempo shown as *sostenendo molto*.

The repetition of the first main phrase of the aria as an orchestral postlude is an admirable instance of Puccini's characteristic and apparently instinctive understanding of theatrical demands. Whether one ever hears it all, or indeed any of it, in practice is another matter, of course; it depends on the audience's reaction to the singer who is appearing as Butterfly. But, audible or not, the instrumental unwinding of the tension created in the aria and the gentle diminuendo to encourage the listener to relax is a typical stroke of Puccini's genius for theatrical timing.

As the orchestral postlude dies away Butterfly and Suzuki embrace and the maid leaves the scene. Goro now enters bringing with him Sharpless, whom Butterfly is delighted to see again after three years. Puccini's reiteration of the Consul's theme—Ex 103—at a leisurely Andantino restores a prosaic conversational atmosphere to the music after the intense lyrical outburst of "One Fine Day". It is an atmosphere maintained for a considerable period of the action from this point onwards, and it is created largely by the use and development of themes familiar to us from the beginning of Act I—including a speeded-up version of the phrase in "The Star Spangled Banner" which fits the words "by the dawn's early light"—and the introduction of one or two new and very Japanese-sounding tunes of the same 2/4 conversational stamp.

Butterfly fusses around the American, offering a pipe, cigarettes and always changing the conversation in an excited and irrelevant manner whenever he tries to get to the point of his visit.

Sharpless takes a letter from his pocket; it is from Pinkerton. Butterfly interrupts to ask Sharpless if robins make their nests in America at the same time of the year as in Japan. Before the Consul can give an answer to her puzzling question, however, Goro, who has been hovering in the background and overhears Butterfly's story of Pinkerton's promise, appears and bursts out laughing.

The appearance of the marriage broker sets Butterfly off on another tack; she begins to talk of something else, but decides first to settle the question of the robins. Sharpless has to admit that he does not know the answer at all.

Butterfly now reverts to the subject brought to mind by the appearance of Goro. As soon as Pinkerton had gone, she says, Goro came round with a proposal that she should marry again.

"To the rich Yamadori," explains Goro, adding that Butterfly is penniless and her relations have disowned her.

At this moment Prince Yamadori arrives, borne on a palanquin and followed by servants carrying flowers; as he enters Butterfly greets him with a broad, oddly passionate tune which, to save space, I will not quote literally but which, for the purpose of identification, I will give in a contracted form:

What Butterfly sings, to a crescendo phrase which always seems to me to have a touch of out-of-character ecstasy about it, is an expression of surprise that Yamadori has not yet realized that his suit is hopeless. It is a faintly perplexing context for this kind of tune.

The Prince repeats his proposal of marriage and, backed up by Goro, points out that a deserted wife is free to marry again whenever she likes.

"That may be the law of Japan," says Butterfly, "but I am bound by the laws of *my* country—the United States." She gives a comical account of how in America you go to a court and say you are tired of married life; and the magistrate throws you in gaol at once. Butterfly ends the conversation abruptly and turns aside to order Suzuki to bring tea for her guests. While Butterfly is busy—to the strains of a remarkably inappropriate and undistinguished Molto moderato *quasi Valzer lentissimo* filled with augmented triads and their arpeggios—the three men whisper together: Sharpless to say that he is grieved by her obstinate faith and blindness, Goro to say that Pinkerton's ship has already been sighted, and Yamadori to remark significantly—". . . and when she sees him again . . . ?"

Sharpless tells the two men that it is precisely for that reason that he has come to see her: Pinkerton does not want to see her again. Butterfly comes back into the action to offer tea. Yamadori rises to leave and bids her "addio" with a sigh accompanied *lamentoso* by cor anglais and bassoon. The Prince leaves on his palanquin with the orchestra playing the tune of Ex 121; he is followed by his servants and Goro.

The Consul is left alone with Butterfly once more; he takes a letter from his pocket and when Butterfly has kissed it and pressed it to her heart he begins to read it, first to the pizzicato accompaniment and then

to the tune of what later becomes the well-known Humming Chorus, now
anticipated by a solo violin and a solo viola:

Butterfly constantly interrupts, and it is obvious that she does not
understand the meaning of the letter. When she greets his reading of "I
ask you to prepare her carefully—" with "—for his return!" and claps her
hands excitedly when he continues ". . . for the blow", Sharpless resigns
himself to defeat and gives up. He puts the letter back in his pocket. He
rises and gravely asks Butterfly what she would do if Pinkerton were never
to come back.

There is a terrible silence, and then Butterfly stammers a reply "with
childlike submission": she could go back to being a Geisha girl and
singing for people, or—better—she would die. Sharpless is deeply moved
by this simple declaration; he takes Butterfly's hands in his and begs her
to marry Yamadori. Accompanied by clarinets and bass clarinet in their
lowest registers, bassoon, muted horns and a low, accented note repeated
by the harp, Sharpless sings his advice to an elegiac melody which Puccini
builds up by simple repetition into a poignant episode:

Butterfly draws herself up stiffly at Sharpless' suggestion and calls
Suzuki to show the Consul the way out. In a moment, however, she
relents and drags him back. Her thoughts of death have passed "as clouds
pass over the sea". She makes up her mind suddenly and cries, "Am I
forgotten?"

Butterfly runs from the room and returns at once carrying her child on
her shoulder—a fair-haired, blue-eyed boy. Proudly, and with a note of
triumph, she asks Sharpless: "And this one? Can *he* be forgotten?"
Butterfly's appearance with the child is accompanied by the first *ff*
statement of a theme which is used with great pathos and dramatic effect
from now onwards:

Sharpless is amazed to learn for the first time of the existence of Pinkerton's child, as also indeed will Pinkerton be, for the child was born after he had left Butterfly.

Placing the child on a cushion Butterfly kisses him tenderly and pointing to Sharpless says: "Do you know what that man had it in his heart to think? That your mother should take you in her arms and go forth to be a Geisha again."

Butterfly's song to her child brings the first unadulterated suggestion of sadness we have heard in the music so far with a characteristically melancholy Puccini melody—"Che tua madre dovrà prenderti in braccio . . ." ("That your mother should take you . . ."):

As Butterfly comes to sing in detail of what it would mean to return to the shame of her former life, to sing and dance before strangers, a second and important subject is heard for the first time. It is a theme heard always in unison punctuated, but not accompanied, by occasional chords and which in this episode is the climax to Butterfly's desperate cry that she would rather die than become a Geisha again:

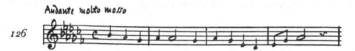

This is scored with much imagination and ingenuity in the course of Butterfly's scene, particularly in the sequence where it is heard across three octaves with the oboe taking the highest part, flutes an octave lower, bass clarinet an octave lower still, the bassoon in the lowest octave of all, and the harp doubling the oboe part with one hand, the bassoon with the other; the strings, also across three octaves, play the tune col legno, an effect still novel enough for Puccini to explain at length in the score that it meant "striking the strings with the wooden part of the bow". This whole passage is played pp and is a wonderfully imaginative passage of colourful orchestration.

Sharpless is deeply moved by Butterfly's resolution; he pulls himself together (an orchestral touch to note at this point is the harp's tuneful counterpoint to the clarinet's quotation of the Sharpless theme of Ex 103), and kisses the child tenderly.

"What is his name?" he asks.

Butterfly turns to the child and says: "Answer him: today my name is Trouble. But tell him that on the day of his return my name will be Joy!" ("Trouble" is the name used in the official English version of this line, and derives from John Luther Long's original story. The Italians, having no equivalent for "trouble" in this particular sense, translate the child's name by the more poetic "Dolore".) Butterfly's cry of "Joy!" is accompanied by a *ff* echo by two horns of "One Fine Day" and as the tune dies away Sharpless promises that Pinkerton shall be told of his son, and leaves hurriedly.

There is a sudden change of tempo and the introduction of a vigorous agitated figure as Suzuki is heard shouting off-stage. She enters dragging Goro roughly with her. The marriage broker protests to Butterfly that all he had said to Suzuki was that in America Pinkerton's child would be treated as an outcast. Butterfly rushes to the shrine, and taking down the sword that hangs there threatens to kill Goro. Suzuki intervenes and Goro flies for his life.

Butterfly stands motionless for a few seconds to recover from the excitement, then returns the sword to its place in the shrine. She turns to her child and says: "You will see—your father will come back and take you far away to his own country."

There is a distant cannon shot and Suzuki rushes in excitedly to say that it is the gun firing in the harbour. The two women run to the terrace and look through a telescope: it is a warship, it is white, and flies the Stars and Stripes. As Butterfly makes her excited running commentary the orchestra echoes the first sixteen bars of "One Fine Day", but without any feeling of excitement. The tune starts *ppp* played by a single flute, violins and violas, not rising above *pp* even though the number of instruments playing is gradually increased, until in the last couple of bars of the phrase the volume matches the excitement of Butterfly's recognition of the name "Abraham Lincoln" on the bows of the ship.

"They all lied!" she cries. "I was the only one who knew! He has returned and he loves me!", and a triumphant quotation of "The Star Spangled Banner" leads to a *fff tutta forza* orchestral proclamation of one of the elaborated forms of Ex 107 heard in the Love Duet that ended Act I.

The atmosphere changes at once to one of busy excitement. Butterfly tells Suzuki to collect flowers and blossoms of every kind and together they decorate the house in the scene known as the "Flower Duet" which begins with the elated little theme:

Some of the scoring of this scene has great charm; some of the melodic invention, on the other hand, is very much below Puccini's best and a great deal of music is heard that scarcely rises above the café chantant level of the earlier *Valzer lentissimo* until the slow tune which brings the duet to an end is reached with Butterfly and Suzuki singing:

When the duet is ended the sun begins to set and Suzuki places two lamps on Butterfly's dressing table. Before she starts to adorn herself, Butterfly tells Suzuki to bring in the child, an action which is accompanied by five bars of quite exquisite scoring for two flutes in their low register doubled by harmonics on the harp, and punctuated by a descending pizzicato run in octaves by divided double basses, the higher part of which is played in an unusually high position. As she sits at her dressing table Butterfly studies her face sadly in a hand-mirror: too many sighs have passed through her lips and her eyes have stared too long into the distance. She paints her face with carmine and because he will look pale in the morning, puts a few dabs of colour on the baby's cheeks as well. Then she smiles as she wonders what people are going to say—Uncle Bonze and poor Yamadori. When her toilet is finished she tells Suzuki to bring her the dress she wore at her wedding, and she puts it on as the orchestra echoes the opening phrases of the first act Love Duet.

As a final touch Suzuki puts a flower in Butterfly's hair, and then at her mistress's bidding she draws the *shosi*, the huge paper screen which serves as a window.

It is now almost night and the moon is beginning to rise. Butterfly makes three holes in the screen—one high up for herself, one lower down for Suzuki, and between the others a third still lower down for the baby, whom she places on a cushion and motions to look through the hole. Suzuki, having brought two lamps and placed them by the screen, settles down and stares through the hole in the *shosi*. Butterfly stands motionless and rigid as a statue and watches through the highest of the three holes. The child, standing between his mother and Suzuki, looks through the *shosi* "curiosamente". Butterfly's vigil has begun.

The moon begins to shine and light up the screen from behind. From back-stage comes the sound of humming; a chorus of sopranos and tenors in octaves, accompanied by a solo viola d'amore behind the scenes and the orchestral strings playing pizzicato, hums the tune we heard when Sharpless was reading the letter (Ex 122).

This closing music, with its long, slowly rising tune, makes one of Puccini's most brilliantly effective curtains. And as usual the effect is achieved with characteristic simplicity of means—the addition of a solo violin to the melody line, or two flutes in their low register, the use of single notes from the harp to reinforce a horn part, or two solo double basses to play with the bow after the rest have been pizzicato for so long. Though it is hackneyed, this drowsy, wordless music still remains one of the most original and evocative sounds ever heard in the opera house.

ACT II

PART TWO (sometimes called Act III)

Scene: The same.

The rise of the curtain is preceded by a long orchestral introduction which starts off well, and ends well, but which I have always found most unsatisfactorily Teutonic and uncharacteristic in the middle. This middle section, with its chromaticism, the dynamic clichés of the *piano-crescendo, piano-crescendo* routine, and its indistinct orchestral texture caused by the busy part-writing, sounds more like the climax-building of a Richard Strauss symphonic poem than the music of one who had heeded Verdi's warning: "Opera is opera, symphony is symphony; and I don't think it is a good idea to insert a symphonic piece into an opera just for the pleasure of letting the orchestra loose once in a while."

As there was no Italian symphonic tradition for Puccini to follow it is perhaps not surprising that if he felt impelled to "go symphonic" in this introduction, as in the passionate *Steigerung* of the *Manon Lescaut* intermezzo (the German word springs to mind automatically), he should have had to make use of the superficial conventions of German "symphonic" opera.

But where in *Manon Lescaut* the essential Puccini is always distinguishable, in *Madam Butterfly* the application of these alien methods results in a passage so lacking in distinction that it might have been written by anybody, and it is only when the climax is reached with a *ff* form of Ex 108 that we are mercifully returned to the familiar world of Puccini opera once more.

When the curtain rises we see Butterfly, still standing rigid and motionless as we left her at the end of the previous scene. Suzuki and the child are asleep. Dawn is breaking, and from the harbour below come the shouts of fishermen and the sound of a ship's chain clanking. The sunrise is accompanied by a horn theme which is built up in a long crescendo as the sunlight grows stronger:

129

It was during this dawn sequence that the bird noises from the auditorium occurred with such unfortunate results at the Scala première of *Madam Butterfly*. "Bird whistles from the garden" are still cued into the orchestral score, but as they are to be played only when one's attention is distracted by perky wood-wind imitation of bird noises based on a rather cynically speeded-up version of Ex 109, one is rarely conscious of this unnecessary touch of realism. (It is interesting to note how this theme, when it is speeded up and scored for piccolo, oboe and pizzicato strings, or for three flutes, becomes thoroughly "oriental", whereas in its first form in Act I and particularly when Butterfly sings it as she tells Pinkerton of her visit to the Mission, it could not sound a more genuinely Puccini tune.)

Suzuki wakes and calls Butterfly by name. "He will come, he will come, you'll see," Butterfly replies. Suzuki implores her mistress to take her child and get some rest; she will call her as soon as Pinkerton arrives. Butterfly, leaving the stage for what, with the exception of the few seconds during her scene with the Consul in the earlier part of this act, is the first time since her appearance in Act I that she is out of our sight, takes the sleeping child in her arms and goes into the next room. It is a scene of quite astounding simplicity, for it consists of little more than a repetition of the tune of Ex 124 twice by muted violins in octaves, four times by Butterfly as she carries her sleeping child and sings to it:

> "Dormi amor mio, dormi sul mio cor,
> 'Tu sei con Dio ed io con mio dolor."

("Sleep, my love, sleep on my heart, you are with God and I am with my sorrow. . . .")

The unfailing dramatic effectiveness of this scene, as Butterfly's voice is heard growing fainter in the distance, is a superb example of Puccini's instinctive sense of the theatre and his equally instinctive choice of the simplest means with which to express it. There is the same masterly touch of simplicity, too, in the two cadences formed by Suzuki's murmured "Povera Butterfly!" There are, in fact, few passages in all Puccini which make their musical and dramatic point more surely and convincingly than the 35 understated bars which make up this scene.

As soon as Butterfly has gone there is one of those typical orchestral anticipations of scenes to come that occur so often in Puccini's operas, when the strings play:

130
Largo

There is a knock on the door of the house. Suzuki answers it and with a cry of astonishment opens the door to Sharpless and Pinkerton, who quickly motion her not to call out. It is an embarrassing meeting, with Suzuki wanting to call Butterfly, Pinkerton being surprised to learn that

Butterfly has been waiting for him, and Sharpless trying to keep diplomatic control so that there shall be no difficult scenes. During the conversation, the second part of which is accompanied by orchestral echoes of the Flower Duet, Suzuki hears a noise in the garden and, looking out, sees a woman walking there. Sharpless explains bluntly that the woman is Pinkerton's American wife. Suzuki breaks down in despair; the Consul takes her gently aside and to the tune of Ex 130 asks her to go and speak to Mrs Pinkerton, who is willing to see that Butterfly's child is properly cared for.

What promises to be Sharpless's only solo becomes first a duet, as Pinkerton wanders around the room soliloquizing remorsefully on the past, and then a trio when Suzuki adds her heart-broken comments.

After some hesitation Suzuki is persuaded by the Consul to go into the garden and meet Mrs Pinkerton.

Sharpless turns to Pinkerton. "Didn't I tell you?" he says, and he reminds his friend how he had warned him that Butterfly trusted him implicitly and that the marriage was not to be taken lightly.

Pinkerton's moral courage is so abysmally low that Sharpless tells him to go. Butterfly will learn the sad truth without him.

Pinkerton stays to sing a farewell to the beflowered retreat where he enjoyed so many happy hours with Butterfly, and then runs away, unable to face the situation. His farewell is the *canzone* which Puccini added after the first performance of the opera—"Addio fiorito asil . . ." ("Farewell, O happy home . . ."):

Even in this little episode the tenor is not allowed to sing entirely uninterrupted. Sharpless continues his "I-told-you-so" remarks and repeats his line that Butterfly will learn the sad truth alone. Lieut. Benjamin Franklin Pinkerton, U.S.N., shakes the Consul by the hand and leaves the scene. Sharpless shakes his head as he watches him go.

Suzuki comes in from the garden followed by Kate Pinkerton. We hear the end of a conversation, during which it has clearly been arranged that Suzuki shall tell Butterfly the worst. She promises Mrs Pinkerton to persuade Butterfly to trust her: Kate is willing to adopt Pinkerton's child.

Butterfly, hearing voices, comes excitedly into the room expecting to find her husband. Suzuki begs her not to come in. Butterfly persists; she searches behind the screen and in every corner of the room, believing that Pinkerton is playing hide-and-seek with her. She sees Sharpless and asks him where her husband is; she receives no reply. Then she sees Kate Pinkerton; still nobody answers her questions.

In desperation she asks Suzuki: "Is he alive?" Suzuki answers: yes.

The music from Butterfly's entrance to this point is simple and magnificently effective "theatre". It begins with the phrase, played by clarinets and bassoons in thirds—

—which Puccini treats in such a way, by distending and slowing up, that he creates an uncannily harrowing atmosphere of growing sadness as Butterfly guesses the truth and all her gaiety and excitement leave her. The orchestration of this whole passage is masterly; the bassoons retire, leaving only the two clarinets to play their major thirds *sempre dim. morendo*, the bass clarinet supplants the second clarinet and as the realization of the truth strikes Butterfly with increasing force what has been the most ominous of all orchestral sounds since Mozart's day—the sound of three trombones—is heard. Unlike the pathos of the final scenes of *La Bohème* the emotional effect in this episode of *Madam Butterfly* is not created by the recollection of moments of happiness at a time of misery. There is none of that reminiscence of earlier themes which made Mimi's suffering so poignant; familiar themes are used, of course, but they are not those with sentimental association. It is as though Puccini intended us to forget Pinkerton as a lover altogether, and to concentrate on what is happening to Butterfly, not what brought it about; and there is little more astonishingly simple and affecting than, for instance, the passage of slowly descending whole-tone scale of major triads played by three solo violoncellos when Butterfly begs Suzuki not to cry, but to answer, yes or no, whether Pinkerton is still alive. On paper this particular sequence for violoncellos is oddly undistinguished, but its impact never fails *in the theatre*.

Butterfly realizes that Kate is Pinkerton's wife and that the strange American lady has come to take her child away. Quietly Butterfly says she will give up the child to Pinkerton, if he will come and fetch him in half an hour's time. She sings these words to the tune of Ex 117, originally associated with the hope of Pinkerton's return ("he will climb the hill") and now ironically associated with Butterfly's sacrifice of all she loves most dearly. Sharpless and Kate leave, escorted by Suzuki who returns at once to support Butterfly, now in tears for the first time and on the point of collapsing.

(As we know, Puccini altered the scene of the meeting between Butterfly and Kate Pinkerton after the first performance of the opera. Neither version, however, compares in dramatic irony with the original John Luther Long story, where Kate and Butterfly meet in the American Consulate. Butterfly is with the Consul and learns the identity of Pinkerton's wife when Kate—or Adelaide, as she is called in Long's novelette—enters to ask Sharpless to send a telegram to her husband who is with his ship at Kobe: "Just saw the baby and his nurse. Can't we have him at once? He is lovely. Shall see the mother about it to morrow. Was not at home when I was there today . . ." As Mrs Pinkerton leaves she sees Cho-Cho-San, and without knowing who she is, exclaims: "How very charming—how *lovely*—you are, dear! Will you kiss me, you pretty—*plaything*!" Butterfly refuses. "Ah well," laughs Adelaide, "I don't blame you. They say you don't do that sort of thing—to women, at any rate. I quite forgive our men for falling in love with you. . . ." Apart from the fatuous dialogue it is a neatly ironic twist to the situation, but operatically impracticable, of course. As it is, Puccini's form is an undoubted improvement. It makes Mrs Pinkerton a more sympathetic character, a little less gushing and feather-brained, and gives us an added glimpse of Butterfly's characteristic dignity and generosity when Kate asks her, "Can you forgive me, Butterfly?" and she replies: "Under the whole arc of heaven, there is no woman happier than you. Be happy always and do not feel sorry for me.")

Butterfly recovers and tells Suzuki to draw the *shosi*; she says the sunlight is too strong, and there is an ironic echo in the orchestra of the theme of the dawn breaking with which the scene began (Ex 129). The shutters are drawn and the room is left in almost complete darkness.

"Where is the child?" asks Butterfly.

Suzuki replies that he is playing outside. "Shall I call him?"

"Leave him to play," says Butterfly, "and you go and play with him."

An effective passage of orchestral detail begins when at Suzuki's refusal to leave Butterfly drags her to her feet and pushes her out of the room, and the timpani have 21 bars of B flats and F's played together:

The dynamics of this figure range through a dramatic crescendo to *ff*—an unnerving, ear-splitting hammering like the violent thumping of a heart—to a distant *ppp*. It is a figure which has the effect of distorting in a curious way what is in fact the violoncellos' quite undistorted and otherwise unaccompanied playing high on the D string of the tune of Ex 108. Against this orchestral background Butterfly remains quite still, lost in thought. On a sudden impulse she goes to the shrine; she lifts the white veil from it and throws it across the screen.

She takes down the dagger and as she kisses the blade reverently violoncellos and double basses play "roughly" (*ruvido*) the theme associated with the death of Butterfly's father (Ex 111). In a monotone Butterfly reads the inscription: "To die with honour when one can no longer live with honour."

Butterfly points the blade at her throat. The door opens and Suzuki's arm is seen pushing Butterfly's child towards his mother. Butterfly drops the dagger and runs towards the child to kiss him passionately. She takes his face in her hands and tells him why she is going to kill herself—so that he may be able to travel across the ocean to a life of happiness. Butterfly's farewell to her child ends with one of the most heart-breaking and characteristic of Puccini phrases:

Those bars, so reminiscent of the death of Manon and of Mimi, and anticipating the death of Liù in *Turandot,* have the composer's fingerprints all over them, for Puccini made peculiar and affecting use of the pathetic properties of the flattened seventh.

Butterfly ends her despairing cry of farewell by telling the child to go and play. She sets him down on a stool, with his face turned away from the screen; she gives him an American flag and a doll to play with, while she bandages his eyes. She takes the dagger, and keeping her eyes fixed on the child, goes behind the screen. These actions are performed to an orchestral passage of great originality and pathos. Violas and cor anglais in unison, *piano* and *lamentoso,* play a long, slowly-descending tune against a solemn two-beats-in-a-bar funeral-march rhythm by timpani, bass drum, gong, the harp in octaves in its low register, violoncellos and double basses. Punctuating this is a solo trumpet with a syncopated and repeated low B played *pp tristamente.*

The music changes and grows more animated as the sound of the knife falling to the ground is heard and the white veil disappears. Butterfly comes from behind the screen and staggers across the room towards the child; the veil is round her neck. She smiles at the child as she drags herself towards him, embraces him and falls at his side. Off-stage Pinkerton's voice is heard calling "Butterfly!" while trumpets and trombones in unison in the same register play *ff* the theme of Pinkerton's return (Ex 117). The door opens and Sharpless and Pinkerton rush in; Butterfly points weakly to the child, and dies. Pinkerton kneels beside her while Sharpless takes the child in his arms.

The curtain falls to an orchestral tutti—a unison reprise (*tutta forza*) of Ex 126, the theme with which Butterfly determined to die rather than live with dishonour.

If Puccini himself was more devoted to Butterfly than to any other of his heroines (and they all had a very real existence for him), then it was not without reason. There are long stretches of uninteresting "plot music" in *Madam Butterfly* as well as passages of such grotesque banality as the

Valzer lentissimo, but in no other Puccini opera does the principal character command the audience's sympathy so completely. Butterfly, who is fifteen when she comes on in the first scene and eighteen when she dies in the last, is the most carefully drawn of all Puccini's Little Girls. The composer gives her immense charm, considerable humour, a great depth of romantic feeling, and succeeds in expressing—in purely musical terms —her unique faith, dignity and pathos. Vocally the part of Butterfly, as I have suggested, is one of the most difficult and exacting in the repertoire; and it is exacting principally because there is no doubt from the moment of her first entrance that she is the heroine. The composer never allows us to sit back and be indifferent to anything she does; she holds our attention the entire time and dominates every minute she is on the stage—whether she is singing in the Love Duet, passing the time of day with Sharpless, snapping petulantly at Suzuki, or standing motionless and silent as she keeps her all-night vigil for the return of her faithless lover.

Puccini wrote musically greater operas than *Madam Butterfly,* but he created no greater, more sympathetic and moving character than that of the little Japanese girl who epitomized the composer's favourite figure— the Little Girl who suffered for her devotion and love. And not until *Turandot* did he again create an orchestral texture so sensitive or so shot through with original, exquisite colour.

THE GIRL OF THE GOLDEN WEST
(*La Fanciulla del West*)

(*Property of G. Ricordi and Co.*)

Opera in three acts, from the play by David Belasco, by Guelfo Civinini and Carlo Zangarini. First performed at the Metropolitan Opera House, New York on 10th December, 1910, conducted by Arturo Toscanini. First performance in England: Covent Garden, 29th May, 1911.

It is symptomatic, I think, of the uncertain position held by the opera itself that *The Girl of the Golden West* should be the one work of Puccini's known by a variety of alternative titles. For the purposes of this study it is only natural that it should be called by its English title; the Italian is, after all, only a translation of what was originally an American play, and to refer to it constantly as "La Fanciulla del West" strikes me as being as unnecessary as thinking of Verdi's projected setting of *King Lear* as "Re Lear". I know it might be argued that in that case we should always refer to Verdi's *Otello* by Shakespeare's English title, but use of the Italian form in this instance leaves no doubt that we are talking about the opera and not the play; I have no doubt that if Verdi had ever written his "Lear" we would have called it by its Italian name to distinguish it from the play. In the case of Puccini's opera, however, which needs no special label to distinguish it from the original play which it has long supplanted, the composer himself always spoke of it as "La *Girl*", or "mia *Girl*", fearing, he said, that the last two syllables of "fanciulla" might be mistaken for *ciullo*, or "stupid", and thought to refer to him.

Although Puccini always identified the opera in his own mind as "La *Girl*" he was for a long time undecided whether its official title should be "La figlia del West" or "L'occidente d'oro" (The Golden West). Perhaps because of Minnie's aria, "Io non son che una povera fanciulla" the more colloquial, less poetic "fanciulla" was chosen as being nearer to Belasco's "girl" who was not, except in a moral sense, the "maid" suggested by "figlia".

Once Puccini had settled on *La Fanciulla del West* some intriguing variants began to appear in other languages. The Germans, for instance, called the opera "Das Mädchen aus dem goldenen Westen"—i.e. "from", not "of", the Golden West, as though Minnie had come from California on a visit to sophisticated relations in New York; while the French, with their alarming habit of introducing Anglo-Saxon phrases wholesale into their exquisite language, called it "La Fille du Far-West". The final variant was thought up by Queen Alexandra, to whom the opera is dedicated and who wrote to thank the composer, in a letter that hangs on the wall at his villa at Torre del Lago, for his dedication of what she called "The Girl of the Wild West".

As he had done with *Tosca* and *Madam Butterfly* Puccini first encountered the subject of *The Girl of the Golden West* in a stage performance, of which he understood scarcely a word, but which impressed him strongly. But on this occasion he took his time over obtaining the musical rights from Belasco. He saw the play on a visit to New York to attend the Metropolitan première of *Madam Butterfly* in 1907, at a time when he was preoccupied with the possibilities of two new operatic subjects, *La Femme et le Pantin* by Pierre Louÿs and the story of Marie Antoinette, and for some time he did not commit himself even in his own mind to more than admitting that the setting and atmosphere of The West attracted him as something novel and different from anything he had encountered before.

Once Puccini had discarded his other projects and decided upon "La *Girl*", negotiations with David Belasco (since *Madam Butterfly* one of the composer's most fervent admirers) were rapid and easy. The composer's progress, on the other hand, was certainly neither rapid nor easy, for in addition to the usual troubles with his librettists—both of them new to him, for Giacosa had died and Illica had been discarded—Puccini's work and peace of mind were brutally disturbed by the tragedy of Doria, the little servant girl driven to suicide by the insane jealousy of Puccini's wife Elvira. This tragic upheaval in Puccini's life, and its consequences, are movingly described in Father Dante del Fiorentino's *Immortal Bohemian*; inevitably they affected Puccini's work, but whether they also affected his inspiration as adversely as some have suggested I am not altogether convinced. *The Girl of the Golden West* has never been a more interesting and gratifying study than it is today, when at a distance of more than 60 years after its production we can see it in a perspective denied to the composer's contemporaries; it was denied to them, not because they were in any way insufficiently educated to appreciate the differences between this opera and the composer's earlier works, but because they could not possibly see the ultimate significance of these differences as we can, who may recognize clearly the unmistakable signs pointing the way not just to the notes and orchestral detail, but to the very style and essence of *Turandot*.

Paradoxically it is not *Turandot* that is better understood if one has heard *The Girl of the Golden West* first, but the other way round. To know *Turandot* is to hold the key to much that is puzzling and unfamiliar in the earlier opera.

CHARACTERS IN ORDER OF SINGING:

JOE ⎤	. . . .	*Tenor*
BELLO (Handsome) ⎬ *miners*	. . .	*Baritone*
HARRY ⎦	. . . .	*Tenor*
NICK, *bartender at the "Polka"*	. . .	*Tenor*
HAPPY ⎤	. . . .	*Baritone*
SID ⎟	. . . .	*Baritone*
TRIN ⎬ *miners*	. . .	*Tenor*
SONORA ⎟	. . . .	*Baritone*
LARKENS ⎦	. . . .	*Bass*
JACK RANCE, *Sheriff* .	. . . .	*Baritone*
JAKE WALLACE, *a wandering ballad-singer*	.	*Baritone*
ASHBY, *agent of Wells-Fargo*	. . .	*Bass*
MINNIE . .	. . . .	*Soprano*
POST BOY . .	. . . .	*Tenor*
DICK JOHNSON (Ramerrez) .	. . .	*Tenor*
JOSÉ CASTRO, *half-caste, member of Ramerrez' gang*	*Basso generico**
WOWKLE, *Minnie's Indian servant and squaw of*	*Mezzo-soprano*
BILLY JACKRABBIT, *an Indian* . . .	*Bass*

Members of the camp.

Scene: A miners' camp at the foot of the Cloudy Mountains in California.

Time: The Gold Rush of 1849-50.

*Another term for *basso caratteristico*—a part in which character of voice is more important than quality.

ACT I

Scene: Interior of the "Polka".

There is a short orchestral introduction to the rise of the curtain, played by a larger orchestra than Puccini had used so far in his career; it includes treble wood-wind as well as cor anglais and bass clarinet, double bassoon, three harps (one of which plays off-stage), tubular bells off-stage, and an instrument called a "fonica" which I will describe later in this chapter.

It is a prelude which may be regarded as getting the opera off to a good and exhilarating start, for it is an immediately arresting opening presenting two themes, both of which are handled with great ingenuity and invention in the course of the opera; once more it is a work constructed out of numberless fragments. The first theme, highly spiced with the flavour of the whole-tone scale and its augmented triads, which are a feature of this score, is heard in a compelling tutti:

This theme leads directly into the second, a tune which is vigorous and passionate one moment, gentle and lyrical the next:

136

The short prelude ends with a brass cadence associated with Ramerrez, the bandit, consisting of Puccini's first touch of "local colour", a phrase unmistakably American in its intentions and suggesting how closely related the earlier forms of "syncopated" music were in their rhythmic pattern to the Cuban habanera. Speeded up and purged of its Latin languor the habanera is recognizable as a far-from-distant ancestor of jazz in Puccini's phrase:

Its most immediate predecessor, of course, is Debussy's *Gollywog's*

Cakewalk, an aspect of the French composer's influence on this opera which is not usually acknowledged.

The curtain rises on the saloon of the "Polka", which is owned and run by Minnie, who is a combination of mother and schoolteacher to the miners' community. It is a scene familiar to all who know their "Westerns", with its bar and card tables, a staircase leading to a balcony which runs the length of one wall and projects over the room. Under the balcony is a short passage leading, according to a large placard, to "The Dance Hall". On one of the walls is a reward notice on which the figures $5000, the name of "Ramerrez" and the firm "Wells-Fargo" are clearly legible to the audience.

Through a big door in the background and a window the valley can be seen with (the stage instructions run) "its wild vegetation of alders, oaks and dwarf pines, brightly lit by the setting sun. In the distance the snow-covered mountains are tinted with gold and purple. The very strong light outside, which is rapidly fading, makes the inside of the 'Polka' seem all the darker. In the gloom the outlines of things can scarcely be distinguished. On the left, close to the footlights, near the chimneypiece the glimmer of Jack Rance's cigar can be seen. Near the staircase on the right, Larkens is seated on a cask, his head in his hands. Suddenly he rises, takes a letter from his pocket, looks at it sadly, goes to the counter, takes a stamp, fixes it on the letter which he puts into the mail-box, and sits down on the cask again."

While all this is going on, the orchestra has quietened down to a gentle swaying movement in which a prominent part is played by a fragment associated, a little improbably, with Minnie's saloon which is scarcely so peaceful a place as is suggested by

138

And we hear, too, a subdued form of the opening theme (Ex 135) played first by a solo flute, then by a solo horn, then by a bassoon, against a *pp* off-beat pizzicato accompaniment by the strings which is especially prophetic of a couple of passages in *Turandot*. While the music is quiet enough for us to hear the off-stage voices of the miners shouting "Hello!" to each other in English, and a baritone in the distance singing the first haunting phrase of a tune which is heard at greater length later in the act, Nick comes in to light the candles and lamps in the bar and the dance hall. When the "Polka" is fully lit the door opens and groups of miners returning to camp begin to come in.

The music changes to a vigorous 2/4 typical of Puccini's "conversation" music; the conversation in this instance consists largely of greetings of "Hello!" (in English) interspersed by an occasional "Hollà!" and a full-blooded "All right!" (spelt in the score "Al right!"). The introduction of these English interjections into an Italian libretto is an odd conceit and not without its charm for the Anglo-Saxon listener, who may be pardoned if he wonders why the librettists did not go the whole hog in their anxiety to create a thoroughly local atmosphere and use nothing but English to do it with. To the Italians, however,—and for all that it was written for the Metropolitan, *The Girl of the Golden West* remains an incorrigibly Italian opera—the odd word of English which makes us smile is an exotic touch of time-honoured attraction, as one would expect of a nation which has delighted in such operatic titles as *Elisabetta in Derbyshire, Emilia di Liverpool,* and *Il birraio di Preston.*

The first miners to enter are Harry, Joe and Bello, followed by Sid, Happy and Billy Jackrabbit, the Indian. Joe, we later learn from the the libretto, is an Australian—"Australiano d'inferno" is what he is called when he fleeces the others at faro. Bello, Joe and one or two of their companions burst spontaneously into a snatch of what the libretto calls "an American refrain", but which the score refers to simply as " a refrain". The words are certainly American—"Dooda, dooda-dooda day . . ."—and one might in consequence reasonably expect to hear a quotation of the familiar strains of Stephen Foster's "Camptown Races". Instead (perhaps because Foster was still in copyright in 1910?), Puccini set the words to a little fragment of a tune which he uses extensively in these cheerful ensemble sequences of the miners:

The action, busily punctuated by cries of "Hello!", is concentrated mainly on getting a faro school going when Sonora and Trin, the last of the miners to answer to a name, arrive on the scene. While the game is in progress Rance asks Nick what is the matter with Larkens. Nick replies that it is his usual trouble: he is homesick and longing for his native Cornwall (Italianized, to avoid overdoing the exoticism, as "Corno-vaglia").

When the game of faro is finished, Sonora gets up from the table and taking Nick aside asks if there is any news of Minnie: has she decided in Sonora's favour? Nick answers certainly; he understands that Sonora is the one she prefers. Sonora jumps for joy and shouts "Cigars all round!", an order greeted with a unanimous "Hurrà!", which is pronounced, for some reason, "hooray" in most performances of the opera. Trin, who had left the card table earlier with an emphatic "Good by!" (*sic*) in English when he lost everything, also takes Nick aside and asking him the same question as Sonora, is given the same answer: Trin is the chosen one. Trin jumps for joy and shouts "whisky per tutti!" and is given the same general reception.

The music suddenly quietens down and the tempo slackens. From behind the scenes a harp is heard playing in the distance, according to instructions in the score, "with paper between the strings in imitation of a banjo.* After a bar of gentle strumming on its own the harp is joined by four solo violins, two solo violas and two violoncellos, all muted, sustaining long *ppp* chords as the voice of Jake Wallace is heard in the distance, singing:

Jake's nostalgic song (for once one may use this over-worked adjective in its literal sense) is an old American tune called "The Old Dog Tray" and is the beginning of a musical scene of great beauty which offers for the first time a glimpse of an entirely new lyrical quality in Puccini's music. It is a quality that is not at all easy to define, for its roots are not in the past of Puccini's music but, as it were, in what is to come. If one has heard the great trio sung by Ping, Pang and Pong in *Turandot* then this episode of *The Girl of the Golden West* will be easily understood and enjoyed. But if experience of Puccini's music is limited to *Manon Lescaut*, *La Bohème*, *Tosca* and *Madam Butterfly* then its whole intention and effect is likely to prove puzzling and unsatisfactory: for Puccini, for the first time, found lyrical inspiration in something that was not Love in its familiar operatic form. He found it in man's yearning for home. Nostalgia was a very real emotion in Puccini's own life and his letters written on his visits abroad were filled with a constant longing for his home at Torre del Lago; but because homesickness is largely a masculine emotion (women are surely never so sentimental about Home as men are) it was not one that came in for much musical consideration in Puccini's operas, which are so essentially concerned with the loves and lives of women.

It was not unnatural, however, that when dramatic opportunity did arise, as it arose with this community of men far from their homes in *The Girl of the Golden West*, and with the three court philosophers of *Turandot*, longing to return to their bamboo forests and lakeside homes, Puccini should have found inspiration in an emotion deeply rooted in his own nature and which found its supreme expression in the superbly sustained lyrical invention of the trio in *Turandot*.

As Jake appears at the doorway of the "Polka" the miners gradually stop playing cards and quietly join in the song, adding their own reflections on the mothers—and dogs—they have left behind them. The words are, frankly, of a quite nauseating sentimentality, but the restraint and extremely personal melancholy of Puccini's music transform this scene into an oddly moving and beautiful sequence which, the composer indicates in the score, "must be sung with much feeling and *never* at full voice".

---

* The harp with paper between the strings has to stand in for many absent friends in orchestral practice—for the mandoline Mozart wants in *Don Giovanni*, the guitar Rossini writes for in *The Barber of Seville*, and the lute prescribed in *Die Meistersinger*. This is the only case I know where the harp is actually *asked* to imitate another string instrument. It is just as well: no real banjo could play the part Puccini has written here.

The atmosphere created by Jake and the miners has an unnerving effect on Larkens, who breaks down in tears, crying in despair that he cannot go on: he must return to his native cornfields and his mother. As the orchestra bursts *fff* into the tune of Ex 140, Sonora takes off his cap and hands it round among the miners collecting money to enable Larkens to return home. The money is raised and with tears in his eyes Larkens thanks the miners and leaves; the music dies away in a final wordless cadence hummed by the chorus.

The tempo changes back to the "conversational" 2/4 of the earlier scene as the miners return to their gambling. This leads to a violent episode in which guns are drawn when Sid is accused of cheating; he is saved by the intervention of Rance, who pins the card Sid has cheated with—the two of spades—on the culprit's breast as a sign that he must never touch cards again; if he does he will be hanged. Sid is thrown out of the "Polka" and never seen again in the opera. This scene is sometimes cut so that in some performances the initial resumption of the miners' card-playing is followed immediately and in an orderly fashion by the entrance of Ashby, the Wells-Fargo agent, whom Rance introduces to "the boys". Ashby asks after "the Girl" and learning that she is well, answers Rance's questions about the bandit—obviously the Ramerrez whose name appears on the notice—with the information that he is still at large, the head of a band of Mexicans who stick at nothing, although their leader "robs like a *gran signore*".

Saying that he is dead tired, Ashby bids everybody goodnight and settles down with a cloak over him under the staircase leading to the balcony, taking no notice (the stage directions tell us) of what goes on around him. What does go on, to be sure, is enough to waken the dead, for when Nick comes on bringing whisky, lemon and hot water with the compliments of Minnie, Rance boasts that she will shortly be "Mrs Rance". This starts a noisy argument between Rance and Sonora, who calls the Sheriff an "old yellow face" whom Minnie is fooling. A serious quarrel develops, Sonora draws a gun, but as he fires his arm is knocked upwards by the crowd trying to separate the two men, and the shot goes in the air. The sound of the revolver shot is the cue for the entrance of Minnie and for this theme:

141

This phrase, which is obviously Minnie's "own" theme, as it were, makes a tremendous impact not only on this first appearance, but virtually every time it is heard during the opera, for Puccini uses it with remarkable reticence and never as a theme for development as, for instance, he uses the theme of Ex 135.

Minnie's entrance, greeted with enthusiastic cries from the miners of

"Hello, Minnie!", has the immediate result of separating Sonora and Rance; she makes them shake hands; the Sheriff does so with ill-grace and then goes over to a table where he sits down to play solitaire.

There follows a quaint little scene in which the miners bring modest offerings to Minnie—Joe gives her flowers picked by the Black River, which grow at his home in Australia; Sonora takes a crimson ribbon from his pocket and gives it her "to match your lips", Harry gives her a silk handkerchief—"blue, like your eyes". Ashby, whose bedding-down under the staircase coincided with the Sonora-Rance uproar and was disturbed beyond repair, comes up to the bar and raises his glass to Minnie, toasting her "with the compliments of Wells-Fargo", a toast to which she replies with the friendly Belascan "Hip! Hip!" of Lieut. Pinkerton (already current, it seems, in 1849), and an offer of cigars. Sonora pays his bar-account with a bag of gold dust which Minnie puts in a barrel where the miners' gold is kept. Ashby, noticing this action, turns to Rance to remark that it seems madness to keep all that gold there, with so many bandits on the road. It would be far safer at the Wells-Fargo office.

The business of this scene completed, the action turns to Minnie and her Bible class—a class consisting of Trin, Joe, Harry, Sonora and those miners—except Larkens and Sid—mentioned by name in the score (the rest have left quietly during the scene when Minnie was receiving her presents of flowers and ribbons).

As Minnie settles down to her reading a charming little theme emerges to be coloured by some exquisite and original orchestration:

Though one half-suspects that it was a delight in the orchestral sounds he could make with this theme that was Puccini's first object, there is a certain air of innocence about it all, created by an ingenious use of piccolo, glockenspiel and celeste, which is in keeping with Minnie's reading of the Psalms. (The violent braying which interrupts the lesson for a moment is Trin's mockery of Harry, who gets confused by the question of David and the jawbones of asses.)

Minnie, after ending her reading of the Psalm with an enchanting cadence, adds a short homily on the meaning of "Wash me and I shall be whiter than snow", which makes a deep impression on her audience, and they sit silently as the orchestra plays the last bars of Jake Wallace's song (Ex 140).

The peaceful atmosphere is disturbed by Nick entering and shouting excitedly, "La posta!" To the naïve sound of galloping horses in the orchestra, the Post Boy arrives, and dismounting* gives the letters to Nick, adding the warning that a half-breed has been seen in the neighbourhood. Nick hands round the mail—letters for Happy, Bello and Joe, a newspaper for Harry, and a despatch for Ashby who opens it and reads it with astonishment. He calls the Post Boy and asks: "Do you know a Nina Micheltorena?"

Minnie supplies the answer. Nina is a fake Spaniard born in Cachuca, a siren who uses lampblack to give herself "a languid eye". "Ask the boys," adds Minnie. Ashby turns to Rance and in a hushed voice says that Ramerrez will be hanged that night; Nina knows where the bandit is hiding, and has sent a message to say he will be at the "Palmeto" saloon at midnight. Rance doubts whether Nina is to be trusted, but Ashby says he will keep the appointment anyway, and leaves with Rance.

The miners discuss the contents of their letters, and the depressing news that his old grandmother has died causes Joe to shout "whisky!" at the top of his voice.

Nick comes in again to tell Minnie that there is a stranger outside, whom he has never seen before. He seems to be from San Francisco and asked for whisky and water, a request that horrifies Minnie: "Whisky and water? What sort of concoction is that?"

Nick makes his announcement to a couple of chords for wood-wind which the student of orchestration will find Puccini has scored with a most intriguing and effective disregard for convention. In the first of the two chords,

the voicing, reading from top to bottom of the chord, is bassoon, oboe, bass clarinet, cor anglais; in the second: bassoon, cor anglais, oboe, bass clarinet. Nick explains that he told the stranger that at the "Polka" (the orchestra echoes the theme of Ex 138) whisky is always drunk straight. "Let him come in, then," says Minnie. "We'll curl his hair for him." Nick goes out.

Rance, who has returned from his conversation with Ashby, and is drinking at the bar, finds himself alone with Minnie. He starts to make love to her, offering her a thousand dollars for a kiss, to the gloomy unison of strings playing this:

* Puccini, knowing the Italians' passion for real horses on the opera stage, indicates in the score that the horse must be visible.

The theme is repeated in consecutive blocks of chords played *ppp* by strings, and wood-wind reinforced by the double bassoon who plays the tune in the lowest register in concert with the double basses. It is a dark, sinister kind of sound which does not rise above *pianissimo* for more than a moment while Minnie holds Rance at arm's length, first by sharp words then with a pistol which she takes from the bosom of her blouse.

She puts the gun back in her dress as Rance moves away from the bar in silence, goes over to the card table where he shuffles the cards nervously. Minnie looks at him and says: "Are you angry with me, Rance? Why? I told you what I think."

Rance throws the cards violently on to the table and turning to Minnie tells her bitterly how when he left his home there was not a tear at his departure; nobody has loved him, he has never loved anybody. His gambler's heart led him in search of gold, the only thing that has never deceived him; and now he is offering a fortune for a kiss—"Minnie, dalla mia casa son partito". The melodic line of this short number again has something of that nostalgic quality which we encounter with increasing frequency in this opera, and for all that Rance is directed to sing in a "harsh and strident voice" there is a lyrical warmth in the music entirely different from anything in the part of Puccini's other baritone-villain, Scarpia:

Minnie answers Rance's plea with a conversational account of her life as a child in her parents' inn ("Laggiù nel Soledad"), of how much her mother loved her father and how she wishes she could find a man like him to love. It is a sequence of great charm and simplicity, with a solo violin that darts in and out of the accompaniment; it is not long enough to rate as an "aria" in any sense of the term, but musically it is more finely drawn than most passages of Puccini narrative.

Nick returns with the stranger, who throws his saddle down on a table and demands to know who threatened to curl his hair. Minnie quickly suppresses a look of recognition as she bids him welcome; the stranger shall have his whisky as he pleases. It is obvious that Minnie and the stranger have met before, and though each takes care not to show any signs of recognition, Rance immediately grows jealous and aggressive, asking the man's name and business. The stranger says his name is Johnson and he hails from Sacramento. "Welcome, Johnson of Sacramento!" cries Minnie, and an angry scowling Rance retreats into the background.

The music now drops to a gentle, swaying 6/8 variant of Ex 137 for the dialogue between Minnie and Johnson, a sequence of unusual warmth and delicate orchestral touches; they recall their earlier meeting on the road to Monterey, which had obviously made a lasting sentimental impression on both of them.

Even at this early stage of the opera it is clear from Puccini's characterization that Johnson has great personal charm and that we are going to like him and be concerned for his well-being. In the general critical confusion that surrounds *The Girl of the Golden West*, it is rarely remembered that there are few more immediately sympathetic Puccini heroes: Dick Johnson is virile without being brash or bone-headed, gentle without being sloppy or hysterical. He has courage and a warm heart.

Rance returns to the scene once more, upsets Johnson's glass and demands to know his business. He is the Sheriff and nobody is going to make a monkey out of him. Johnson, instinctively putting his hand on his revolver, says nothing. Minnie pulls his hand away from the gun; he leans against the bar again and pays no attention to Rance. The Sheriff goes over to the dance hall and shouts to the miners that there is a stranger in the camp who refuses to state his business. Rance's unaccompanied words are sung to a phrase which has no importance at all at this point, but is the basis of a long and imposing tune in the second act:

The occurrence of this tune at this point seems to be entirely coincidental, for neither words nor dramatic situation suggests any connection with what happens to it later in the action.

A crowd of miners come in from the dance hall and make threatening noises at Johnson, but Minnie intervenes; she says she knows Johnson and will vouch for him. The atmosphere changes immediately and cordial relations are established between the stranger and "the boys", who are openly delighted to see the discomfited Rance put in his place. Harry points to the dance hall and suggests Johnson might like to waltz. Johnson offers his arm to Minnie, who laughs at her own confusion: she has never danced in her life. Encouraged by Johnson and egged on by the miners Minnie agrees to try and to a general shout of "Hip! Hooray!" she dances into the adjoining hall with Johnson to the music of a waltz la-la'd by the chorus:

The orchestral accompaniment to this vocal unison is limited first to three clarinets, then to three flutes. When the full phrase has been sung, the strings take over with a "middle section", but instead of returning us to the original tune the music builds up in a big crescendo as cries of "Hang him! Hang him!" are heard off-stage. At a change of tempo to a well-named Allegro feroce, Ashby and a crowd of angry men drag in the unhappy half-caste Castro, who sees Johnson's saddle and thinks his master has been captured. It is quickly apparent to Castro, from Rance's threats, however, that Johnson (or Ramerrez) is still at large, and he offers to lead them (on a false trail, of course) to his hideaway in the Madrona Canyada. Sonora and Trin go to the dance hall door and call for men to saddle the horses. While the door is open Castro is overjoyed to catch sight of Johnson dancing.

During the general commotion and excitement Johnson comes out of the dance hall and Castro manages to speak to him quickly, telling him what is happening. He has allowed himself to be captured to throw them off the scent; he adds that when Johnson hears a whistle he is to whistle back in answer if he is ready: the band are all close by in hiding, and ready to pounce on the "Polka". Rance's men grab Castro, and the saloon is empty except for Johnson, and Nick, who begins to close down and put out the lights. Nick goes into the dance hall and Johnson is left alone on the stage.

Puccini's magical change of atmosphere at this point is typically achieved at a single stroke by the simplest means: the tempo drops, the time changes to 6/4 and an oboe plays a broadened and *dolce* version of the waltz tune against a background of murmuring strings. Johnson wanders slowly around the room, catches sight of the barrel containing gold but "with a gesture of contempt" dismisses the subject from his mind and instead goes over to the card table to pick up his saddle. As he does so Minnie enters and seeing him still there asks him *dolcemente* if he has stayed behind to keep her company and guard the house. Certainly, replies Johnson, if she wants him to. How odd, he reflects, to find her again in these surroundings, where anybody could come in and drink or rob. Minnie assures him she would know how to deal with a situation like that. Even if somebody came to rob her of a kiss? Minnie answers that it would not be for the first time, though no man has ever yet kissed her.

As she clears up the bar and puts the money away Johnson listens "with growing interest". Does she live at the "Polka"? No, she lives in a cabin half-way up the mountain. When Johnson says she deserves something better, Minnie replies that she is happy and contented as she is; she lives alone and is not afraid. At these last words a new phrase makes the first of many appearances in the orchestra:

It is a theme which becomes very much Minnie's personal property. It is not a "love theme" (it is too much of a fragment for that), but we hear a great deal of it in her scenes with Johnson, or where his name is mentioned and affects her.

No, she is not afraid, says Minnie; she trusts Johnson even though she does not know who he is. Johnson replies he does not know himself who he is, but he has loved life and still loves it; just as Minnie loves it but, he says, has not yet lived it to the full.

There follows a little scene of great pathos and simplicity. Minnie reflects sadly that she is only a poor girl, obscure and good for nothing—"Io non son che una povera fanciulla":

With a simple orchestral accompaniment that begins with one and then two oboes, Minnie tells Johnson that he says such beautiful things, that perhaps she does not understand; she cannot explain, but in her heart she is unhappy that she is so small and longs to raise herself up to him "high as the stars, to be near you and talk to you"—an ascending phrase echoed by a solo trumpet and piccolo, violins, violas and violoncellos in their highest registers, in a shimmering orchestral reaffirmation of Minnie's words.

Tenderly Johnson, to the tune of the waltz in the broadened romantic form which began this scene, tells Minnie that while they were dancing her trembling heart against his breast told him all she could not express in words, and he felt "a strange joy, a new peace that I cannot describe".

Minnie is just beginning to say how happy and yet how full of fears she is when Nick enters to warn them that there is another suspicious half-breed Mexican lurking outside. He takes a pistol from under the counter and goes out, shutting the door behind him.

Johnson holds Minnie back, telling her to stay where she is. As he does so the sound of a shrill whistle is heard outside—the signal Johnson was expecting. Minnie instinctively moves towards Johnson for protection. There is a fortune in that barrel, she says; usually one of the boys stays all night to guard it, but tonight—anybody who tries to rob it will have to kill her first. And in a rather melancholy passage Minnie reflects on the miners who have left their homes and families, and have come to die like dogs so that they can send a little gold back to their children and ageing parents far away. "That is why," Minnie concludes, "whoever wants that gold must first get past me!"

Minnie's resolute words are followed by a short orchestral epilogue, a warm, expansive phrase which is partly new, partly a distortion—or perhaps better, an adaptation—of the first theme in the opera (Ex 135):

Whatever the tune's origin it leads logically to the second phrase of the orchestral introduction (Ex 136) and thence into the first theme proper, as though this was, in fact, what the composer had had in mind all along. This passage accompanies Johnson's assurance to Minnie not to be afraid, when he sees her go behind the bar and get two pistols which she places on the barrel; nobody will dare to rob the "Polka".

On a sudden impulse Johnson tells Minnie how much he likes to hear her talk in this way—but he must go; he would have liked to have climbed up to her cabin to say a last goodbye to her there. Johnson's words, "I should have liked to have climbed" ("Avrei voluto salire . . .") are sung to a phrase which, when I first heard it, struck a strong chord in the memory:

The reminiscence in fact turned out to be another of those strong anticipations of *Turandot* which, as I have suggested, give *The Girl of the Golden West* so much of its fascination in our generation. Unfortunately, I cannot tell, having already heard *Turandot* before the earlier work, whether Johnson's phrase is really as arresting in its context as I think. But when the same tune (in a different key) recurs in *Turandot*—not as a theme, as the *Manon Lescaut* tune recurred in *La Bohème* (see Exx 13 and 42)—it is one of the unforgettable moments of what was in so many ways Puccini's masterpiece.

Minnie does not conceal her disappointment that Johnson has to leave; in a near-monotone she says that the boys will be back soon and if he would like to they could continue their conversation in front of the fire in her cabin. Johnson thanks her and after a moment's hesitation accepts her invitation. "Don't expect too much," says Minnie, half gaily, half sadly. "I only had thirty dollars' worth of education." She tries to laugh, but her eyes fill with tears as she adds: "If I had studied more, what might I have been?"

"What might *we* have been! I know, now that I look at you, Minnie!"

The music to this short episode, from the point where Minnie says that the boys will be back soon, is based on the phrase of Ex 150 marked "A", played first in a much broadened form by an unmuted solo violin then together with 8 muted violins against a background of long *ppp* chords sustained by muted strings, with the addition at various times of flutes, muted horns, clarinets, and coloured by occasional octaves from the harp, and the celeste in its lower register. It is a passage with a peculiar magic unlike anything else in Puccini's music, for it has a quality of wonderment which increases as these last moments of the act move towards their climax.

Minnie wipes away a tear, saying "what's the use?", and relapses into her earlier pessimistic mood with two solo violins, against a murmuring figure by flute and violas, playing the first phrase of "Io non son che una povera fanciulla" in octaves (Ex 149). Burying her head in her hands Minnie bursts into tears as she finishes the phrase with "oscura e buona a nulla".

Johnson, with great tenderness, tells her not to cry: "You do not know yourself. You are a creature with a good and pure soul, and you have the face of an angel." As Johnson sings these words the tune of Ex 141 is played *pp* by divided strings and hummed off-stage by 15 tenors whom Puccini uses once more as a sound-effect, as he did in *Madam Butterfly*.

Johnson collects his saddle and goes out quickly. The tune of Ex 141 is repeated by a solo violin and solo violoncello in octaves as Minnie stands dazed in the middle of the room, unaware of Nick's movements in the background as he puts out the light over the bar and goes, leaving his mistress's face lit from above by a single lamp hanging from the ceiling.

As though in a dream Minnie whispers, "He said—what did he say? 'The face of an angel!' " and the orchestra adds its own sigh to match the "long sigh like a lament" that comes from Minnie when, for the first time in her tough life, she has heard tender words from a man:

152

The curtain falls slowly as the final chord grows quieter and quieter, the number of strings gradually diminishing until each note of the chord is played by only one instrument—a total of four violins, two violas and three violoncellos. The last three bars of the act include a part for the instrument described as a "fonica". It took me some time to discover exactly what kind of an instrument this was, but eventually I learned from Ricordi's in Milan that it consisted of six metal strips mounted on a wooden frame and each with a brass box under it to act as a resonator as with the Japanese bells used in *Madam Butterfly* and Mascagni's *Iris*. (So far the instrument is not unlike a vibraphone in principle.) Six felt hammers, set in motion by a handle, strike the metal strips simultaneously and very rapidly to produce the tremolo shown in the score. The report continued: "To listen to the impression is not pleasing; the sound lacks tenderness. In a *dolce* moment like the end of the first act of *The Girl of the Golden West* the fonica is disturbing rather than pleasant. This is no doubt the reason why use of the instrument has been abandoned." That is all I have succeeded in learning about the fonica. When it was invented, by whom it was invented, why Puccini should have written for an instrument which seems to have been so unsympathetic that it was not tolerable even for the only three bars it had to play in the entire opera, I do not know. I cannot help feeling it is a pity that it should have disappeared altogether without leaving even a passing reference to itself in any of the musical encyclopaedias or books on orchestration that I have consulted.

The curtain to the first act of *The Girl of the Golden West* is one of the most effective in all Puccini's operas. It is also the end of one of the most original scenes he ever wrote, for though Minnie and Johnson are on the stage alone for most of the last quarter of an hour or so of the act, it is not a love duet in the accepted operatic sense of the term. If it had been, then I would not have found myself having to refer in such unusual detail to the words of the libretto, for after the initial sallies the words of the average love duet are little more than the sweet poetic nothing provided as a peg to hang music on. In the case of this scene, however, the words are important in the exposition and development of the characters of Minnie and Johnson and in the building up of a situation which comes to its full dramatic climax later in the opera. We see two people slowly growing more attractive to each other—and to us—and both of them revealing unexpected sides to their natures: beneath her rough exterior Minnie, who can keep a campful of unruly miners in order, is shown to be a typically weak and helpless woman in need of protection, while Johnson-Ramerrez, the bandit with a price on his head, has a gentler way with him and a more tender approach to the woman he loves than any of Puccini's tenor heroes. It is, in short, altogether a fine first act, full of invention and vitality and culminating in a sequence of great lyrical beauty.

ACT II

Scene: Minnie's cabin. A single room above which is a loft where trunks and empty boxes are neatly piled up. At the back, centre, with windows either side of it, a door opening on to a small porch. Along one of the walls is a bed. In front of the hearth of a low fireplace is a bear skin.

The curtain rises to rather nondescript music in 6/8 time in which for the only time in the opera I consider Puccini inclined to overdo the whole-tone scale as an exotic colouring. It is not monotonous, as it turns out, but one feels it could have been just a little more interesting. The rocking 6/8, which persists for quite a time in this scene, is justified by the picture we see when the curtain goes up on Wowkle, Minnie's Indian servant, singing a lullaby to the papoose she rocks on her back; it is an authentic Indian tune with an exquisite orchestral accompaniment of flute, bass clarinet, muted trumpet, harp, bassoon, timpani, and four solo violins sustaining octave D's in the high register.

Wowkle is joined by Billy Jackrabbit, and they discuss the question of getting married in language liberally laced with the phrase "Ugh" (pronounced "ooh") and in the form of a fantastic kind of pidgin-Italian in which all definite articles are dispensed with and the infinitive form is exclusively used for all verbs. (It is not quite clear why two Indians should converse together in a foreign language they scarcely speak rather than in their own, which must surely consist of more than "Ugh!")

Billy leaves at the entrance of Minnie who announces to an astonished Wowkle that there will be two for supper. Minnie then begins to titivate herself—roses in her hair, gloves, slippers from Monterey, eau de Cologne on her handkerchief, a coloured shawl over her shoulders; she wants to dress up and look beautiful, she says, as though it were a *festa*. The music to which she tells us this is an altered version of Ex 136 culminating in the first four notes of Ex 148 (a fragmentary phrase heard with increasing frequency in this act), and dressed up in some colourful orchestral clothing in the form of the tune played in harmonics by 1st violins, violas and violoncellos, and *sul ponticello* by the 2nd violins.

Minnie is just looking at herself in the mirror and wondering whether she has not made herself "troppo elegante", when there is a knock on the door and Johnson's voice is heard outside—inevitably calling "Hello!" A moment later he comes in and, after another "Hello!" asks Minnie whether she is going out—a piece of uncharacteristic facetiousness that throws the poor girl in confusion.

What follows now is a long sequence of dialogue which gradually expands into a love scene. Minnie, to a gentle 6/8 version of the waltz tune, begins by suggesting that Johnson had come to the "Polka" that evening only because he had lost his way to Nina Micheltorena's. Johnson changes the subject, first by trying unsuccessfully to kiss Minnie, then by observing what a nice place she has here—how strange her life must be, he adds, high up on the mountain alone and so far away from the world. Minnie replies that he has no idea how exciting her life is ("Oh se sapeste come il vivere è allegro"), and in artless terms she describes how she rides down to the valley and the river with its flower-covered banks, and when she returns to her mountains near the sky she feels as if she can knock on the threshold of heaven. It is a naïvely enthusiastic recital more remarkable for the sparkling orchestral accompaniment, in which an *ostinato* solo violin is featured, than for its musical substance.

Minnie ends her tale by telling Johnson that in the winter she runs the "Academy"—her school for the miners. The atmosphere and the colour of the music change when Minnie matter-of-factly offers Johnson a "biscotto alla crema" (which is not a cream biscuit, but of all unlikely dishes to find in the circumstances, a *charlotte russe*) and we hear one of Puccini's characteristic and quiet orchestral anticipations of a vocal tune to come, with violins playing the curious descendant of Rance's phrase in Ex 146:

The small-talk continues in spite of this sudden hint of lyricism with Johnson almost literally asking Minnie if she has read any good books lately. He learns that she is fond of reading love stories and promises to send her some; she teases him when he says there are some women "with whom one longs to have just one short hour—and then die!"

"Indeed?" is Minnie's comment. "And how many times have you died?" and she gives him a cigar.

At last Minnie manages to get rid of Wowkle, who has been hovering around serving coffee and embarrassing Johnson by her presence. (In passing, the "supper" seems to have been a gastronomically quaint sort of meal altogether. At least, there is no mention in the score of anything more than coffee and the *charlotte russe*, which in the original Belasco play Minnie called a "charlotte rusk.") The Indian cannot go home, because of the snow which is now falling thickly, but she is sent off to lie in the hay —presumably in the stable where Minnie keeps her pony. Johnson and Minnie are alone at last and she throws herself in his arms to give him the kiss he has begged for since he first entered her cabin. Their embrace coincides with a *fff* whole-tone version of Ex 136 as a great gust of wind blows the door open and snow drifts into the room. The lovers remain in each other's arms, oblivious of everything. The door closes itself and the tumult subsides; the same theme (Ex 136) continues, in a tenderer, more leisurely form with the roughness of the recent climax taken out of it.

Johnson tells Minnie that he has loved her from the first moment, but on a sudden he is afraid and overcome with remorse. He kisses her and goes quickly to the door to leave. He opens the door and closes it again; the blizzard outside is now thick, and is described in an orchestral passage that makes original and remarkably effective use of tubular bells. Minnie tells him he cannot possibly go; it is Fate; he must stay. Three rapid revolver shots are heard outside. "Listen!" cries Minnie. "Perhaps it's a bandit. Perhaps it's Ramerrez. What does it matter to us? Stay here! It is destiny!" Johnson stays, and the tune of Ex 146 bursts forth exuberantly as a fully-bloomed theme for a love duet as he sings, *con grande passione*, "I shall never leave you again!":

Minnie joins in and for the first time there is melodic unanimity between the lovers. When they have sung the word "eternamente" a cut is usually made which is one of the most necessary cuts made in any opera, for it spares us fifteen bars of probably the worst music Puccini—or indeed any other composer of genius—ever wrote. It is music of such banality that it is incredible any composer, having started his duet so convincingly, could possibly have ended it so disastrously.* The student with masochistic inclinations may enjoy this passage in the score beginning at 14 bars after Fig. 31 and ending at Fig. 32, where normal performances resume. For those who do not have the score I quote the melody, the triteness of which is fully matched by that of the harmony:

Minnie makes up her bed for Johnson and wraps herself up in the bear skin in front of the fire, and at this safe distance apart they chatter a little while the blizzard rages outside.

* The passage in question was in fact an afterthought of the composer's, added for a new production of the opera in Rome in 1922—to supply, he said, "warm bars which were lacking." The singers in Rome, however, found the phrase too difficult, and it was not until 1923 that a modest company, performing at Puccini's local theatre, the Politeama at Viareggio, introduced the new climax to the duet for the first time. How often those fifteen bars were performed thereafter I do not know; but today their omission is, rightly, such universally accepted procedure that it is as though they had never existed.

Minnie now learns for the first time that Johnson's name is Dick; in a whisper they swear eternal fidelity and say good night.

The peace and quiet which Puccini has so expertly created is now shattered by shouts of "Hello!" coming from Nick outside, who adds that Ramerrez has been seen on the trail. Minnie hides Johnson behind the curtains of the bed; he stands there, pistols in hand, while Minnie opens the door to let in Rance, Nick, Ashby and Sonora who have been anxious for her safety. "That Johnson of yours", she is told with obvious glee by Rance, is Ramerrez. Sid, the card sharper who is now an absent friend, reported having seen him head along the trail to this cabin. Who told them Johnson was Ramerrez? asks Minnie. His woman, replies Rance—Nina Micheltorena; she gave them Johnson's portrait, and the Sheriff shows it to Minnie, who—not very convincingly—feigns a careless laugh as she hands it back. She bids "the boys" good night and sends them away closing the door behind them.

There is a moment's pause before Minnie turns on a saddened and dejected Johnson with all the fury of a woman deceived.

Johnson is at last able to get a hearing; when Minnie shows him the door, he refuses to go before he has explained, though not excused, his career as a highway robber.

Against a figure in the orchestra based on the cakewalk "Ramerrez" theme of Ex 137, Johnson declares passionately that he would not have robbed Minnie. He did not know that he was born the son of a bandit until, six months before, his father had died leaving him as his inheritance a band of robbers. He had accepted the legacy; it was his destiny. But then one day he had met Minnie and he had dreamed ever since of taking her away with him to a life of love and honest work. The music changes from the roughness of his recital of fact and reverts to the tender lyrical mood of the duet with Ex 136 played *Largo e calmo* as Johnson tells Minnie how he has always prayed she would never learn of his shame. His plea ends passionately with a *fff* orchestral echo of the tune of Ex 154.

This impassioned declaration of Johnson's is a scene which I find more satisfying at each hearing, and one which I am surprised is not more often sung as a solo "number" by tenors, if not in preference, at least in addition, to "Ch'ella mi creda libero", which is normally the only excerpt from this opera to be heard out of its context. Beginning at Fig. 52 in the score (that is, 9 bars earlier than the section, sometimes referred to as an "aria", which begins with "Or son sei mesi"), it is a sequence of such vigour and lyrical warmth, leading to the climax of a high B flat which should certainly appeal to the normally uninhibited tenor, that one can only suppose that either tenors have never heard of *The Girl of the Golden West*, or, having looked at the score, they are filled with an uncharacteristic respect for the composer's intentions that they regard Minnie's immediate continuation of the plot as a hint that Johnson's scene is not to be studied separately. My own belief, however, is that the average tenor has simply never looked any further into the score than

"Ch'ella mi creda libero".

Minnie certainly steps smartly on Johnson's last notes with the bitter words: God may forgive you for being a thief, but you have taken my first kiss. And she tells him to go: they will kill him, but what does it matter to her? Johnson, according to the directions in the score, "desperate, resolute, unarmed, opens the door ready for sacrifice, like a suicide, and goes out quickly". A shot is heard outside.

Instead of a dramatic outburst from the orchestra, which one might have expected here according to common operatic usage, a breathless syncopated *ppp* and *staccatissimo* figure is heard played by cor anglais, clarinet, bass clarinet, bassoons and double bassoon, muted horns, three muted trumpets in unison, muted trombones, timpani in thirds, bass drum, and strings—all in their lowest and "darkest" registers. It is an orchestral reaction that provides an unusually tense background to Minnie's powerful dilemma. Her first instinctive feeling is one of anxiety: they have shot the man she loves. But within a moment she is shrugging her shoulders again and asking what does it matter, as she bursts into tears and buries her head in her hands. The sound of a body falling with a heavy thud against the door breaks down Minnie's defences. She rushes to the door and drags in the wounded Johnson, who tries to staunch the flow of blood from a wound in his side with his handkerchief. He resists Minnie's assistance as hard as he can, gasping that he must go, the door must not be closed. Minnie exerts all her strength and cries that he must stay; she loves him—"You are the man who gave me my first kiss—you cannot die!"—and with a superhuman effort she manages to get him up the ladder into the loft to hide. Minnie's desperate struggle and words of encouragement are accompanied by a repeated four-note phrase, played *pp* by the entire orchestra:

There is a loud and repeated knocking at the cabin door. Minnie comes down from the loft, quickly removes the ladder, and opens the door to let in Rance who enters cautiously, pistol in hand, and searches the room thoroughly to an orchestral echo of Ex 144. Minnie, addressing him as "Jack", asks what's new. Rance snaps back that he is not "Jack"; he is the Sheriff looking for Johnson-Ramerrez, and he continues his search. Minnie tells him to look where he likes and then be off and out of her sight for ever. Rance surprises Minnie by turning to her suddenly, saying, "Tell me that you don't love him!" Minnie replies that he must be mad. Yes, says Rance, mad for love of her; and he grabs her and tries to kiss her. Minnie picks up a whisky bottle and brandishes it over Rance's head, telling him angrily to get out and stay out. The Sheriff goes; as he reaches the door he turns and exclaims: "Yes, I'll go. But I swear he shall never have you!"

What are intended to be Rance's parting words introduce a theme used by Puccini as a typical means of raising the dramatic tension. It is a menacing theme, closely related in character to the sombre phrase heard in the second act of *Tosca* (Ex 85):

It is a phrase played seven times consecutively, beginning with its initial statement by violas and horns, rising to a *fff* echo by brass playing *con tutta forza* and dying away as a pale echo by a solo bassoon; it is never heard again. But the dramatic impact of its brief appearance is tremendous; its dynamic climax coincides with Rance's threatening oath that Johnson shall never possess Minnie, and it subsides immediately to a sinister quiet when a drop of blood falls from the loft on to the Sheriff's outstretched hand.

Minnie quickly explains that she must have scratched him; Rance points out that there is no scratch, and another drop of blood—this time accentuated by the harp—falls on his hand. Rance, drawing his gun, shouts at Johnson to come down out of the loft. Minnie pleads with Rance to wait: Johnson is seriously wounded and cannot climb down the ladder. Rance repeats his order and Johnson, helped by Minnie, comes slowly and helplessly out of his hiding place to the sound of a weary reprise of Ex 156, but with the addition this time of a poignantly accented string figure reminiscent of so many of Verdi's musical expressions of weeping and anguish. Rance's sarcastic greeting of Johnson misses its mark when Minnie points out that he has fainted.

After a moment's reflection Minnie proposes to Rance that the whole situation should be decided by a game of poker—the best of three hands. The stakes: her life and Johnson's. "If you win," she tells Rance, "you take this wounded man and me. But if I win, this man is mine!" Minnie issues her challenge to a melancholy reprise of Ex 156 by a solo oboe. Rance's acceptance is made to a short sequence of unusual dissonances which for a moment introduces a sudden element of sinisterness to the character of the Sheriff, which it has not had before and which, of course, it does not deserve: Rance is as ordinary and unsinister a villain as they come. Puccini's little excursion into new harmonic spheres is over and done with so soon, however, that it has no lasting dramatic effect and one is left with the impression that the composer was enjoying a private technical experiment just to see what it sounded like.

Before she sits down to play, Minnie goes to the cupboard, ostensibly to fetch a new pack of cards, and can be seen hiding something away in her stocking. The game of poker and its preliminaries begin to the sound of music oddly reminiscent in its scoring of small-orchestra Ravel, with much use made of divided and solo string instruments, and the colourful variety of solo wood-wind. As Minnie and Rance declare their first hand —which Minnie wins—an *ostinato* figure begins in the double basses which persists in the rhythm, if not always in the identical notes of:

As the second hand is played, which is won by Rance, and the final hand is dealt, this figure provides the only orchestral accompaniment for a period of immense and growing tension. Rance looks at his cards and shouts triumphantly: "Three kings! Look! I have won!" Minnie seems about to faint; she asks Rance to get her a glass of whisky, and while his back is turned quickly exchanges the card she hid in her stocking for one in her hand which she tucks into her blouse. The tension is built up during this by a steady rising crescendo of the persistent Ex 158 (with the basses now fortified by timpani and violoncellos) and the repetition of a harsh phrase of bare fifths and octaves which leads to the climax of Minnie's victory with three aces and a pair. Rance looks at Minnie's cards and with a sharp good night goes out into the night, leaving an exultant Minnie laughing hysterically and crying "He's mine! He's mine!" to a *tutta forza* reprise of the theme of Ex 156. As the curtain falls Minnie bursts into tears and throws her arms round the unconscious Johnson.

The second act curtain of *The Girl of the Golden West* is another wonderfully effective climax to an act which is full of drama and (with the exception of the unbelievable passage I have quoted in Ex 155) rich in lyrical invention. Like so much of this opera it is as interesting for what it anticipates in Puccini's music as it is in its own right, and there are in the theme itself (Ex 156) as well as in its use at the fall of the curtain strong hints of the typical clashing of unrelated minor chords which gives *Il Tabarro* much of its savage character. In its own right, I find this second act ending as surely and superbly well-timed as anything in any Puccini opera—above all in the theatre, where it is not merely "effective", but can often be uncommonly moving as well.

ACT III

Scene: A clearing in the Great Californian Forest at early dawn in winter.

Puccini raises the curtain with an unusually sombre and evocative sound—a gloomy North American equivalent of the dawn that introduces the third act of *La Bohème*. It is a mood, a smell almost, created by the simplest and most immediately effective means: a phrase by three bassoons echoed distantly by three horns, over a repeated two-in-a-bar figure by double basses whose lowest string is tuned down a semitone to E flat:

Rance is discovered, tired and dishevelled, sitting over a fire. Nick, thoughtful and worried, is sitting opposite him. Ashby is lying on the ground near his horse, listening; Billy Jackrabbit is asleep at the side, while the figures of miners lying sprawled asleep can be discerned here and there in the background. Ashby's horse, tethered to a tree, is the first of many horses the audience may expect to see in any properly conducted production of the last act of *The Girl of the Golden West*. (The Italian delight in real live horses in the opera house probably reached its highest pitch of satisfaction in this opera at the New York première when no fewer than eight animals took part.)

What conversation there is takes place between Nick and Rance, who reflect acidly on the change Johnson has brought to their lives. The Sheriff curses the bargain he made with Minnie that prevents him saying where the bandit is hiding; Nick permits himself the cynical observation on the unpredictable nature of love that even Minnie should have been struck down by it.

Further discussion is prevented by an abrupt change of tempo and the first of many alarums and excursions raised by members of the manhunt who appear to be being led something of a dance by their quarry Ramerrez, alias Dick Johnson. According to scraps of narrative we learn that Johnson has been thwarting them right and left with the agility of the Scarlet Pimpernel. The music to all this is characteristically active and exciting and has in it an element of virility which, one realizes, one has not encountered before in Puccini's music for chorus. For the first time, in fact, the chorus is not just adding local colour or commenting on a situation: it is taking part in the action as a composite force, as the voice of an active all-male mob. Puccini's treatment of the chorus in this last act, indeed, is another feature strongly foreshadowing the style of *Turandot*. Not only do we find the mob shouting for blood, as it does in the later opera, but it does so to an almost identical musical phrase. The phrase which first announces the approach of the off-stage chorus, and which in the course of this scene in *The Girl of the Golden West* is declaimed to words "A morte! A morte!",

becomes, in a similar situation in *Turandot*, where the crowd is clamouring for blood,

A great deal goes on, both in the libretto and in the music once the depression of the opening scene has been dispelled, and Rance finds time, between all the galloping of horses that goes on in the background, to gloat—to his tune of Ex 144—over what he predicts will be Minnie's discomfiture when Johnson is finally caught and hanged. It is Sonora (shouting "Hollà!" instead of "Hello!") who gallops on to the stage and announces that Johnson has been captured and will be with them in a moment—an announcement ironically made to the main tune of the Johnson-Minnie duet in Act II (Ex 154). The excitement among the chorus of miners increases with every moment they anticipate the joys of execution, and how they will pump lead into the dancing body of Ramerrez as it swings from the highest branch ("We'll teach him to dance!"). So great is their delight in the end that the crowd breaks into dancing and jumping for joy while it sings the old refrain from the first act, "Dooda, dooda-dooda, day!" and goes off into the distance shouting "Hooray!"

The music stands still for a moment for Nick to take Billy Jackrabbit to one side. Billy has been going around trying out the most suitable trees on which to hang a rope. Nick gives him a handful of money and thrusting a gun in his ribs tells him to take his time about making a noose. Billy makes no reply, but clearly understands; Nick leaves the scene hurriedly.

The mob returns with Johnson, his shirt torn, his face scratched and his hands tied behind his back. Ashby hands over the prisoner to Rance and rides away with a sarcastic expression of good wishes for "my fine gentleman".

The crowd arranges itself into groups in the form of a tribunal, the horses fastened to the trees and Johnson alone in the middle. Rance lights a cigar slowly and to show us what kind of a *gentiluomo* he is goes over to Johnson and deliberately blows smoke in his face. Johnson looks at him contemptuously and tells him to get on with it—"that's all I want".

"And that's what everybody wants, isn't it boys?" shouts Rance, turning to the crowd. The miners turn on Johnson once more, demanding his death and accusing him and his gang of robberies and killings which they specify in detail. Johnson, standing fearlessly proud and defiant, denies their accusation of murder. "A thief I may have been, but a murderer never!"

A new *ostinato* begins at this point, a two-in-a-bar phrase on the alternating chords of G minor and E flat which is played for 39 bars:

The miners bring a new accusation against Johnson: he has robbed them of Minnie's love, and their fury rises once more in another vigorous suggestion of the crowd scenes which were to come in *Turandot*. The *ostinato* of Ex 162 slows down and takes an elegiac turn when Johnson begs the crowd to spare him all the mockery; he is not afraid of death. All he asks is that he may be allowed to speak to them about the woman he loves. The miners shout impatiently, but Sonora quietens them down: the prisoner has a right to speak. Johnson thanks Sonora (who, according to the score, looks fixedly at Johnson with the conflicting emotions of "hate, admiration and jealousy") and asks the crowd that Minnie shall not be allowed to know how he died. Let her believe that he is free and far away on a new road to redemption, and that he will come back one day— "Ch'ella mi creda libero e lontano":

This extremely effective and simple aria in the best and happiest tradition of its composer consists of one melodic phrase of eleven bars played twice. The first time it is sung in full by Johnson to one of the most original and remarkable of Puccini's orchestral accompaniments. Muted strings, including the double basses, solo flute, a solo clarinet, bass clarinet and solo horn, play the tune in unison with the harmonic background meagrely supplied by bassoons, clarinets, horns and muted trombones. The first violins and violas, the flute, first horn and bass clarinet are all instructed to play "come un organo"—an instruction, which it would be charitable to remember, was probably meant well by a composer who did not know the dreadful implications the phrase "like an organ" would have for a later generation nurtured on the horrors of the electrically impelled cinema organ and its kind. To want an orchestra to sound like an organ at all—let alone in this context—is something which, in any case, one can only put down to a sudden eccentricity on Puccini's part. In practice, the passage sounds exactly like what its composer has written—a unison tune across three low octaves with a minimum of harmonic support, which one would never have dreamed had anything to do with an organ unless one had seen it written in the score.

In the second part of the number, the orchestra—dominated by violins—plays the tune *dolcissimo espressivo*, while Johnson, in a way very characteristic of Puccini, seems to sing the tune all of the time, whereas he sings only some of the time until the climax. (The division of labour between voice and orchestra in a Puccini aria is worth a study on its own. Again and again the composer created a wonderful illusion of constant singing of a tune when in fact the soloist very often contributed little more than a monotone descant against a rich orchestral version of the melody.)

Johnson's last passionate words about Minnie are greeted with a slap in the face by Rance who with his customary old-world charm asks if Johnson has anything more to say. He receives the haughty reply: "Nothing. Let's go."

A curious fanfare-like passage begun by trumpets and trombones in unison (which seems to me distantly related to the riddle scene and the Emperor in *Turandot* with its *funebre* interjections for timpani, bass drum and side drum), and repeated by wood-wind and horns, accompanies the silent action beginning with Johnson's answer to Rance, and leads to the elaborate preparations for the execution. Billy Jackrabbit delays the fixing of the rope by deliberate non-co-operation: he sits playing patience and smoking. After being kicked by Rance and pushed about by Sonora his rope is taken away from him and he returns to his game of cards. Johnson stand silently and unflinchingly as the noose is put round his neck.

Suddenly the sound of a galloping horse approaching from the distance and Minnie's voice is heard—Minnie singing a wordless phrase "like a wild cry", as the orchestra begins to whip up an excited version of her "own" theme (Ex 141). At once all activity stops; the miners drop everything and turn their eyes to where Minnie is going to appear on horseback. Only Rance, his fury growing as nobody heeds him, shouts "Hang him!" seven times. At the seventh time the Sheriff is confronted by Minnie, who gets off her horse and stands between Johnson and the crowd. She ignores Rance's threats and when one or two of the miners approach menacingly she draws a gun and holds them at bay. At this point a broad and *fff* version of the whole of Ex 141 is proclaimed by the orchestra, the dynamics subsiding from time to time enough to enable us to hear Rance inciting the mob to remove Minnie and get on with the hanging.

The miners rouse themselves again and shout "Enough! Hang him!"

Some of them grab Minnie by the shoulders in an attempt to get her away from Johnson, but she points her pistol defiantly at them and cries "Let me go, or I will kill him and then kill myself!" Sonora suddenly intervenes and placing himself between Minnie and the crowd cries "Leave her alone!" The crowd retreats and Rance, "pale and grim", goes silently and sits on a tree trunk by the fire.

With her theme still undergoing various key-changes (Ex 141 is one of those tunes like the trumpet tune in the Grand March in *Aida* which can go on modulating upwards indefinitely) Minnie reproaches the men: "None of you ever said 'Enough' when I gave up my young life to you." And she reminds them how she has always shared their troubles with them "and you never said 'Enough' ". The miners stand silently and guiltily before her. "This man is mine!" she tells them. "Mine from God! The bandit is dead—he was killed in my cabin. You cannot kill him!" At this point, according to the stage directions, "a rough feeling of emotion steals into their hearts. No one offers any further protest." With a sob in his voice Sonora says, "But Minnie, he has stolen more than gold: he has stolen your heart."

Minnie smiles affectionately at Sonora: "My dear good Sonora will be the first to forgive—as you will all forgive." There are half-hearted and *pianissimo* dissentient voices, but they carry no weight. Minnie has her audience in the palm of her hand and she starts to work on her listeners' most vulnerable point: their homesickness. To the strongly nostalgic themes of Exs 138, 140 and a suggestion of the second part of Ex 150, which lead to Ex 136, Minnie reminds Joe, Harry, Trin, Happy and Bello of their families, the flowers they have brought her, of their first hesitant letters home written when they had first learned to write under her guidance. She throws her pistol away and what has developed into a moving ensemble, in which the miners' resistance is slowly beaten down, rises to a climax as Dick Johnson, freed from his bonds, kneels at her feet and receives (for some extraordinary reason) a gesture of blessing on his head from Minnie—as though she were a bishop.

The music changes to the tune of the waltz (Ex 147) as Sonora goes towards Minnie, and saying that her words are from God, formally and touchingly hands over Johnson to her keeping and bids them both godspeed. Minnie kisses Sonora, then with a cry of joy buries her head in Johnson's shoulder. The miners, deeply touched, and many of them in tears, sing their sad farewell to Minnie to the tune of Jake Wallace's ballad (Ex 140), the words restricted to "You will never return again, no never again". Minnie and Johnson sing their own farewell in a monotone as they slowly move away, arm-in-arm, into the distance—"Addio mia California". The miners, *pp*, *sotto voce* and *con grande melanconia*, repeat their last and tearful words which, since *Aida*, have always been among the most immediately moving phrases in Italian opera—"mai più, mai più. . . ."

The curtain falls slowly with the orchestra no more than a whisper of a high, sustained diminuendo chord for divided strings, a triad for the celeste and an almost inaudible note for the bass drum. Billy Jackrabbit alone remains unmoved. He continues to play his game of patience and smoke his pipe, unconcerned.

The final curtain of *The Girl of the Golden West* is, I believe, characteristic of the whole problem of this opera; and there is no doubt that it is a problem, just as there is no doubt that it is a far more interesting and attractive work than its detractors would have us believe, but unfortunately not quite so good as those of us who admire it could wish.

The most frequently encountered criticism of the opera is that Puccini was ill at ease with a happy ending. Certainly, hero and heroine survive to ride off to a better life together, and there is consequently no opportunity for Puccini to indulge in his effective dramatic device of recalling happiness in times of misery, for the very good reason that the only time anybody—apart from poor Larkens—is miserable in *The Girl of the Golden West* there had not yet been any happiness to recall. But is it an entirely happy ending? Is true pathos to be found only in the tragedy of young love? To me the final moments of the last act have a peculiar and affecting pathos not found elsewhere in Puccini's operas; the voices of Minnie and Dick Johnson fade away in the distance, but in the foreground there remains the sadness of the tough and lonely miners at the loss of the woman whose love and companionship has been taken from them by a stranger. And it is Puccini's music that makes this sadness real and pathetic.

It would be an exaggeration to say that "the boys" and the chorus in general are the central figures of the action of *The Girl of the Golden West*, but, as I have suggested, the crowd plays a larger and dramatically more important part in this work than in any of Puccini's operas hitherto, and it is the crowd which in the end commands one's sympathy. The chorus, in fact, experience a considerable variety of emotions, one way and another—ranging from the high spirits, homesickness and gentle demonstration of affection in the first act, to the mob-anger, and final change of heart in the third.

It is—as we have been told for years—a libretto of quite appalling sentimentality. But it is a sentimentality that affects the music to a remarkably small degree. The indefensible banality of the phrase I have quoted in Ex 155 is one of the lowest depths to which the composer ever sank; but at least it can be, and usually is, cut; which is more than can be said for the dreadful little afternoon-tea-trio waltz in the second act of *Madam Butterfly*. In every other respect, however, the music of *The Girl of the Golden West* rises consistently higher than the melodramatic level of the libretto. The three "curtains" are not only dramatically, but musically extremely effective and unconventional. One has only to consider the love-duet finishes to the first acts of *La Bohème* and *Butterfly* for instance, to appreciate the novelty of the first act curtain of *The Girl of the Golden West*, or to reflect on the impact of the end of the second act to know that it is equalled only by the second act curtain of *Tosca*. The third act curtain, too, as I have suggested, is unlike anything else Puccini ever wrote.

And in between, since an opera does not consist only of curtains, there is an unusual wealth of exhilarating and original music—the sustained lyrical breadth and warmth of the long scene between Johnson and Minnie which ends the first act, the dramatic characterization of the chorus throughout, the charm and passion of the second act duet for the lovers, the tremendous tension and excitement of Minnie's desperate poker game with Rance, the violence of the lynching party and the gentle music with which Minnie wins them over.

There is, in fact, very little wrong with the music of *The Girl of the Golden West*; it is a score full of melodic invention, harmonic adventurousness, superbly executed dramatic touches and brilliantly assured, audacious orchestration. Its only real fault, one begins to realize, is that the opera as a whole is "different". It is not the Puccini we know. And for this very reason it is musically perhaps the most interesting, because it is the most tentative, of all Puccini's operas.

Frankly, I have little time for those who dismiss the whole work as virtually negligible because, in the words used by the Vienna-born-and-bred George Marek in his book on Puccini, "to American audiences, *The Girl* is an impossibility." One might as well say that to Scottish audiences, *Lucia di Lammermoor* is "an impossibility"; or that *Die Entführung aus dem Serail* is "an impossibility" to Turks, *The Pearl Fishers* to Singalese, or *Carmen* to Spaniards. As it happens, *Carmen* very nearly *is* "an impossibility" to the Spanish; but that can hardly be said to detract from its merits as they are regarded by a great number of non-Iberians. The important thing about *The Girl of the Golden West* is not whether it seems an impossibility to the nation in whose country the action is laid and its first performance happened to take place, nor even that some of the more nauseating features of the libretto are relics of the American original, but whether it carries any musical conviction as an opera to those of us who are not over-sensitive to the importance of local colour in the action or exotic colloquialism in the text, and are not any more perturbed by the spectacle of Italian choristers dressed up as Wild West frontiersmen or what have you, than we are by the thought of English choristers dressed up as Happy Shades in the Elysian Fields.

I do not consider, as some do, that the music shows signs of a decline in the composer's powers. On the contrary, it seems to me that Puccini had reached a new high point in his artistic development and was re-disposing a remarkably strong group of forces in order to embark on a new and unfamiliar adventure—an adventure which we, in our time, can see was to lead to *Turandot*. It was a first and determined attempt to get away from the small-scale sentiment of Manon, Mimi and Butterfly, and to explore a wider, rougher field. Minnie, of course, is not a large-scale heroine by any stretch of the imagination, even though she packs a gun and can keep a turbulent crowd of miners under control; she is as weak and feminine at heart as any of her predecessors. But the surroundings in which she lives are harsher and the prevailing mood of the music is on an altogether tougher, more masculine note. Though there is considerable lyrical beauty and tenderness to be found in the detail of the score, the general effect of *The Girl of the Golden West* is of a work on a larger and more ambitious scale than anything Puccini had hitherto conceived.

It is tempting to regard *The Girl of the Golden West* as a failure; certainly, its libretto is unusually poor and conventional melodrama, and the absence of a death at the final curtain militates against its universal popular acceptance, for opera audiences are notoriously cynical and do not consider love is worthy of operatic attention unless it all ends in tears. But as an operatic experiment, as an essential step in the composer's development, it cannot be counted as a failure. At its best, the opera contains some of Puccini's most inspired dramatic writing and much lovely and highly personal music. At its worst, it is an important preliminary process, an incomplete experiment, if you will, which opened the way to *Turandot*. Perhaps *The Girl of the Golden West* is more of a musician's opera than anything else, for the musician, in studying the multitude of fascinating and original detail in the score can shut his eyes to the weaknesses of the libretto. But the ordinary opera lover, if he feels disappointed that Puccini did not give him what he had grown accustomed to, and even after closer acquaintance with it does not develop the affectionate feeling for the work which I myself have done over the years, can still be grateful for "La *Girl*". Not only did it point the way to *Turandot*; but the way led through the three one-act operas, at least one of which ranks as a masterpiece, called *Il Trittico*.

IL TRITTICO

Puccini was still busy following the fortunes of *The Girl of the Golden West* by personal attendance at the European premières of the opera, when he decided that instead of continuing another exhausting and possibly fruitless search for a libretto for a new full-length opera he would compose a triple bill of three short and strongly contrasted one-act operas. In 1913 Puccini had made up his mind that the *Trittico* or Triptych would consist of one opera with a libretto by D'Annunzio, another with a libretto by Tristan Bernard, and a third based on a French play called *La Houppelande* by Didier Gold.

Only the last of these projects came to anything: as the work known nearly always by its Italian title, *Il Tabarro* ("The Cloak"), which Puccini began in 1913 and finished in 1916. Search for the two companion pieces to *Il Tabarro* was interrupted by the composition and production of *La Rondine* ("The Swallow"), a title which I was intrigued to hear pronounced by a BBC Third Programme announcer as though it were a French word, a kind of musical version of the film, *La Ronde*. Although there have been sporadic performances of *La Rondine* during the past few years, and there exist complete recordings of the opera, I do not think its inclusion in this study could have been justified, for it cannot be said to qualify as a "famous" Puccini opera. As an incident in Puccini's life *La Rondine* might, of course, rate as a "notorious" opera, but that is a matter of no great relevance at the moment; the inquisitive reader, however, can learn more about it from any of the published biographies of the composer.

The *Trittico* was completed by the addition of two operas composed to librettos of a kind rarely encountered by Puccini: both were "originals". Hitherto only *Le Villi* among Puccini's operas had not first been adapted from a novel, a short story or a play. Both *Suor Angelica* and *Gianni Schicchi*, however, were conceived by Giovacchino Forzano as operatic subjects custom-built for Puccini right from the start, and in consequence the composer seems to have had far less trouble writing the music for these two one-acters, far fewer delays and arguments over dramaturgic and poetic details of the libretto than ever before in his career.

In the intervening years, since its first performance at the Metropolitan Opera House in New York on 14th December, 1918, the *Trittico* has disintegrated as an operatic unity. First, *Suor Angelica* was dropped from the bill, then *Il Tabarro*; only *Gianni Schicchi* survived to earn frequent and regular performances all over the world. As time passed, however, *Il Tabarro* has gradually come back into favour to be performed in conjunction with one-act operas by other composers, or as the other half of a double bill with *Gianni Schicchi*, as it has done at Sadler's Wells. Since the

Second German War, *Suor Angelica* has been played with increasing frequency, though curiously enough not always with the other two parts of the *Trittico*. In the seasons immediately preceding the Puccini Centenary Year, however, *Suor Angelica* was reinstated and the original triple bill is now heard more often in the way its composer intended.

Although each of the three operas has qualities which, as I believe, enables it to stand up on its own it is as a comprehensive view of three aspects of the composer's genius that the *Trittico* is best studied and enjoyed. Few things have been more encouraging to note in my own lifetime than the ever-increasing popularity of *Turandot* and the growing popular, as well as professional, regard for the once neglected *Trittico*.

IL TABARRO

(*THE CLOAK*)

(*Property of G. Ricordi and Co.*)

Opera in one act, after *La Houppelande* by Didier Gold.* Libretto by Giuseppe Adami. First performed at the Metropolitan Opera House, New York, on 14th December, 1918. First performance in England: Covent Garden, 18th June, 1920.

CHARACTERS IN ORDER OF SINGING:

GIORGETTA	*Soprano* (25)†
MICHELE, *bargemaster, her husband* .	*Baritone* (50)
LUIGI, *a stevedore*	*Tenor* (20)
IL "TINCA" (the Tench) *a stevedore* .	*Tenor* (35)
IL "TALPA" (the Mole), *a stevedore* .	*Bass* (55)
A BALLAD-MONGER	*Tenor*
LA FRUGOLA, *wife of Il Talpa* .	*Mezzo-soprano* (50)
TWO LOVERS	*Soprano and Tenor*

Stevedores, midinettes, an organ grinder.

Scene: Paris   Time: *Circa* 1913‡

* Didier Gold must be unique in having translated into French the Italian libretto of the opera made of his original play. It would be interesting to compare the two versions.

† For some reason I have not discovered in my orchestral score of *Il Tabarro* there is no indication what type of singers the characters should be. All we are told is how old they are.

‡ The time of the action is not specified but according to purely musical evidence one supposes it to take place in the days of the Paris Puccini knew when he was writing the opera. The score provides for a distant motor horn (in B flat) which precludes use of the convenient tag "The Present", which has hitherto appeared in the programme. Motor horns have been forbidden in the French capital for some years now.

Scene: A corner of the Seine where Michele's barge is tied up. In the background the outline of the older parts of Paris is visible, particularly the silhouette of Notre Dame which shows up against a bright red sky. The vessel itself, connected by a gangway to the quayside, is typical of the brightly painted barges found on the Seine; it is decorated with a clothes-line, pots of geraniums and a bird in a cage. It is sunset on a September evening.

As one comes to study each succeeding Puccini opera so one realizes that few composers have ever equalled his gift for the creation of an immediate and unmistakable atmosphere in the space of a couple of notes. Only the instrumental prelude to *Madam Butterfly* seems to me to make no dramatic impact comparable to the superbly arresting and evocative first bars of *Manon Lescaut* and *La Bohème*, *Tosca* and *The Girl of the Golden West*. The curtain of *Il Tabarro* rises to what is perhaps Puccini's most successful piece of musical landscape-painting, a picture exotically coloured with the distant sounds of a motor horn and a tug's hooter which add discreet and telling overtones to the undulating theme of the opening sequence:

164

The orchestration of this theme, accompanied by a steady pizzicato figure in the double basses, is particularly effective, with a solo violoncello prominently doubling the melody in the same register as either muted violins or a solo flute.

The gentle swaying motion of this first theme forms the background to what may be called the "atmosphere" action—the setting of the general scene and also the first suggestion of the main dramatic situation.

As the curtain rises (which is a moment or two before the music actually begins), Michele is seated by the tiller, gazing steadily at the sunset, his unlighted pipe hanging from his lips. Stevedores unload the barge, carrying heavy sacks from the hold to the quayside (where, true to Italian operatic tradition, a real horse and cart are asked for in the stage directions). Giorgetta comes out of the cabin, and without seeing her husband, takes the washing down from the line, waters the flowers and cleans the bird-cage. When she finally sees him we sense from their conversation that Giorgetta's relations with her husband are strained. Michele's feelings for her have not cooled; he does not want any of the wine she proposes to give the stevedores whose work is just ending: he wants her love. But she turns away as he tries to kiss her and gives him her hand to kiss instead of her lips. Michele says nothing, and goes below into the cabin.

From time to time during this short scene between husband and wife the stevedores are heard singing a little *chanson* invented by Puccini which has all the characteristic simplicity and charm typical of his "French" music and is the first of several instances of this expertly handled local-colouring in an opera crammed full of atmosphere.

The languid tempo changes to Allegretto con vivacità when Luigi, the youngest of the three principal stevedores, greets Giorgetta's appearance carrying wine and glasses, with a vigorous little ditty in praise of wine and their hostess, which is taken up in turn by Il Talpa and Il Tinca:

During the singing and drinking Luigi catches sight of an organ grinder on the towpath and beckons him over, addressing him as "Professore". Giorgetta quickly observes that the only music she understands is music that makes you dance. She addresses her remark pointedly to Luigi "as though to seduce him to dance with her", but laughingly accepts Il Tinca as a partner when he pushes forward and asks her to dance a waltz with him.

These brief preliminaries to the dance are conducted to the first appearance of a theme associated with what we later recognize is the love affair of Giorgetta and Luigi. This consists of a sinister pizzicato phrase first heard on its own—

—which continues as an accompaniment to a broader tune:

The waltz played by the organ grinder is a wittily scored little impression, its imitative orchestration for two flutes, two clarinets and bass clarinet openly modelled on the organ grinder's music in Stravinsky's *Petrouchka*. But whereas Stravinsky's played on a well-tempered instrument, Puccini's organ grinder has an instrument that has grown sadly out of tune. Stripped of its excruciating "octaves" (a major seventh apart) the waltz in *Il Tabarro* is a delightful tune which one feels has in it all the elements of a thoroughly successful French *java*.

Il Tinca's dance with Giorgetta (he turns proudly to his companions and announces "I'm dancing with the *padrona!*") is the subject of ribald comment for the onlookers until Luigi cuts in and Giorgetta "languidly abandons herself in his arms". The waltz is interrupted by the appearance of Michele. Luigi gives the organ grinder some money, and goes down into the hold with the stevedores to resume the unloading of the barge.

Conversation between husband and wife is as strained on this occasion as on the first; Giorgetta keeps up a flow of small-talk: are we leaving next week? will Talpa and Tinca stay on? She learns, too, that Luigi is going to stay on although only yesterday Michele had not expected him to.

From time to time during this dialogue a ballad-monger is heard in the distance selling the words and music of his songs. As he approaches, Giorgetta suddenly changes the subject of conversation to the beauty of the sunset. Michele receives his wife's comparison of the setting sun to a large orange in silence, and for the first time Giorgetta is disturbed by her husband's attitude. Why is he in such bad humour? What is the matter? What is he looking at? And why is he so silent?

Our attention is distracted for a moment when the ballad-singer arrives on the scene, followed by a companion with a small harp under his arm who settles himself down on a folding stool on the quay. The singer and his accompanist are joined by a group of midinettes who stop to listen on their way home.

As the harpist prepares to play, Michele suddenly speaks: "Have I ever made scenes with you?"

"No," admits Giorgetta, "you don't beat me."

"Would you rather I did?"

"I would prefer it" she replies, "to your eternal silence."

The ballad-monger begins his song, two verses about spring and "who lives for love, shall die for love" to another typically "French" tune of great charm:

168

The song, we learn, is "the story of Mimi" and each verse ends with a cadence quoting the theme of Ex 45 on page 58—not at the original wistful tempo that it was heard in *La Bohème*, but in the sprightly Allegretto of the rest of the ballad-monger's song, accompanied by a solo string quartet of two violins, viola and violoncello.

Between verses Giorgetta pleads with Michele at least to say what is the matter with him. All she receives in reply is a sullen "Nothing! Nothing!"

The singer and his harpist move off; the midinettes, reading the words and singing the music from the copies of the song they have bought, disappear into the distance repeating the tune in two-part harmony (Since the Mimi of this little ballad dies of a broken heart when her lover does not return it is obviously not the Mimi of *La Bohème* that the singer tells us about. The lighthearted and unpathetic quotation of "Mi chiamano Mimì" was purely a piece of fun and a natural association of ideas on the composer's part.)

A new scene begins with the appearance of La Frugola,* a ragpicker who has come to fetch her husband, Il Talpa. She greets Giorgetta and Michele as "eterni innamorati" and when Michele goes below shows Giorgetta the contents of the sack—the fruit of her day's scavenging. La Frugola's demonstration of a remarkable variety of objects (among them a brand new comb, which she gives Giorgetta) is made to the accompaniment of a reiterated 3/8 figure:

The orchestral colouring of this is deliberately grotesque and harsh—three muted trumpets in unison, strings playing with the wood of the bow (*col legno*) and so on. The harmonic structure, with its consecutive blocks of chords, is also very characteristic of this opera and is one of the devices Puccini borrowed from Debussy to put to his own peculiar use in *Il Tabarro*.

The rigorous repetitiveness of La Frugola's catalogue of her finds is interrupted for a moment when the tempo, but not the rhythm, relaxes as she explains that a packet containing a bullock's heart is for her cat "Caporale". There are quaint little mewings from two oboes and two solo violoncellos in the same register, as the old woman grows lyrical about the pet that keeps her company when her husband is at work. The first tempo returns to accompany La Frugola's exposition of her cat's simple and unspectacular philosophy of life: better to be master of your own tumble-down hut than a servant in a palace, and better still to eat two slices of heart than to wear out your own in the chains of *l'amore*.

The predominance of colourful and more or less irrelevant episodes over any serious development of plot continues, after Il Talpa joins his wife, with the appearance from the hold, and eventual departure for the nearest *bistro* of Il Tinca, an inveterate toper who takes the company's criticism of his habits in good part. Why shouldn't he drink, he asks; it stops him thinking and when he thinks he cannot laugh. Luigi agrees with him and embarks on an unexpected little diatribe against social conditions and the workers' lot, which works up almost in a monotone to a powerful and dramatic cadence: "It's best not to think. Just lower your head and bend your back":

* "Frugolare" means to rummage, or to root, like a pig; "frugola" is a woman willing to undertake anything.

The sudden introduction of this rather heroic note has a strangely dramatic effect: for the first time the prevailing atmosphere of low life by the Paris riverside is momentarily dispelled. Luigi, we can guess, is no political agitator; but his outburst suddenly focusses our attention on his importance as a character in the drama by musical instead of purely visual means.

Il Tinca wanders off, repeating "Follow my example: drink!" When her husband suggests they should go home, he is dead tired; La Frugola sighs for her dream cottage in the country where she can rest, with her husband lying in the sun and her faithful cat at her feet. La Frugola tells us of her dreams in a busy, restless sequence largely on one note which is echoed from time to time by a chirruping solo oboe and accompanied by a steady march-like four-in-a-bar of strings playing pizzicato and *col legno* as before.

When La Frugola has finished her quaint little tune, Giorgetta confesses that her dreams are different. She was born and bred in Paris and all she longs for are the bright lights and the sound of footsteps on the pavements; those born in cities cannot live on the water, cramped in a dingy cabin, living a life bounded by the bed and the stove. Giorgetta sings the praise of her native city enthusiastically to a tune of great warmth:

171

After a short and charming lyrical interlude in which Giorgetta reflects on the joys of the Bois de Boulogne (with a distant cuckoo heard in the orchestra, played by a horn in a register which suggests that cuckoos are tenors in the Bois), the main tune returns and Luigi, also a native of Paris, joins Giorgetta in an ecstatic climax. The libretto says that "the lovers remain awhile as if transfigured, hand in hand, as if spellbound by the same thought, one soul; then realizing that others are present, they let go of each other's hands." The score is less concerned with what happens to the lovers at this point: at the end of the duet "they remain as though in ecstasy" and are left to their own devices to get out of it.

La Frugola concedes that there is something to be said for Giorgetta's feelings about Paris and taking Il Talpa's arm, husband and wife disappear into the distance singing their little monotone song about their dream-cottage.

The mood of the opening of the opera returns momentarily when a soprano and then a tenor voice are heard off-stage singing wordlessly the tune of Ex 164.

We have now reached the point that marks the end of a long preliminary setting up of "audible scenery", as it were, and the real beginning of the action that is to take place against Puccini's expertly established background. Luigi and Giorgetta are alone and the whole atmosphere changes in an instant with the sound (marked, a little superfluously, *misterioso*) of Exs 166 and 167 which, now in 6/8 time, is repeated with dramatic insistence and quite remarkable effect.

The new scene begins with Giorgetta begging Luigi to be careful and not to take her in his arms. Michele may appear at any moment. In hushed tones the lovers discuss their unhappy circumstances—if only they were alone, and far away and together for always.

Michele emerges from the cabin, surprised to find that Luigi has not yet gone. Luigi explains that he wanted to talk to the bargemaster alone, to thank him for the work he has been given and to ask if he might travel in the barge as far as Rouen and leave Michele's employ there. Michele is astonished by the idea; there is nothing but misery to be found in Rouen; Luigi would be far worse off. In that case, Luigi decides, he will stay on. Michele bids him good night and goes below to fix the vessel's riding lights.

As soon as her husband has gone, Giorgetta asks Luigi agitatedly why he wanted to leave the barge at Rouen. "Because I can't share you with him!" he replies. Giorgetta reflects again on the hopeless circumstances of their love affair, but a short duet develops on the theme that when they are in each other's arms everything is forgotten. Luigi changes the mood with a passionate tune which, divided between singer and orchestra, takes this over-all form:

The furtive theme that began this second part of the opera is heard again now as the lovers arrange to meet later. The signal will be the same as the night before: Giorgetta will strike a match "as though to light up a star, the flame of our love, a love that never sets". As Giorgetta sings these last words we hear in the orchestra a fragment of a theme which plays an all-important part in the climax of the work. We have several times encountered Puccini's practice of anticipating a theme which later blossoms out more fully; we have also encountered his effective use, once a theme has been established in full, of harmonic or melodic distortion. This is the first time, however, that we have heard a theme distorted *before* it has been established. As a result we get a strangely grotesque preview of a phrase which, while it is never exactly tender in feeling,

never again sounds quite so acid (in spite of the description "dolce") as
on its first appearance in the wood-wind:

(The orchestral voicing of those three chords is interesting: the highest
and lowest notes are played by flutes, the other two by clarinets, while a
solo viola doubles the 2nd flute part an octave lower.)

The music becomes passionate again with Luigi's reaffirmation of his
love, and the sequence ends with his promise that he would not hesitate
to use his knife to gain Giorgetta and to fashion a jewel for her from
drops of blood. These last words form the climax of the scene, reiterated
on the tenor's high G sharps, while the lower register of the orchestra
repeatedly thunders out the tune of Ex 166 (without the appendant Ex
167). Luigi leaves quickly, hurried away by Giorgetta who is frightened
and apprehensive. As the theme subsides gradually in a lengthening
rallentando Giorgetta wearily passes her hand over her forehead and
sighs "How difficult it is to be happy!"

There is no greater, or less expected change of tempo and atmosphere
in the music of *Il Tabarro* than the change to the intensely *cantabile* tune
played by the violoncellos which now occurs as Michele, carrying the
lighted lanterns, emerges from the cabin. The change is unexpected,
because so far we have been carefully led to regard Michele if not as the
villain of the piece, at least as a rather sinister figure. Certainly we could
not have counted on his being *musically* the sympathetic character that
Puccini now develops from the theme:

It is a matter-of-fact passage of dialogue that follows Michele's
appearance. Why doesn't Giorgetta go to bed? Why hasn't Michele
gone to bed? Perhaps it was unnecessary to keep on Luigi; two men would
have been enough. But Il Tinca is a drunkard, objects Giorgetta. Yes,
replies Michele meaningfully, he drinks to drown his sorrows. He has a
strumpet for a wife and he drinks to avoid killing her. Giorgetta is
obviously disturbed by this pointed remark; what is the matter, asks her
husband. "They are all stories that don't interest me," replies Giorgetta.

Michele turns sadly to his wife and asks her "Why do you not love me
any more?" ("Perchè non m'ami più?"). It is this phrase that begins one
of Puccini's most effective duets. The tune of Ex 174 continues in the
orchestra while Michele plays on Giorgetta's memories. Does she not
remember how happy they three had been—he, she and the baby that
died not long ago? And how she rocked the baby and fell asleep in

Michele's arms? Giorgetta begs him to stop; but Michele goes on. There had been evenings like this and he had wrapped Giorgetta in his old cloak when the wind had grown cold. At the mention of Michele's cloak we hear for the first time the whole of the theme hinted at in Ex 173, a "dark" theme marked by the composer, when it is first heard, to be played *con dolore*:

Michele recalls how happy he had been with her, but now his grey hair seemed an insult to her youth. Giorgetta begs him to calm down; she is tired and wants to go to bed.

"But you won't sleep", says Michele bitterly.

"Why do you say that?" Giorgetta asks with surprise.

"I don't know—but I know that you have not slept for a long time now." Michele tries to draw Giorgetta towards him and pleads with her to stay with him. Does she not remember other nights like this? Why does she shut her heart to him?

Michele's plea is made to a gentle rocking rhythm which leads to a rough repeated figure of characteristically bare, harsh fifths and octaves on which Puccini builds his climax:

Giorgetta remains unmoved by all her husband's pleading. We are growing old, she says; they are not the same people they were. The music dies away, a distant clock strikes nine; Giorgetta bids Michele good night and goes below. Michele watches her go and angrily spits out the one word "Harlot!"*

There now follows one last and superb sequence of "atmosphere". Over a repeated *ppp* chord of A minor in the lower strings, the voices of two lovers are heard as they walk with their arms around each other along the river bank singing an entrancingly simple song in Puccini's most effectively "French" vein. When their voices have faded into the distance, the sound of a cornet sounding the retreat comes from a distant barracks.

Michele, who has been putting the riding lights in position on the barge, goes slowly and cautiously to the cabin and listens. As he does so the orchestra plays *misterioso* the theme (Ex 175) which virtually dominates the opera from this dramatic soliloquy until the final curtain. Michele hears nothing—"Nulla! Silenzio!" He peers through the window of the cabin. Giorgetta is still there; but she is not asleep. She is waiting—for

---

* The official English version of *Il Tabarro* transforms the expressive word *sgualdrina* into the magnificently fatuous and genteel "Flirt!".

what? for whom? Perhaps for Michele to fall asleep. This last thought occurs to Michele to a cadence which in fact is the cadence that rings down the curtain on *Il Tabarro*. I would like to quote it fully in this first context, however, as it is characteristic of so much of the harmonic construction of this Puccini opera. The jarring false relations which made the second act curtain of *The Girl of the Golden West* so grimly effective, have been developed by the composer with great skill and effect in this one act thriller, and are typical of his genius for making familiar major and minor chords in unfamiliar juxtaposition, or at unexpected moments, do his dramatic work for him, so that he does not have to resort to extravagant dissonance to make a point or surprise the listener:

In his soliloquy Michele puzzles over the change in his wife. Who is responsible? Not Il Talpa; he is too old. Il Tinca drinks. Luigi? No; he wanted to leave the barge at Rouen. Who then? All Michele desires is to be able to lay his hands on the throat of the deceiver and shout at him: "It's you! You! You!"—and the music rises to a tremendous and unnerving climax on the reiteration and relentlessly increasing dynamic intensity of the "cloak" theme (Ex 175).*

At the final words of his monologue Michele sinks back on the verge of collapse. Mechanically he takes his pipe from his pocket and lights it. As the match flares, Luigi moves cautiously towards the gang plank and jumps on to the barge. Michele, seeing the shadow, is surprised, and hides; then, recognizing Luigi, he throws himself upon him and catches him by the throat.

The action, which takes place to a greatly speeded-up form (Allegro vivo agitato) of the "cloak" theme, still in C minor but now repeated over and over again in a crescendo unison by the lower strings, is swift and horrifying. Michele tightens his grip on Luigi's throat and when he has made him confess again and again that he is Giorgetta's lover he strangles him.

The music subsides as Luigi "remains holding on to Michele in his death contortion". From the cabin Giorgetta's voice is heard calling "Michele! Michele! I am afraid, Michele . . ." Hearing his wife's voice Michele quickly sits down, throwing his cloak over the corpse which is

---

* "Nulla! Silenzio!" was not written until 1921 when Puccini asked his librettist Adami to provide him with words to replace the original monologue "Scorri, fiume" ("Flow on eternal river") which the composer said was "too academic altogether and weakens the end of the drama". Some of the musical features of the first aria remain, but the dramatic character is completely changed. "Scorri, fiume" was a contemplative ode to the Seine mingled with Michele's desire for peace or death, and in Puccini's own words it "chilled and choked the close".

still clinging to him. Giorgetta comes out of the cabin and goes slowly towards Michele, looking around her anxiously as we hear a sinister echo of Luigi's theme (Exx 166 and 167), the first part of it played mysteriously by violoncellos and basses pizzicato, the second part hinted at by the voices.

"I was right," says Michele, "you couldn't sleep."

"I am sorry I was so horrid," replies Giorgetta meekly.

"It was nothing," Michele assures her. "It was your nerves."

Giorgetta moves closer. "Don't you want me nearer to you?"

"Where? Under my cloak?"

"Yes, close—close. You told me once that 'every man carries a cloak which hides sometimes a joy, sometimes a sorrow'."

"And sometimes," says Michele grimly, "a crime! Come under my cloak!"

He rises and throws open the cloak. Luigi's dead body rolls over at Giorgetta's feet. With a terrible cry she draws away, horror-stricken. Michele seizes her, drags her back and throws her violently on the body of her dead lover. The curtain falls to a savage (Puccini marks it *selvaggio*) final reiteration of the "cloak" theme, ending —*tutta forza*—with the harsh cadence of falsely related major and minor chords first heard in Michele's monologue (Ex 177).

In its way *Il Tabarro* is a little masterpiece of operatic craftsmanship and, to my mind, musically by far the finest and most fascinating of the three parts of the *Trittico*. In spite of the absence of a typical Little Girl, or of any conventionally romantic interest, it is a wonderfully compact synthesis of Puccini's peculiar genius. In the course of forty minutes or so, and in a compact form which is a miracle of economy of means and concentration of ideas, we have immediately effective, inimitable touches of "atmosphere" and local colour, swift and brilliant thumbnail character-sketches, moments of humour and fun, great charm in the fleeting episodes of the lovers, the ballad-monger and midinettes, and throughout it all a gradually increasing air of tension and overwhelming suspense. It is also the only opera of Puccini's with anything at all to offer a baritone singer in the way of a "selection". Scarpia has no tunes; Rance has only one. Marcello shares a duet with a tenor; so does Sharpless. Michele on the other hand, dominates a duet to which he contributes a share distinguished by some of Puccini's most tender lyrical sequences, and has a soliloquy of immense dramatic force and intensity which one is astonished to realize is performed far too seldom as a separate number that would add considerable variety and opportunity to the repertoire of the operatic baritone.

As drama the subject of *Il Tabarro* is frankly grand guignol, and in consequence is often rather haughtily dismissed as having no roots in reality, as lacking in characters that come to life convincingly, and so on. The object of grand guignol, of course, is that its characters should come to death convincingly, and if the final outcome of the action is inevitably a little macabre, it is far less so than the things that happened, for instance, in the all-too "real" 20th-century world of Buchenwald and Belsen, where man-made truth was infinitely more horrible and incredible than any man-made fiction ever devised.

Perhaps *Il Tabarro* is more of a "musicians' opera" than any of Puccini's earlier works in that the listener who has had an average musical education may derive more immediate pleasure from it than one who has not. But for the listener who may not be aware of the subtleties of Puccini's superlative craftsmanship, whose feeling for historical perspective may not run to discovering the fascination of the signs, already apparent in *The Girl of the Golden West*, of the development of a new musical style and greatly extended harmonic range pointing more clearly than ever the way ahead to the magnificence of *Turandot*, the "old", familiar Puccini is still recognizable beneath the strange technical clothing. His highly personal and original gift of lyrical melody is there, as it had been in his other operas, but it is put to unfamiliar uses: a hymn of praise to Paris, a husband saddened by his wife's infidelity, a bitter outburst on working-class conditions. Luigi's passionate declaration of love for Giorgetta is the only passage in which the familiar Puccini means is used to a familiar Puccini end.

In the more than fifty years that have elapsed since *Il Tabarro* was first performed, however, there have been signs that the opera is beginning to have a more general appeal than is suggested by the description of the work as a "musicians' opera". The growing popular acceptance of *Il Tabarro* has been due largely to the gradual recognition that the work is not "different" Puccini after all, but that, like Verdi's *Falstaff*, it is composed of familiar ingredients assembled in a different way and used in unfamiliar proportions. The final result is a superbly effective and stimulating essay in musical drama which is a masterpiece of its kind.

SUOR ANGELICA
(*SISTER ANGELICA*)

(*Property of G. Ricordi and Co.*)

Opera in one act. Libretto by Giovacchino Forzano. First performed at the Metropolitan Opera House, New York, on 14th December, 1918. First performance in England: Covent Garden, 18th June, 1920.

WHEN he first encountered the subject of *Suor Angelica*, Puccini is reported to have been overjoyed to find "the mystic subject of which he had so long dreamed". It was a reaction which, in view of his profitable predilection for the grim realities of violent death in his operas, may appear a little surprising, to say the least. It was also, I think, a reaction which examination of the opera will show to have been a pity.

Puccini was by no means an exceptionally religious man. He had had a practical grounding in the performance and composition of church music as a boy in his native Lucca, and his eldest sister, Iginia, lived to become Mother Superior of a convent in Vicopelago; but even the combination of these two circumstances was scarcely enough to make a mystic out of one who was very much a child of his time and who, in spite of the characteristic bouts of melancholy often suffered by artists, was at heart an extremely practical man. Puccini was a realist, in short, whose adoption of the cloak of mysticism in *Suor Angelica* was a disguise that deceived nobody. Nobody, that is, but himself.

CHARACTERS IN ORDER OF SINGING:

SISTER ANGELICA	*Soprano*
THE SISTER MONITOR . . .	*Mezzo-soprano*
MISTRESS OF THE NOVICES . .	*Mezzo-soprano*
SISTER OSMINA	*Soprano*
SISTER GENEVIEVE (Suor Genovieffa) . .	*Soprano*
SISTER DOLCINA	*Soprano*
NURSING SISTER	*Mezzo-soprano*
TWO ALMS SISTERS . .	*Soprano and mezzo-soprano*
THE ABBESS	*Mezzo-soprano*
THE PRINCESS, *Angelica's aunt* . . .	*Contralto*

Sisters, novices, postulants.

Scene: A convent in Italy.   Time: The end of the 17th century

Scene: The interior of a convent, with a small church (chiesetta) *and cloisters. In the background, beyond the arches on the right, is the cemetery; on the left, the garden. In the centre of the scene there are cypresses, a cross, herbs and flowers. In the background, right, a fountain. It is sunset on an evening in spring.*

Before the curtain rises we hear the sound of bells coming from what proves to be a considerable complement of back-stage instruments which includes—in addition to six bells—a piccolo, two pianos, an organ, three trumpets, cymbals, and various effects in the way of bronze doorbells. The tune played by the bells—

—is taken up, when the curtain rises on an empty stage, as a reiterated accompaniment to the nuns' singing of the "Ave Maria" which is heard coming from the church. The back-stage piccolo provides bird noises as two postulants, late for prayers, cross the stage, and after pausing to listen to the bird singing, enter the church. Sister Angelica, who is also late, enters and goes towards the church. She opens the door and makes the act of penance customary for late-comers (which was not done by the two postulants), that is to say, she kneels and kisses the ground; she goes inside and closes the door.

The libretto of *Suor Angelica* is divided by sub-headings into separate sections—The Prayer, The Penances, Recreation, Return from the Collection of Alms, and so on, ending with The Miracle. These divisions are not noted in my small orchestral score of the opera, but in fact the character of the music changes at those points indicated by the librettist. Remembering the *Andante religioso* in the first act of *Tosca* and the Requiem in the Scala museum* it is not surprising to find that the opening sequence of *Suor Angelica*—The Prayer—is in F major.

When the nuns have come out of the church the Sister Monitor announces the penances incurred by the two postulants (who were late, the Mistress of Novices explains to her charges), and the silent Sister Lucilla (who laughed and made others laugh in the choir), and by Sister Osmina, who denies firmly that she carried roses into church in her sleeves, but is sent to her cell nevertheless. Sister Osmina's exit is accompanied by the first appearance of a theme later associated with the prayers of the nuns and the idea of the convent in general. On this first occasion, accompanied only by three muted trumpets, six of the nuns sing the words "Regina Virginum, ora pro ea . . ." to the phrase:

* See page 88.

The whole little episode, particularly the part played in it by the two postulants, is dealt with by Puccini with a great charm that echoes the passages for women's voices in the first act of *Manon Lescaut*.

Charm, indeed, is the most noticeable quality of these early scenes and a great deal of it emanates from the gay and youthful Sister Genevieve, whose observation that the sun has turned the water in the fountain to gold leads to a delightful sequence in which the nuns give thanks for the spring and the orchestra makes ingenious and varied instrumental use of the phrase:

It is during the treatment of this little figure that we first encounter some of the beautifully effective wood-wind writing in which this score is peculiarly rich, and which is characterized by a gentle translucence rarely found elsewhere in Puccini's operas.

Sister Genevieve suggests that some of the sunlit water from the fountain should be sprinkled on the grave of Sister Bianca Rosa, who died a year ago. "She would like that!" answer the other nuns.

This is the cue for Sister Angelica's first solo passage, in which she reflects that desires are flowers for the living that do not blossom among the dead—"I desiderî sono i fiori dei vivi". The climax at the words "Death is beautiful life!" ("La morte è vita bella!"), comes with an impassioned orchestral tutti (the loudest music so far) in a phrase which occurs once more later on:

The conversation turns to the question of desires. The Monitor and three other nuns declare they have none: Sister Genevieve confesses that she has one surely pardonable desire: she was a shepherdess before she became a nun and longs to hold a lamb in her arms again. Wouldn't the Lamb of God forgive her?

Sister Genevieve's short and telling confession, which has a touch of Butterfly's tone of voice to it, is made to a charming accompaniment of wood-wind with a few notes from a string quartet, in the rather melancholy key of E flat minor and includes a characteristically naïve imitation of a bleating lamb (Puccini could never resist onomatopoeic reference to animals in his scores).

A fat and cheerful nun, Sister Dolcina, is rebuked for her obvious and incurable desire for good food and drink. And Sister Angelica, has she any wishes? None, she replies, and turns to water the flowers. "May Jesus forgive her!" whisper the nuns. "She lies!", and they discuss

Angelica's yearning for news of her family. She has been in the convent for seven years and has heard no word. And yet she was rich and noble— a Princess, the Abbess had said. She had become a nun in penitence. Why? What was her sin?

The question is still unanswered when the Nursing Sister enters to ask Angelica for some herbs. Sister Clara has been stung by a wasp. This sad little recital of poor Clara's sufferings provides Puccini with yet another opportunity for his celebrated animal imitations, the wasp in this case being characterized by piquant sounds from three muted trumpets and pizzicato figures from the strings. Angelica picks a herb and a flower and gives them to the Nursing Sister to take to her patient.

No sooner has the Nursing Sister gone and the wasp noise died down in the orchestra than the sound of a donkey is heard in the music and the animal itself (as a change from the traditional horse of Italian opera) is driven on to the stage by two nuns returning from the collection of alms. The donkey is relieved of its load, which consists of food of various kinds, including a lot of fruit which delights the perpetually ravenous Sister Dolcina. The two alms collectors announce excitedly that a carriage is standing outside the convent. Angelica turns suddenly and asks anxiously whether it is a rich-looking carriage; she is told that it is. It is at this point that we hear for the first time another theme which becomes important later on and is associated with Angelica's family and her past, though of course there is no knowing that at this stage:

Angelica can learn no more from her questioning than that it is a magnificent carriage; the nun did not notice what arms it bore. General speculation is cut short by the ringing of the bell at the convent gate. At the sound of it Angelica, "raising her eyes to heaven", prays fervently to the Virgin and there is heard the first of the several tunes characteristic of the peculiar pathos which now begins to be felt in the music:

Sister Genevieve goes over to Angelica and "with great sweetness" tells her how much they all hope the visitor is for her. The Abbess appears, and motioning the rest of the nuns away (we hear them off-stage a little later chanting a phrase of the Requiem for the soul of Bianca Rosa), calls Angelica by name. Angelica begs the Abbess to tell her who has called; she has been waiting for seven years without seeing or hearing a word from anyone. These few bars are scored with considerable skill and effect for a solo viola playing the tune of Ex 183 (in the register shown in the illustration) with a solo flute an octave below it and half the first violins doubling the viola part pizzicato. It can be an exquisite sound.

The Abbess tells Angelica that her aunt, the Princess, has called to see her—words which bring an austere unison theme for the strings in the orchestra. This is played four times altogether, punctuating the Abbess's words and increasing the tension as the last two notes of the phrase are raised a tone on the third and yet another tone on the fourth playing:

The effect of this passage is immediate in its creation of what can only be described as a mood of deep depression, and it prepares one for that part of the opera which the librettist labelled "The Princess"—in the original Italian the gracious "La zia Principessa" for which there is no idiomatic English equivalent. After "queen mother" and "dowager duchess" we tend to run out of terms for royal or noble relations.

The Princess enters, an old lady of sombre and forbidding appearance who walks with a thin ebony stick. Angelica is deeply moved by her aunt's arrival but when she moves towards her the Princess coldly gives her only her outstretched hand to kiss.

With her eyes carefully avoiding Angelica's in a fixed stare ahead of her, the Princess explains why she has come to the convent. Ever since Angelica's parents died 20 years previously the Princess had administered their ample estate. She has come to get Angelica's signature to a document. Angelica is more affected by the event of seeing one of her family again after seven years than by her aunt's matter of business.

The Princess continues. The reason the document has to be signed is that Angelica's young sister Anna Viola is getting married.

"Married?" cries Angelica, excitedly. "Little Anna Viola getting married? To whom?"

Coldly the Princess answers: "To one whose love has enabled him to overlook the dark stain you have cast upon our honour."

Angelica, in a sudden moment of vehemence, reproaches her aunt for being so cruel and merciless. The Princess replies that often when she prays she sees the spirit of Angelica's mother—"How painful it is to hear the dead mourn and weep!" and she repeats her condemnation of Angelica's sin in a solo passage which begins with the austere phrase, repeated several times:

This little scene has its climax in the words "Espiare! Espiare!", and is a skilful thumbnail sketch of the old lady's adamantine character and has one or two noticeable moments of effective scoring, particularly in the use of the piccolo in *pianissimo* legato phrases.

Unless we have studied the synopsis found in opera house programmes or on the record sleeves which usually tells us the situation from the very start, it is only at this stage that we begin to guess the reason for the Princess's harsh and unrelenting attitude towards her niece. Angelica pleads passionately with her aunt to give her news of her son, the baby that was taken away from her when she had seen it and kissed it only once. How is the child? What does it look like? What colour are his eyes? Angelica's plea is constituted mainly of a short urgent phrase repeated again and again in the orchestra:

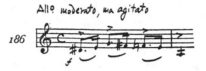

The phrase is played sixteen times in this key and twice—to increase the dramatic intensity—a minor third higher; it is a superb instance of Puccini's genius for achieving a maximum of effect by a minimum of means. The theme dies away as the Princess sits watching her niece in silence. "Why don't you speak?" asks Angelica in desperately anxious tones. Then in a violent outburst she cries: "Another moment of this silence and you will be damned for eternity. The Virgin hears you and she judges you!"

The Princess answers coldly, without emotion, that the child was taken ill two years ago. Everything was done to save his life.

"Is he dead?" asks Angelica.

The Princess bends her head and says nothing.

Angelica, with a heart rending cry, falls to the ground face downwards. Her aunt gets up to help her, thinking she has fainted; but hearing Angelica's sobs she suppresses the only sign of compassion she has shown and goes over to a sacred image on the wall and prays in silence before it. The Abbess and the Portress enter with pen and ink; Angelica drags herself to her feet and with a trembling hand signs the document. The two nuns and the Princess leave. Night has fallen and in the cemetery nuns can be seen lighting the small lanterns on the tombstones. Once more the theme of Ex 186 is repeated to die away slowly into a wonderful silence.

Angelica is alone and sings what has for many been the only music at all familiar from *Suor Angelica*—her lament for her dead child who has died motherless, without her kisses: "Senza mamma, o bimbo, tu sei morto!"

Except for the unnecessary banality of a section, to the tune of Ex 182 in Puccini's "religious" key of F and with words to the effect that "now you are an angel in heaven you can see your mother,"* this scene of Angelica's is one of the most moving, most characteristic and full of pathos that Puccini ever wrote. Apart from the opening section (musically the simplest, most immediately effective and harmonically ingenious part of the whole aria), the number is constructed from tunes and phrases we have already heard. What I can only continue to think of as the *religioso* section is followed by a broad and affecting repetition of the tune of Ex 183 which ends the scene.

Even the *religioso* movement is redeemed by scoring which repays the musician's study; it is rich in details such as the effective use of the harp playing the tune in the same register as the horn (the only arpeggios are supplied by divided violins). Taken as a whole, "Senza mamma" is Puccini very nearly at his best, as a composer who seems to have understood and been able to express the unhappiness of women with quite remarkable sensitivity and skill. The only difference between Angelica and Puccini's other heroines is that the little nun laments the loss of her child instead of her lover (the father of the child is never once mentioned or even thought about); it is still, whatever its cause, the pathos of a woman's broken heart that moves us as it clearly moved the composer.

At the end of Angelica's monologue Sister Genevieve comes on with the other nuns to reassure her that the Virgin has heard her prayer. Angelica rises "as if under the spell of a mystic exaltation" and the music tells us plainly that for the first time since *Le Villi* a Puccini opera is concerned with the supernatural as Angelica gives thanks to the Virgin Mary for her new-found happiness in another *religioso* theme, this time exploiting an almost endless sequence of consecutive fifths:

188

Music like this, with a chorus to help it towards its climaxes, is conventionally the kind of thing that leads to scenes of apotheosis or transfiguration in opera. Angelica's first high C, however, proves to be merely a hint of things to come. The nuns, including Sister Angélica, return to their cells; the stage is left empty for a moment and their singing (with another top C by Angelica) is heard coming from behind the scenes.

The orchestra now plays a purely instrumental version, slightly broadened in places, of "Senza mamma" beginning at the second part— i.e. where we heard Ex 182 again—as an accompaniment to the action which follows. Angelica comes out of her cell, carrying in her hand an earthenware jar which she fills with water from the fountain and places on a fire she makes at the foot of one of the cypresses. She then picks a

---

* The whole text of this number comes perilously close to a literal expression of the classic sentiment of *East Lynne*—"Dead! And never called me mother!"

handful of herbs and flowers and puts them in the jar singing, as she does so, to the persistent elegy of Ex 183, that the flowers will now repay her for all the care she has lavished on them: for through them she is going to die.

Angelica then turns towards the cells of the convent and bids farewell to the nuns, to the little church where she had so often wept and prayed: her child has summoned her and she will meet him again in heaven. As the orchestra plays *ff* the tune of Ex 181, Angelica kisses the Crucifix on the shrine and drinks the poison. There is a moment's pause, then Angelica, realizing what she has done, that she has committed a mortal sin, throws herself in despair on her knees, her cries punctuated by a full orchestral outburst of Ex 186 as she prays to the Madonna for help.

The whole focus of one's ears now has to be adjusted to take in the important contribution to the score by the group of instruments behind the scenes already alluded to. Where, before, the back-stage bells and piccolo were introduced for the sake of realism, Puccini now uses his piano and three muted trumpets, to which are eventually added a second piano, an organ and a pair of cymbals, as a means of suggesting the supernatural.

In addition to the off-stage instruments, there is the off-stage chorus consisting in the first instance of boys and sopranos whose prayer to the Virgin is heard approaching from the distance accompanied in the "prayer" theme (Ex 179) by trumpets and a piano, whose playing of spread chords in its highest register gives the music a tinkling quality which does not leave it from now on. We have reached the final section, The Miracle.

The libretto suggests that Angelica "seems to hear" the voices of angels interceding for her to the Mother of all Mothers; the score states more categorically that Angelica's invocation "is answered by the voices of angels". This passage includes some intriguing orchestral detail. The second piano is added, so that we have arpeggios as well as an *arpeggiato* version of the tune of Ex 188; the organ plays (also in its higher register), and a curious duet goes on between the cymbals off-stage, played *pp* on the strong beats of the bar, and the cymbals in the orchestra pit played *pp* on the weak beats. (Later the stage-cymbals player performs his part *pp* on the weak beat, but there is no strong-beat response from his colleague in the pit.)

At the direction, "The Miracle begins", the size of the chorus singing the hymn to the Virgin is increased by the addition of tenors and basses, the only broken male-voices to be heard in this otherwise exclusively treble-clef opera. The little church is suddenly lit by a dazzling light. The door opens slowly and through a mystic haze the church is seen to be crowded with angels. "Over the door the Queen of Comfort appears, solemn and with a sweet expression; in front of her there stands a blond child, dressed in white. The Virgin, with a gentle gesture, pushes the child towards the dying woman." The orchestral climax is reached at this moment in a blaze of musical-box scoring; a powerful minor version of Ex 179 is coloured by glockenspiel, celeste, harp and triangle all in the pit, in addition to the off-stage band with cymbals.

There is a pause and an ecstatic cry from Angelica. She holds her arms out towards the child. The hymn to the Virgin continues *pp* against a background of the tune of Ex 188. In the final cadence the theme of Ex 179 returns, with bells and much arpeggio-playing and *tremolando* by the two off-stage pianos. The child takes one step slowly towards Angelica, then another. At the third step Angelica falls gently and lifeless to the ground. The curtain falls on a long and fading high C in the chorus and a scene filled with light.

There is little doubt, I think, that *Suor Angelica* is the problem child of Puccini's triplets. Like *The Girl of the Golden West*, it is a work which proves on experience to be by no means as bad as one had previously been led to believe, but unfortunately not quite so good as one hoped it might nevertheless have proved to be. It is certainly the least popular of the *Trittico* operas, but not, I believe, for the reasons usually given. The physical objection that it is for women's voices only, for instance, seems to be no more valid as music criticism than the objection that the first act of *Siegfried*, which is very much longer than *Suor Angelica*, is for men's voices only.*

In the case of *Suor Angelica* the experiment was unusual, but it was by no means unsuccessful. There is a quite remarkable degree of contrast and variety in the vocal writing—as anybody who has actually *heard* the opera instead of just reading it will recognize. Puccini was too skilled a craftsman to permit the monotony which some commentators lead us to expect as inevitable. In the theatre, if not from conclusions hastily drawn from perusal of the vocal score, *Suor Angelica* is extremely effective, and there is little to compare with the grim tenseness of the characterization of the Princess, little so disarmingly innocent and happy as the music for the nuns in the earlier sequences, while the genuine pathos of Angelica herself is in its way as tenderly moving as anything found in *Madam Butterfly*.

The objection that there is no conventional romantic interest is also one that does not strike me as valid. *Suor Angelica* was conceived as part of a triptych, as a centre panel to contrast with a thriller on one side of it and a comedy on the other. Both *Il Tabarro* and *Gianni Schicchi* have "conventional romantic interest" after their fashion, but in neither of them does it touch the heart as the (operatically) unconventional emotion of mother love. Torn from its context it is conceivable that *Suor Angelica* might lack box-office appeal for want of sex-appeal; but in the surroundings in which its composer intended it to be heard the absence of Passion, in the Hollywood sense of the term, is not only right: it is impressive and touching.

To me, disappointment with *Suor Angelica* sets in from the moment the

* As a matter of statistics it is altogether 630 pages of miniature score before the Forest Bird is heard in the second act of Wagner's opera, a part intended for a boy's, not a woman's voice, and—when it comes—consisting of fewer than 50 bars all told. The first real woman is not heard until Erda's arrival out of a hole in the ground at the beginning of Act III on page 800—which is a very long time. The total number of pages of the miniature score of *Suor Angelica* is 102.

composer and librettist change musical and dramatic gear from the natural to the supernatural. Up to that point, when the off-stage choir of angels is first heard and the *café concert* piano's spread chords flatly dispel any preconceived notion that the harp is the instrumental basis of all heavenly music, the listener is in a familiar world. The people on the stage look real, sound real, behave and suffer like human beings we know. Suddenly, however, we are asked to accept an entirely different, unreal standard of behaviour. We are confronted with visions, mystic lights, angels, celestial choirs and a general operatic foreshadowing of the worst kind of Technicolored transfiguration. One does not question the sincerity of Puccini's religious feelings. But sincerity, unfortunately, has never been a guarantee of artistic merit. However affecting it may have been to the audience of nuns moved to pray for the soul of the fictional Sister Angelica when Puccini played over the score at his sister's convent, the finale of *Suor Angelica* lacks musical conviction when it is heard in the theatre. It is not enough to label this final "The Miracle", to have celestial choirs sing Latin hymns to a medley of tunes we have heard earlier in the opera and hope that an elaborate stage lighting-plot will do the rest.

It might help if by some trick of production the focus of the final scene could be altered so that the audience were not expected to feel involved in Angelica's experience but were merely disinterested witnesses of a young woman suffering hallucinations as she dies. If this could be done then I believe "The Miracle" would be more convincing—or at any rate, less embarrassing. The audience must not be asked to believe in the supernatural, though there is no reason why we should not be moved by other people's belief in it.

In the end, however, what is needed is a miracle in the music and it just does not occur. Verdi might have supplied it; Puccini was not of such a calibre. In the end, the finale of *Suor Angelica* is the musical expression of the Italian village church filled with tinsel and oleographs, wax flowers and mass-produced plaster images of the saints. It is touching; it is sincere, and charming in its simple sentimentality; but it is not really very inspiring as a work of art. And least of all—as Puccini of all composers should have known—does it belong in the theatre.

GIANNI SCHICCHI

(Property of G. Ricordi and Co.)

Opera in one act. Libretto by Giovacchino Forzano. First performed at the Metropolitan Opera House, New York on 14th December, 1918. First performance in England: Covent Garden, 18th June, 1920.

THE final panel of Puccini's Triptych is remarkable in at least two respects. It is the composer's only comic opera, and he had so little trouble with the libretto that he composed the music in two months. Neither of these aspects of the opera is really so surprising, of course, if we consider Puccini's musical character and the circumstances in which he composed *Gianni Schicchi*. He had shown a highly developed sense of comedy and high spirits in *Manon Lescaut* and particularly in *La Bohème* which, except for its unhappy ending, might well be a romantic comedy; it was present in the first act of *Tosca*, in *The Girl of the Golden West* and in *Il Tabarro*. There was a hint of it in the episode of the wasp in *Suor Angelica*; even in *Madam Butterfly* there are moments which cause at least the flicker of a smile. It was obvious on reflection, therefore, that Puccini had the temperament as well as the technical equipment to write a comic opera. The first and second acts of *La Bohème* alone showed that he was a master of that variation and contrast of speed which is essential to the musical construction of operatic comedy.

When, in 1917, Giovacchino Forzano brought Puccini his ideas for the two one-act operas the composer needed to complete his projected *Trittico*, he set about the writing of the librettos in the order in which they were to take their places in the triple bill. Forzano had scarcely started work on *Suor Angelica* than Puccini begged him to drop everything and finish *Gianni Schicchi* first. Puccini's enthusiasm was understandable. Apart from the desire to write a comic opera which had long obsessed him, and his feeling that the only possible antidote to the depression of the First German War was to write something to make people laugh, he perceived at once that Forzano's idea was what would nowadays be termed "a natural".

For some time I was firmly convinced that *Gianni Schicchi* had been based by the librettist on a story by Boccaccio, and in doing so, of course, unwittingly paid its author the compliment he deserved. In fact the plot comes originally from half a dozen far-from-comic lines in Canto XXX of Dante's *Inferno*, in which the poet encounters Gianni Schicchi in that compartment of the eighth circle of hell reserved for impostors who have "counterfeited the persons of others, debased the current coin, or deceived by speech under false pretences".

Schicchi's crime, according to Dante, was that he used his great gift of mimicry to personate Buoso Donati, just deceased, and dictate a will in the son's favour by which he himself received a beautiful mare known as "The Lady of the Stud". Dante's indignation was naturally a little influenced by the fact that his wife Gemma was a Donati, and the affair of Gianni Schicchi de' Cavalcanti became in consequence very much a matter of personal and family umbrage. What Dante carefully neglects to tell the reader, however, is that Schicchi committed the fraud at the instigation of Buoso Donati's son, Simone, and that, with the exception of Schicchi's modest and justifiable perquisite in the form of the mare, the new will benefited nobody but the son. But perhaps complicity before, during and after the fact was not regarded by Dante as more than a misdemeanour—in the family, that is.

Forzano took no more than the bare facts mentioned by Dante and elaborated and developed the situation into a comedy of great wit and ingenuity which in its first form evidently satisfied the composer so thoroughly that no revision or modification seems to have been necessary, and there is significantly almost no correspondence on the subject to be traced between Puccini and his librettist. It was in every respect a unique and happy occasion in the lives of all concerned.

CHARACTERS IN ORDER OF SINGING:

The Relations of Buoso Donati

ZITA, *called "The Old Woman", cousin of Buoso* Contralto (60)*

MARCO . . . . . . *Bass* (45)

LA CIESCA, *his wife* . . . *Mezzo-soprano* (38)

SIMONE, *cousin of Buoso and Marco's father* *Bass* (70)

RINUCCIO, *nephew of Zita* . . . *Tenor* (24)

GHERARDO, *nephew of Buoso* . . . *Tenor* (40)

NELLA, *his wife* . . . . *Soprano* (34)

BETTO DI SIGNA, *brother-in-law of Buoso, poor and raggedly dressed* . . . *Baritone* (*age indefinable*)

GHERARDINO, *child of Gherardo and Nella* *Boy* (7)

GIANNI SCHICCHI . . . . *Baritone* (50)

LAURETTA, *his daughter* . . . *Soprano* (21)

MASTER SPINELLOCCIO, *a physician* . . *Bass*†

AMANTIO DI NICOLAO, *notary* . . . *Bass*

PINELLINO, *a shoemaker* . . . . *Baritone*

GUCCIO, *a dyer* . . . . . . *Baritone*

Scene: Florence Time: 1299

* As in the case of *Il Tabarro* the characters in *Gianni Schicchi* are described in my orchestral score only by their ages, not by the type of voice required for each part.

† The physician and the remaining three characters listed are given neither voice nor age in the cast list.

Scene: Buoso Donati's bedroom. On the audience's left, the main door beyond which is a landing and the staircase. There is a tall glass door leading on to a terrace. In the background, on the left, a large window through which can be seen Arnolfo's tower of the Palazzo Vecchio. Against the right-hand wall there is a small wooden staircase leading to a gallery where there are a chest of drawers and a door. There is another small door under the stairs. On the right, at the back, a bed. Chairs, chests and cabinets are scattered around the room; there is also a table with various silver objects on it.

The rise of the curtain is preceded by a short and vigorous orchestral passage full of characteristic high spirits, but noticeably more brilliantly and harshly scored than the gay introductions to *Manon Lescaut* and *La Bohème*. Two themes are heard in this short prelude which play a considerable part in the opera. The first consists of the phrase, marked by the composer "tumultuoso":

—while the second is no more than a fragment which Puccini treats with great ingenuity in the course of the work as a theme associated with the influence of Gianni Schicchi on the action in general:

The initial Allegro begins to sag; the tempo slows to a lugubrious Largo version of Ex 189 as the curtain rises on music and action which give an immediate and unique indication of the character of the opera we are to hear—unique because no other comic opera in the repertoire that I can think of (not even *Falstaff*) begins by being funny at once.

The mourning relatives of Buoso Donati are discovered keening and praying around the death bed. At the four corners of the bed, the stage directions tell us, are four tall candlesticks with four lighted candles. In front of the bed, a three-branched candelabra, unlighted. There is sunshine and the glow of candles. It is nine o'clock in the morning. Through the half open curtains of the bed can be seen a red drapery covering a body.

The mumbling and moaning that comes from the gathering of relatives has an extremely hollow ring, and though the muffled funeral note of a drum persists through the dirge-like orchestral reiteration of Ex 189, the assembled company is easily distracted by Betto, the ragged and obviously poorest of poor relations, who begins to repeat what "they say in Signa . . ." What they say in Signa, we eventually learn, is that Buoso Donati has left all his money to the Church—one rumour says to a monastery, another says to a convent. The mere idea of such a tragedy, whether it is true or not, strikes the mourners with horror. There is a moment's incredulous silence. The funereal drum-beat is resumed, more frequent and clearly marked this time, while the melancholy tone of the cor anglais at its most *doloroso* takes over the tune of Ex 189. In despair the relatives turn to Simone, who has ceased to be Buoso's son in Forzano's treatment and has become his cousin.

"You speak," says the Old Woman. "You are the oldest."

"And you've been mayor of Fucecchio too," adds Marco with emphasis.

Simone reflects for a moment. Then he says gravely: "If the will is in the hands of a lawyer—who knows? That could be bad luck. But if it has been left somewhere in this room, then that will be bad luck on the monks and hope for us."

The relatives solemnly intone Simone's last words in unison, Rinuccio adding an aside addressed to the absent Lauretta to suggest the importance of his uncle's will in their lives.

The tempo changes suddenly and to a busy and extremely unmournful Allegro vivo form of Ex 189 the hunt for the will begins. Every drawer and cupboard in the place is ransacked. There are moments when first Simone, and then Zita think they have found the will; but it proves to be a false alarm and the search is resumed more frantically than before. Only Betto takes no active part in the search: he is too busy pocketing the silver that is lying about.

At length there is a triumphant cry from Rinuccio who has found the will in the chest at the top of the stairs, and the orchestra anticipates a theme (a characteristic practice in this opera) which is later associated in a fuller form with the two young lovers, and which on this first appearance accompanies Rinuccio's fervent prayer that now the will has been found he will have Zita's permission to marry Lauretta:

Zita, taking the will from her nephew, replies that if everything goes as well as she hopes Rinuccio can marry whom the devil he pleases. While his aunt is busy tearing apart the ribbons that are tied around the will (Betto has purloined the scissors), Rinuccio takes Gherardino on one side and giving him a couple of coins, sends the child off to fetch Gianni Schicchi.

Zita opens the will and reads the opening sentence: "To my cousins Zita and Simone." This moves Simone so deeply that he solemnly lights the three candles in the candelabra in front of the bed. As she unfolds the parchment of the will still further Zita is surrounded by the relations pressing on top of each other, their lips moving in silence as they read over her shoulder, while in the orchestra we hear the wonderfully simple and mock-serious "will" theme proclaimed in a stately fashion first by a group of wood-wind, then by a solo bassoon, followed—in B flat—by a solo horn:

An echo yet another tone lower (in A flat) by bass clarinet and violoncellos is marked in the score as an optional cut and the four bars are usually omitted—a little unnecessarily as I think. The libretto describes how "suddenly a cloud overshadows all faces . . . until they have a tragic look". The gloom and stupefaction are reflected in a mournful figure by cor anglais and horn, and the tune of Ex 189 played pizzicato by violoncellos and basses. The comic melancholy of this passage has an unfailing effect in the theatre when it accompanies the actions of Simone, who "turns round and seeing the three candles he had lighted a moment before, blows them out; he closes the bed curtains completely and then blows out all the remaining candles".

There now follows, at a vigorous Allegro vivo, a scene of anger and indignation started off by Simone's "So it was true! The monks will get fat on Donati money!" Each of the disinherited relations has a harsh opinion to express and the scene ends in a climax of bitter laughter to a theme first heard as Rinuccio's personal lamentation that all his happiness has been stolen from him to support a church:

As the indignation and exasperation of the relatives subsides into dejection ("Who would have thought that when Buoso was taken to the cemetery we'd be shedding real tears!" wails Zita), this theme broadens to create an ingenious impression of hopeless exhaustion as the choristers sink speechless and rigid into their chairs. There is a moment's pause.

Is there nothing to be done about the will, they ask. Can't it be changed or twisted? Once more Zita appeals to Simone: he is the oldest (and has been mayor of Fucecchio). Simone makes a gesture of helpless despair. Rinuccio suddenly pipes up: there is only one person who would possibly save them.

"Who?" ask the relatives.

"Gianni Schicchi!" replies Rinuccio to a perky little phrase which is from now on firmly attached to the name:

Zita retorts crossly that she doesn't want to hear any more about Gianni Schicchi or his daughter. The boy Gherardino rushes into the room and shouts: "He's coming!"

"Who?" ask the relatives.

"Gianni Schicchi!" answers the child, to the same little phrase as before.

"Who sent for him?" asks Zita. Rinuccio replies that he did; he had hoped—— But we do not hear what it was he had hoped because he is interrupted by the general opinion that this is a fine time to have Gianni Schicchi around. And furthermore, says Simone, who is backed up by Zita, the very idea of a Donati marrying the daughter of a peasant!

Rinuccio tells them they are all mistaken. Schicchi is a fine and astute man who knows all the ins and outs of the law, a quick-witted jester; if a new trick is needed it is always Gianni Schicchi who can do it. Reference to Schicchi's ingenuity and quick-wittedness introduces a new theme closely associated with his gifts as a joker and first played by wood-wind and three muted trumpets—a distant and rather mysterious sound when a few bars later, it is heard without the voice:

Rinuccio continues his enthusiastic description of Schicchi's character, his shrewd, cunning eyes, the smile on his quizzical face, his great big nose, which throws a shadow like a high tower. He comes from the country? What does that matter? Rinuccio sings a vigorous song in praise of Florence, the flowering tree with strong roots in the countryside— "Firenze è come un albero fiorito":

Puccini indicates in the score that this aria is "in the manner of a Tuscan popular song"; to the listener not acquainted with the popular songs of Tuscany, however, the sequence sounds the purest Puccini, especially when, probably to his surprise, the first stanza ends with a phrase familiar to millions who have never been inside an opera house but who recognize it as coming from an opera called *Gianni Schicchi*:

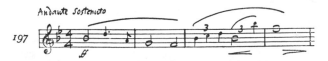

This is instantly identifiable, of course, as the opening phrase of

"O mio babbino caro" which comes later in the action. I have always been slightly puzzled by what it is doing in the context of Rinuccio's aria for, as we know, its principal function in the opera is as Lauretta's plea to her father. At this point, however, it does not appear remotely connected with Lauretta, her father, or even with Rinuccio, for it bursts forth as he describes enthusiastically how Florence blossoms and new towers and palaces rise upwards to the stars. It would be interesting to know what was in Puccini's mind with this first hint of a tune later used for an entirely different purpose. Was he anticipating Lauretta's aria? Or was Lauretta's aria intended as a reference to this first appearance of the phrase? If so, then in either or both cases: why? Whatever the reason, the four-bar theme seems to have taken Puccini's fancy.

Finishing his stirring recital of the greatness of Florence, with instances of its famous men who have sprung from the country soil—Arnolfo, Giotto, the Medicis—Rinuccio makes a final powerful call for an end to snobbish distinctions and a "Viva!" for the new people like Gianni Schicchi. And he does so with that first phrase of Lauretta's aria audible in the lower part of the orchestra.

The enthusiastic tones of Rinuccio's Tuscan song die down (also to the tune of Ex 197 in the bass). There is a knock at the door; Rinuccio goes over to it to let in Gianni Schicchi and Lauretta. Schicchi stands by the doorway and looks at the dejected company of relatives before him. "How desolate they all look!" he says to himself. "Buoso Donati must have got better!" Rinuccio and Lauretta whisper greetings to each other and Ex 197 returns for a brief moment played *dolce* by a clarinet and a solo violin.

Gianni advances slowly into the room and notices the candelabra by the bed. To the accompaniment of the familiar mourning music he sympathizes hypocritically with Donati's unhappy relations in their loss. "But there you are," he reflects philosophically. "In this world you lose one thing and find another. You lose Buoso, but there is his legacy." The mention of the subject of Buoso's will is the signal for a renewal of the "indignation music" launched with characteristic disgust by Zita whose hatred of the monks is matched in intensity by her sudden determination that her nephew Rinuccio shall not marry Schicchi's dowerless daughter. An admirably conceived slanging-match ensues (with Ex 193 playing its inevitable part, as before, in the development, and evoking memories of Act II of *La Bohème*). Gianni and Zita, hurling insults at each other, try to drag Rinuccio and Lauretta apart while the unfortunate lovers struggle and in despair bid farewell to their hopes of marrying on the First of May —those hopes which were anticipated musically by Rinuccio in Ex 191 and which, in spite of everything, have now expanded into a more romantic and warmly orchestrated form:

198

un po' sostenuto

Ad - di - o   spe - ran - za bel - la,   spe - ran - za bel - la

The voices of the onlookers are added to this incipient Montague-and-Capulet feud, when the relatives join in to complain (not without reason) that this is a fine moment to be having a dispute over young lovers. What about the will?

The ensemble comes to a sudden stop as Gianni Schicchi takes Lauretta to the door and starts to leave. Rinuccio holds him back, begging him to stay for a moment; and turning to his aunt, tells her to give Schicchi the will instead of creating an uproar. Rinuccio is sure Gianni can find a brilliant way out. "For this lot?" says Schicchi scornfully, pointing at the relations. "Niente! Niente! Niente!"

Schicchi's fierce refusal is not quite as final as his words and attitude suggest: the phrase ends on a chord that traditionally leads to the key of A flat and a change of subject. This is just what happens. Lauretta kneels before her father and pleads with him to help, otherwise she will throw herself into the Arno; and we hear the Puccini aria (marked *Andantino ingenuo*) which in recent years has come to rival the familiar show-stoppers in *La Bohème*, *Tosca* and *Madam Butterfly*—"O mio babbino caro":

This little aria, a beautifully simple and exquisitely fashioned tune with a remarkably restrained and effective orchestral accompaniment, is commonly stated by critics to have been written by Puccini with his tongue in his cheek as though mocking his own sentimental manner. I don't know how this legend started, nor what evidence there is that the composer regarded the aria in this light, but it is a point of view to which the public, at any rate, has resolutely refused to subscribe for over fifty years. It is a pretty and touching little tune that Lauretta sings and it melts the heart of the audience as it melts the heart of her father on the stage. If the composer really did mean to satirize his own lyrical style then it is a musical joke that has completely misfired so far as the ordinary listener is concerned.

There is a pause. "Give me the will," says Gianni Schicchi shortly. He takes it from Rinuccio and paces up and down the room reading it. He comes abruptly to a stop. "There's nothing to be done," he says.

"Addio, speranza bella", sing Lauretta and Rinuccio, bidding farewell again to their chances of marriage in May. Schicchi resumes his walking and reads the will once more; and once more he says, "There's nothing to be done."

Lauretta and Rinuccio sing their farewell once more (*con dolore*) but end on a more optimistic note as Gianni Schicchi interrupts with a hopeful "And yet . . ." Schicchi stands motionless and silent and a smile of triumph slowly spreads across his face.

"Well?" ask Buoso's relations, breathlessly.

Schicchi sends Lauretta out on to the terrace to feed the bird in its cage, and turning to the relatives asks whether anybody but themselves knows of Buoso's death. No, nobody else; and to the accompaniment of a funereal figure played by side drum, the harp in its low register, violoncellos, and double basses divided into three parts (a total sound which reminds one strongly of the off-stage drum in the second act of *Tosca*) Schicchi gives his instructions.

Buoso's body and all the candelabra are taken into another room, the bed is newly made up. A sudden knock at the door scares everybody nearly to death. It is Maestro Spinelloccio, the doctor, who gets as far as the door but is allowed in no further by the Donati family. Gianni hides himself behind the bed-hangings while Betto pulls the shutters over the windows to make the room dark. The relations greet Maestro Spinelloccio of Bologna (the doctor from Bologna is a stock figure of Italian comedy), who asks after the patient in a nasal Bolognese accent, in which the "z" in words like "potenza" and "scienza" becomes softened to "potensa" and "sciensa".

Buoso is much better, the doctor is told. "What heights science has attained," comments the doctor with satisfaction. "Well, let's see him, let's see him."

"No, he's resting," say the relatives.

"But——"

"He's resting," the relatives repeat firmly.

A thin, frail voice comes from behind the curtains: "No, no, Maestro Spinelloccio——" Gianni's imitation is so good that for a moment the relatives think it is Buoso himself speaking; Betto drops the silver tray he has been hiding in his sleeve with the shock.

(We have to take the accuracy of Gianni Schicchi's imitation on trust, of course, for we have never heard Buoso's voice for comparison. The relatives' reaction is purely visual, the execution of a stage instruction with no counterpart in the music to indicate the exact nature of their astonishment. I am surprised, indeed, that Puccini did not add an incredulous *sotto voce* exclamation of some kind to make certain that the facial expressions of the characters were understood. As it is, it seems to me to be expecting rather a lot that a single rapid gesture should convey all that Forzano tells us in the stage directions it should.)

"I want to rest," continues Schicchi. "Perhaps you would call again this evening?" The doctor agrees to do so; as he leaves he turns proudly to the relations to tell them that no sick patient of his ever died—oh, he takes no personal credit for that, of course: the glory all belongs to the Bologna school of medicine.

As soon as the door is shut on the doctor, Betto opens the shutters and Gianni, resuming his natural voice, asks if his imitation was successful. When he is told it was perfect (punctuation by the "impersonation"

theme of Ex 195) he cries joyously "Vittoria!" The relatives look blankly
at him. "What fat-heads!" exclaims Gianni, and he begins to explain
what seems to him to be the extremely obvious. The tempo reverts to the
familiar busy Allegro 2/4 and a new thematic fragment, six notes long, is
heard for the first time, a phrase associated from now on with the making
of the new will:

All they have to do, says Schicchi, is to go to the notary and tell him
to come quickly. Buoso Donati has had a relapse and wants to make a
will—quickly, or it may be too late. The notary comes, continues Schicchi;
the room is in semi-darkness (funeral drums and Ex 189 in its solemn
form). In the bed lies the form of Buoso who, Schicchi describes
with great deliberation, wears a night cap on his head and a scarf
over the lower part of his face. Between cap and scarf there is visible
a nose, which instead of being Buoso's nose is Schicchi's; and as he
goes on to explain the details of the scheme Gianni grows increasingly
ecstatic over the idea of all time, working up to an oddly fierce
climax which seems to have strayed from one of Michele's scenes in
Il Tabarro.

The relatives finally understand the point of the plan. Rinuccio goes
out to fetch the notary while the rest excitedly surround Gianni Schicchi,
kissing his hand and his garments in their delight, so excitedly, indeed,
that they grow a little light-headed and begin to sing the praises of Love
Among Relatives. Simone restores order to the scene by raising
the question of how the legacy should be divided. The florins left
in ready money, for instance? In equal parts, is the unanimous reply.
Gianni nods in approval. There is a return to a faster tempo and a new
theme to which the relatives stake their claims to the properties they
covet:

To the tune of this (first played by muted horns "con voce nasale")
Simone says he wants the farms at Fucecchio, Zita those at Figline, Betto
those at Prato; Gherardo the lands at Empoli, Marco those at Quintole.
There is an ominous pause. "There remain," says Zita portentously,
"the mule, this house and the mills at Signa." Slowly, with feigned
ingenuousness, Simone says: "Ah, I understand. As I am the oldest and
have been mayor of Fucecchio, you want to give them to me! I thank
you!"

"Just a moment!" exclaims Zita. "If you are old then that's bad luck on you"—and a first class general uproar starts up with each of the relatives individually laying claim to the mule, the house, and the mills at Signa. The din, which includes Schicchi's hearty laughter at this display of Love Among Relatives, is suddenly silenced by the tolling of a passing bell.

"They know!" whisper the relatives. "They know that Buoso is dead!" To the rather naïvely illustrative effect of a rapid descending chromatic scale Gherardo dashes out of the room and runs down the stairs to find out what has happened. Lauretta comes in from the terrace to say that the bird won't eat any more. "Then give him something to drink," snaps Schicchi, who has been slightly unnerved by the implications of the passing bell. Lauretta goes back to the terrace as Gherardo, accompanied this time by an ascending chromatic scale, returns breathlessly to say it is all right: it is only the captain's converted Negro servant who has suddenly died. "Requiescat in pace!" pronounce the relatives with unseemly cheerfulness.

Simone proposes magnanimously that the question of the mule, the house and the mills should be left to the honesty of Schicchi to decide, a proposal accepted unanimously and commented on by the wood-wind with a brief reference to the end of Rinuccio's song in praise of the great men of Florence. Schicchi agrees, and with the help of the three women begins to assume his disguise as Buoso. While he is being dressed he is approached one by one by Zita, Simone, Betto, Nella and La Ciesca who offer him (sotto voce) handsome rewards if only he will leave them the mule, the house and the mills at Signa. To each of them Gianni Schicchi replies "All right!" When he is dressed the three women gather round him to praise his perfect disguise and begin to put him to bed with some rather arch baby-talk in a wheedling little trio which begins with the gentle lilting phrase:

A charming, unexpected lyrical interlude ends with an impassioned tribute to Schicchi the Saviour. The relatives push Gianni towards the bed, but he stops them with a solemn gesture to remind them of the law: whosoever shall substitute himself for another in wills and legacies shall have his hand cut off and be exiled. Gianni points through the open window towards Arnolfo's tower of the Palazzo Vecchio. "Farewell to Florence," he sings, "farewell to its lovely sky—I salute thee with this handless arm—and wander homeless like a Ghibelline."

Schicchi sings this to a most captivating phrase which is repeated after him in unison by a very subdued and deeply impressed chorus of relatives, and which I quote here in a form to show how Puccini hovers

between the two keys of D and G and how peculiarly effective his sense of
the right harmony could be:

203

Schicchi's first recital of the farewell to Florence is punctuated three
times by a short *pp* phrase for two muted trumpets which sounds like a
very distant fanfare. The same orchestral punctuation occurs during the
relatives' repetition, but scored twice for two oboes and a bassoon, and
the third time for oboes and cor anglais.

There is a knock on the door. Schicchi jumps hurriedly into bed, the
relatives close the shutter, place a lighted candle on the table where the
notary is to sit and the door is opened to Rinuccio, the Notary, and
the witnesses Pinellino the shoemaker, and Guccio the dyer.

The action which follows is accompanied by a musical commentary of
great wit and simplicity, constructed of themes we have already heard—
among them the "will" theme (Ex 192), the tune of Ex 200 slowed up to
conform with the Notary's reverence and admiration for his client, the
mourning music (Ex 189) and the cynically recurrent fragment Ex 190.

Gianni Schicchi explains to the Notary that owing to paralysis of his
hand he will be unable to write the will and will have to dictate it instead;
he also asks that the relatives should be present during the preparation of
the will. The music settles down to a long passage for strings based on the
"will" theme (Ex 192), which has always reminded me a little of an
organ voluntary (suitable, of course, for the offertory). After the lawyer's
long Latin preamble, which he interrupts by a timely interjection—also
in Latin—revoking and rendering null and void all other wills ("What
foresight!" comment the relatives with approval), Schicchi makes the
smaller bequests.

For the upkeep of Buoso's favourite church: five lire, a modest sum
which comes as a great relief to the relatives and which Schicchi justifies by
saying that if you leave a large sum to the Church everybody thinks the
money must have been stolen. To Simone, Zita, Betto, Gherardo and
Marco, he bequeathes those lands they asked for earlier. There is a sudden
tension in the music, achieved by the simple device of a string tremolo,
as "through their teeth" the relatives mutter: "Now we come to the
mule, the house and the mills at Signa." Slowly, deliberately prolonging
the agony, Schicchi extolls the virtues of the mule ("which cost 300 florins
and is the best mule in Tuscany") and leaves it to "my devoted friend,
Gianni Schicchi"—the name sung with malicious relish to the tune of
Ex 194.

The relatives are staggered—and when the Notary repeats the bequest
in Latin can only stammer "But——!" Simone speaks up and angrily

asks what Gianni Schicchi could possibly want with a mule. Schicchi rebukes him with "Please behave, Simone. I know what Gianni Schicchi wants!" and bequeaths the next item, the house in Florence, to his "dear devoted, affectionate friend, Gianni Schicchi!" The relatives explode with fury and indignation to the sound of an unexpected reprise of the very first boisterous notes of the opera, but their spirit is completely dashed by Schicchi's high-pitched reminder of the Farewell to Florence (Ex 203).

Schicchi comes to the mills at Signa, alternating a matter-of-fact *quasi parlato* with the tune of "Addio Firenze."—"The mills at Signa (farewell, dear Florence!) I leave to my dear (farewell, divine sky!), affectionate friend, Gianni Schicchi (I salute thee with this handless arm—la-la-la-la-la). That is all!" This passage is accompanied by a funeral drum beating ominously against a sinister *ostinato* of most un-Puccini-like discords:

The Notary and witnesses are a little surprised at the abrupt ending to Schicchi's testament but are reassured by his request to Zita to give 20 florins from her purse to the witnesses and a hundred to the good Notary. As they move towards the bed Gianni Schicchi waves them away with a trembling hand: "No farewells, please." Maestro Amantio di Nicolao, Pinellino and Guccio, deeply upset, move slowly to the door, reflecting to the slow version of the tune (Ex 200) with which they greeted the testator on their arrival, "What a man! What a loss!" and, with genuine sadness, bidding the shortly-to-be-bereaved relatives have courage, leave the room.

There is a moment's pause. Then, with the exception of Rinuccio who has gone out to join Lauretta on the terrace, the relatives turn on Gianni Schicchi in all their fury. They tear his nightgown to pieces, but he retaliates by grabbing Buoso's stick which hangs beside the bed and lays about them. The relatives grab everything of value they can see and rush out of the room, with Gianni Schicchi shouting at them to get out of *his* house and at the same time pursuing them to recover his belongings. The din subsides and the stage is left empty.

The door leading on to the terrace opens slowly to reveal Florence in all the glory of its sunlight and Rinuccio and Lauretta in each other's arms, singing of Florence and the beauties of Fiesole where they first kissed and in the valley far below them the city looked like Paradise. This warm lyrical passage is sung to the familiar tune of Ex 198, now an expression of hopes fulfilled and rich with the promise of that enchantment that perhaps only those know who have ever spent a honeymoon in Fiesole.

To the cynic this little duet may appear nothing more than conventional "love interest"; to the musician it is the touch of genius needed to contrast with the acrimonious activity and vigour of the action, to relax the great comic tension that has dominated the opera up to this point. The spirit of farce is revived for a moment when Gianni Schicchi returns, his arms filled with the loot he has recovered from the relatives. He drops the bundles on the floor, and seeing the two lovers, is touched by the sight and smiles. Then, taking off his cap, he turns to the audience and addresses them in a spoken *envoi*: "Tell me, ladies and gentlemen, could Buoso's money have ended up in a better way than this? For this little escapade I was hounded to Hell—well, so be it. But with permission of our great father Dante [with delicious irony two clarinets echo the final theme of Rinuccio's ode to the great men of Florence], if you have been amused this evening—then perhaps you will return a verdict of extenuating circumstances."

Gianni Schicchi claps his hands to lead the applause and bows to the audience as the curtain falls to a *fortissimo* echo of Ex 195—the musical symbol of Schicchi's ingenuity and wit.

The success of *Gianni Schicchi* and the public's preference for it over the other two operas of the *Trittico* is easily understood. It is a work which makes an immediate appeal and in doing so I think reveals all its secrets. I do not find, at least, that like its companion operas *Gianni Schicchi* holds more for the listener at a second or third hearing than at a first. One's enjoyment of it and one's affection for it may increase every time one hears it, but it is music that wears its heart on its sleeve, as it were—which is all, surely, one wants of any comic opera not by Mozart.

Puccini's comedy is not a subtle conception, but it is unusually rich in that quality not always abundant in comic opera—namely, comic suspense created by music which is in itself funny. The mock solemnity of the scenes with the doctor and the notary is admirably effective, because the composer's wink is barely noticeable. An Italian critic has said somewhere that of all Puccini's operas *Gianni Schicchi* alone lacks a distinctive atmosphere, that we are aware of being in Florence only because the characters keeping telling us we are. This may be so, for as we have seen there is nothing immediately recognizable as peculiarly Florentine, for instance, about Rinuccio's song, as far as the average listener can detect. But the atmosphere of *Gianni Schicchi*, to me at any rate, is not in any case a physical or geographical one as it is in *Il Tabarro*, *La Bohème* or *Suor Angelica*. Its atmosphere is a purely musical one, created by the hard brightness of the orchestral colouring and the expression of that rather malicious gaiety and exuberance which was so characteristic of the composer's nature.

It is a paradox of the *Trittico* that what is in the end musically the least interesting of the three operas should so surpass the others in popularity. Puccini conceived his triptych as an entity of three strongly contrasted works, and while *Gianni Schicchi* has enough musical and dramatic appeal to exist in its own right, it is only in the context of the triple bill that it makes its true effect, not only so far as its own music and drama are concerned, but because in this way both *Suor Angelica* and *Il Tabarro* can be seen in their proper light. Sentimental and tragic relief are just as important dramatic devices as comic relief, but like all such devices depend for their effect on contrast. If we regard the sentiment of *Suor Angelica* and the stark realism of *Il Tabarro* as forms of emotional relief from each other, and the comedy of *Gianni Schicchi* not only as a relief from both, but in itself providing the element from which *Suor Angelica* and *Il Tabarro* in turn also provide relief, then I think the *Trittico* takes on a new and more satisfying significance. Complete performances of the triple bill in the theatre are still unfortunately rare, but the gramophone provides one with a wonderful opportunity to judge a fascinating and unique artistic conception in its proper perspective.

TURANDOT

(*Property of G. Ricordi and Co.*)

Lyric drama in three acts and five scenes by Giuseppe Adami and Renato Simoni.
First performed at La Scala, Milan, on 25th April, 1926, conducted by Arturo Toscanini.
First performance in England: Covent Garden, 7th June, 1927. First performance in the
United States: Metropolitan Opera House, New York, 16th November, 1926.

No opera ever gave Puccini such heartaches or caused him to suffer such
agonies of frustration as the opera he never lived to finish. It was not so
much that he died before he could finish *Turandot* as that he did not
finish *Turandot* before he died. The time between the completion of the
Trittico and his death was longer than he had needed to write any of his
other operas, but the years Puccini spent in the creation of *Turandot*
were abnormally filled with periods of despair and loss of self-confidence,
with second thoughts, with exasperating moments of complete deadlock
between composer and librettists, and long weeks when Puccini, with the
composition behind him, was left without words to set to music. "This
infamous *Turandot* terrifies me and I shall not finish it"—"I have no desire
to work"—phrases like these recurred again and again in his correspondence as he faced the problems of a work which he feared he would not
do well and at times did not want to do at all. There was even a time
when he dropped the project of *Turandot* altogether and begged Giovacchino Forzano, who had been his librettist for *Suor Angelica* and *Gianni
Schicchi*, to find him a new subject.

The idea of *Turandot* as a theme for an opera was decided upon early
·in 1920. Renato Simoni, who had been commissioned by the composer to
find a suitable operatic subject with Giuseppe Adami, the librettist of *Il
Tabarro*, suggested in a moment of desperation that Puccini might find
something possible among the plays of the 18-century Venetian, Carlo
Gozzi—"something fantastic and unreal," said Simoni, "but interpreted
with human feelings and presented in modern colours."

It is usually said that Puccini made his very first acquaintance with
the subject of Turandot through an Italian translation of a German
version of Gozzi's play. This may well have been the rather roundabout
way in which he came to know Gozzi, but he could hardly have failed to
have known something of the character of Turandot before that, if only
because his own teacher at the Milan Conservatiore, Antonio Bazzini,
had composed a *Turanda* which had been performed at La Scala in 1867
and, described as a "solemn fiasco", had once and for all convinced the
former violin virtuoso that the lyric drama was not his true métier. It was
Bazzini's only opera.

Nor can we imagine that Puccini was wholly ignorant of the play
written by his own and greatest librettist, Giuseppe Giacosa, whose
Trionfo d'amore was inspired by the figure of Turandot. Finally there was

Busoni's two-act *Turandot*, based on Gozzi, dedicated to Toscanini, and performed in a double bill with *Arlecchino* at Zürich in 1917, which Puccini did not hear but which he certainly heard about, and with his well-known interest in the music of his contemporaries, might well have studied in score.

In one respect *Turandot*, as Puccini first envisaged it, resembled Busoni's opera in being in two acts, and for some time the composer worked along these lines. But as the libretto developed it was obvious that the more acceptable three-act form would have to be adopted in order to accommodate the abundance and richness of Puccini's musical invention. (One mentions this original form of Puccini's opera with some trepidation lest the administrators of Covent Garden get to hear of it and in their endless zeal for staging what they consider to be What The Composer Really Meant add a two-act *Turandot* to a repertoire already eccentrically distinguished by a *Traviata* bearing the names of Dumas' characters instead of Verdi's, an almost continuous, interval-less *Butterfly* and the longest *Boris Godunov* on record.)

Gozzi's *Turandot*, written in 1762, was in five acts, a play he described as a *fiaba*, or fable, in which the improvised comic features of the commedia dell'arte were combined with a main plot of a simple, romantic fairy-tale nature. The extent to which the composer and his librettists transformed Gozzi's model into the magnificent and original work of art that is Puccini's *Turandot* is something which I hope will become clear in the course of this analysis. Since Puccini's opera may still be unfamiliar to some readers of this book, little purpose would be served in drawing attention to the differences between the play and the opera at this point. Such questions as the significance of the "Masks" and the character of Liù are best considered, I feel, when we know what and who these characters are.

CHARACTERS IN ORDER OF SINGING:

A MANDARIN	*Baritone*
LIÙ, *a young slave girl*	*Soprano*
THE UNKNOWN PRINCE (Calaf), *son of* .	*Tenor*
TIMUR, *exiled King of Tartary* . . .	*Bass*
THE YOUNG PRINCE OF PERSIA . .	*Tenor*
PING, *Grand Chancellor of China* . . .	*Baritone*
PANG, *The General Purveyor*	*Tenor*
PONG, *Chief of the Imperial Kitchen* . .	*Tenor*
THE EMPEROR ALTOUM	*Tenor*
PRINCESS TURANDOT	*Soprano*

The Executioner, Imperial Guards, the Executioner's assistants, children, priests, Mandarins, Dignitaries, The Eight Wise Men, Turandot's attendants, soldiers, standard bearers, musicians, Spirits of the Dead Suitors, the crowd.

Scene: Peking   Time: Legendary Times

ACT I

COLUMBIA–ANGEL, SIDE I

DECCA–LONDON, SIDE I

Scene: The stage is almost entirely enclosed by a semi-circle of the massive wall of the Imperial City. On the right, the curve is interrupted by a high loggia at the foot of which a heavy "sonorissimo" bronze gong is suspended from two arches. Impaled on stakes at intervals along the wall are the heads of the executed. In the distance the city of Peking is bathed in the golden light of a glorious sunset.

The curtain on *Turandot* is raised by a few bars of some of the most immediately, dramatically arresting music Puccini ever wrote. A harsh barbaric sequence of four notes, thundered out in a tremendous orchestral unison is the first statement of a theme that plays an important and exciting part in this first act:

A moment later—and it is at this point that the curtain rises—we hear for the first time a chord which is one of the unmistakable harmonic characteristics of the opera:

This particular mixture of major and minor harmonies may not have been invented by Puccini, but once it is heard in *Turandot* it becomes almost as much the composer's personal property as the famous "*Tristan* chord" was Wagner's. Puccini makes varied and effective uses of the chord in the course of the opera. When we first hear it, in this abrupt, crisp form, it is associated with the official dignity of the Mandarin. From the heights of the bastions he reads a decree to the motionless and attentive crowd below him. In the words of the decree we have a brief summary of the whole dramatic situation that prevails as the story begins. The Mandarin addresses the crowd: "People of Peking! The Law is this: Turandot, the Chaste, shall be the bride of him of Royal Lineage who can solve the three enigmas she will propound. But he whose attempts are unsuccessful shall pay for his failure with his noble head. The Prince of

Persia has not been favoured by fortune: at the rising of the moon he is to die at the hand of the executioner."

In the short course of this proclamation we have our first experience of the rich and varied colouring of the orchestral texture of this last score of Puccini's. It is an orchestral texture, however, which is woven from far more than the more obvious exotic threads of xylophone, Chinese gongs and the rest, though these naturally play a considerable part in giving the score its peculiar character. For the discerning student it is Puccini's ingenious use of the more conventional instrumental possibilities of the orchestra that is so fascinating and original, and the score is full of endless imaginative touches such as the accompaniment to the Mandarin's words "al sorger della luna" (three bars before Fig. 3 in the score), when the ascending chords of C sharp major are given to violas divided into four parts, three muted trumpets, flute and piccolo in octaves, and violins, divided into four parts, playing tremolo near the bridge of the instruments (*al ponticello*) to produce that peculiar sound so hard to describe but so unmistakable when you hear it.

At the Mandarin's mention of the executioner the crowd immediately comes to life—"tumultuosamente", the libretto says—and we have our first major experience in Puccini of the chorus as a dramatic *character*. Hitherto in his operas, with the exception of *The Girl of the Golden West*, the chorus has played a conventionally operatic role—commenting on the action, creating atmosphere, but doing nothing that one can honestly say affects the action; the absence of a chorus in *Manon Lescaut*, *La Bohème* or *Tosca* would not have altered the fate of Des Grieux, Mimi or Cavaradossi. But in *Turandot*, the importance which we first encountered in "La Girl" of the chorus as a factor in the story, whose actions affect the lives of other characters, is something we are made conscious of by muscial means from the first notes they sing. The opening theme of the opera (Ex 205), quickened up in an Allegro 2/4, becomes firmly associated with the chorus's impatient lust for blood—"Fetch the executioner! Quickly—if he doesn't appear, we'll wake him!", and shouting the name of the executioner, Pu-Tin-Pao, the crowd tries to storm the bastions with cries of "To the Palace! To the Palace!"

They are driven back roughly by the guards. In the resulting panic and confusion people are knocked down, children are trampled on and a short musical sequence begins which is based on the two-bar pattern:

This theme is introduced with the tune played in a unison tutti except for two of the three trumpets, the trombones and double basses who supply the harmony. It is a simple and admirably lucid lesson in effective, straightforward orchestration—one of the many such lessons in which this score abounds.

Above the tumult of the crowd the voice of the young slave girl

Liù is heard crying for help. The old man she is accompanying has been knocked down in the crush. A young man goes to her aid—the Unknown Prince, who recognizes the old man as his father, Timur. The theme of Ex 207, in a gentler orchestral form, now becomes the accompaniment to the tender reunion of father and son. Each had feared the other was dead; but when Timur addresses him as "my son" the Prince silences him quickly. "The usurper of your crown," he tells his father, "is looking for us both. There is no refuge for us in this world." This short sequence is another that is rich in ingenious orchestral writing, particularly in the two bars accompanying Timur's words "T'ho cercato, mio figlio, e t'ho creduto morto!" ("I searched for you, my son, and I believed you dead") where a wonderfully "dark" sound is produced by wood-wind (no horns), a trumpet, three trombones, violas and divided violoncellos and basses.

The scene between father and son is interrupted for a moment by the crowd greeting the appearance of the executioner's twelve assistants with renewed delight at the prospect of another death. It is at this point that we hear the phrase anticipated in *The Girl of the Golden West* in a somewhat similar blood-thirsty situation (see Exs 160 and 161 on page 165). Timur continues telling his story to the Prince; in a long and lovely phrase, in which the vocal melody is doubled by bass clarinet, bassoons, violoncellos and eventually violas, and the ceremonial arrival of the executioners is punctuated by funeral drumming, the old King relates how when the battle had been lost and he was preparing to escape he heard a voice say: "Come with me and I will be your guide." The voice was Liù's. "And when I fell exhausted," Timur continues, "she dried my tears and begged for me." The Prince turns to Liù and asks who she is.

"I am nothing," the girl replies. "Only a slave."

"Then why have you shared so much suffering?" asks the Prince.

"Because one day in the Palace you smiled at me."

This little scene of question and answer, which lasts less than half a minute, is the first of the peculiarly moving passages of music with which Puccini characterizes the figure of Liù, perhaps the most convincing *musical* character he ever created. Even more than Madam Butterfly's, Liù's music is intensely personal and since she takes part in no love duet she never shares her music with any one. She is a figure apart, not only in *Turandot*, but in all Puccini's operas, her whole character summed up in the spirit of devotion expressed in the single phrase: "One day in the Palace you smiled at me." The strength and consequence of this devotion is something we learn in the course of the story. Its first manifestation is made to a delicate and typically graceful little tune that is in no sense a "theme"; it is not heard again, though a phrase from it occurs by coincidence and without dramatic significance later in the opera:

The scoring of this short sequence is exquisite, with the tune played across two octaves by a piccolo, an oboe, a clarinet and celeste, with a simple counter-melody played by cor anglais with a solo viola an octave below it (a solo violoncello and a solo double bass supply the bass part). At one point the celeste abandons its companions and doubles the cor anglais in the same register with magical effect. The score of *Turandot* as a whole features the piccolo, cor anglais and celeste with rare skill and originality and presents an altogether fascinating study of the character and capabilities of these instruments.

While Liù is answering the Prince's questions, voices off-stage are heard crying "Turn the whetstone!", a menacing monotone which is continued as more people anxious to enjoy the execution come in to swell the crowd. A tremendous and exciting choral scene builds up as Liù's last note dies away—a fierce, vigorous and gruesome scene with the twelve assistants urged on by the crowd as they sharpen the executioner's huge sword on the whetstone and proclaim with gleeful satisfaction that there is never any fear of unemployment where Turandot reigns. The music to this is in the same vein as the Allegro 2/4 with which the chorus greeted the Mandarin's decree, but intensified and assisted by off-stage trumpets and trombones in the relentless reiteration of phrases such as that which recurs to the words "dove regna Turandot" ("where Turandot reigns"):

We hear, too, the tune anticipated so unmistakably during the torture scene of *Tosca* (see Ex 87 on page 98) which now, powerfully orchestrated with the horns instructed to play with the bells of their instruments raised, beginning deliberately and returning to the original tempo of the movement, takes the form:

Each time the original tempo returns there is an intensely shrill, speeded-up reminder of Ex 205—piccolo and flutes in their highest register and first violins playing pizzicato considerably higher than the textbooks of orchestration consider desirable or practicable.

At the climax of the scene the sky has darkened, and the crowd fall to their knees in invocation of the moon which has not yet appeared and has therefore delayed the execution. The transition from the crowd's barbaric ferocity to this invocation is one of Puccini's master-strokes achieved with his infallible harmonic instinct, which amounted to genius, for exactly the right chord at the right moment. The din of the crowd's chorus is ended by the notes of Ex 205 in an orchestral unison played *tutta forza* which leads to a long *piano* sustained chord of D major. In an instant the whole colour and feeling of the music and the drama changes; for the first time since the rise of the curtain there is silence in the music— that silence, or impression of silence, created by audible musical means which Puccini, like Verdi before him, was able to suggest to such wonderful dramatic effect again and again in his operas.

The Invocation to the Moon is another superbly conceived choral sequence, and like so much of the music of *Turandot* it is utterly unlike anything of Puccini's we have heard before, not only in its evocative colouring but in its melodic and harmonic characteristics. The orchestration, with its little arabesque runs for clarinet, of flute and celeste in unison, is rich in exquisite and ingenious detail achieved by the simplest methods. Throughout it the chorus keeps its distinctive personality, the only chorus in all Puccini (with the exception of the off-stage humming chorus in *Madam Butterfly*, which merely takes the place of an orchestral interlude) that contributes anything in its own right to the gramophone catalogues. "Gira la cote" ("Turn the whetstone") and this Invocation to the Moon were first recorded many pre-LP years ago, long before there was such a thing as a complete recording of *Turandot*.

The *musical* status of the chorus in this opera, indeed, is perhaps the greatest single departure from the composer's former familiar path. There were already clear signs of a change in the *dramatic* status of the chorus in *The Girl of the Golden West*, but its participation in the action was not accompanied by any great musical individuality; the rank and file of the gold miners behave in the same musical way as Happy or Joe or Harry. In *Turandot* the chorus stands musically apart from the other characters.

The Invocation builds up slowly from its opening murmured monotone and as the first silver light from the rising moon is visible the crowd call out joyfully for Pu-Tin-Pao, the executioner. The cries die away as the execution procession approaches, preceded by a choir of children whose voices give a peculiar pathos to the sound of the dirge they sing:

211

This theme, with its characteristic flourish in the third and fourth bars, is associated with the figure of the Princess Turandot. It is something of an all-purpose tune, for it is heard in varied contexts during the opera, and it is one of the numerous genuine Chinese tunes Puccini made use of in *Turandot*. When it is first heard, sung by children, the orchestral accompaniment of this theme features two extremely un-Chinese—and, indeed, un-Puccinian—instruments behind the scenes: namely, two alto saxophones, which double the tune in unison with the children while wood-wind, Chinese gongs, glockenspiel, harp, celeste, and the humming of the women and basses of the chorus contribute towards the harmonic background.*

The procession, which moves slowly along the city wall above the heads of the crowd, is led by the executioner's assistants, followed by Mandarins and priests who bear funeral offerings. After them walks the handsome, almost childlike young Prince of Persia. At the sight of the victim, who walks in a daze with his white neck uncovered and a far-away look in his eyes, the ferocity of the crowd is changed to an unutterable feeling of pity. As soon as the Prince of Persia comes on the scene the executioner appears—a gigantic, horrifying figure with the huge sword resting on his shoulder.

The appearance of the Persian prince is accompanied by a passage of great beauty which Puccini marks *Andante triste* (*Tempo di marcia funebre*). It consists of a single tune, played three times, over a repeated E flat in the basses:

212

To this tune the crowd's heart melts and its admiration for the young Persian's proud bearing changes into a passionate plea to Turandot to spare the Prince's life. The melody of the funeral march undergoes some quite lovely instrumental treatment, varying from a solo muted trumpet and violas an octave apart, to strings divided into eight parts.

The Unknown Prince, who is deeply moved by the spectacle of the Persian prince's walk to his execution, adds his plea for mercy to the crowd's and finally, as his feeling of pity turns to anger, he cries out: "Let me see thee, that I may curse thee!"

Repeating their appeal for mercy, the crowd turns expectantly towards the loggia: "Principessa! Principessa!" Trumpets and trombones both sides of the footlights thunder out *fff* the tune of Ex 211 as Turandot appears "like a vision", high in the imperial loggia. The light of the moon falls on her face; the crowd prostrate themselves before her. Only the Prince of Persia, the Unknown Prince and the executioner remain standing. Turandot raises her hand with an imperious and decisive gesture that indicates sentence of death. The procession moves on its way once more as the crowd despairingly repeats its plea for mercy. The tune and tempo of the funeral march are resumed, this time with the piccolo, *piano* and *dolente*, playing a prominent part in the performance of the tune. In *Turandot*, Puccini uses the piccolo with astonishing and uncon-

* The coda to the children's chorus contains the repeated phrase first heard in *Tosca* (Ex 99).

ventional effect in moments of great sadness. It is not an instrument one would normally regard as having markedly elegiac qualities, but, as we shall see, the piccolo is entrusted with a vital part in the emotional climax of the whole opera—at least, as it was left at Puccini's death.

As the cortège moves off, followed by the crowd, the Unknown Prince stands motionless, stunned by the sight of Turandot's beauty. Instead of cursing her cruelty, like so many unhappy young men before him he has fallen completely under her spell. "O heavenly beauty! O wonder! O dream! O heavenly beauty! O wonder! O dream! O wonder! O heavenly beauty! O wonder!"—the words he sings, which seem to have strayed from the Pyramus and Thisbe interlude in *A Midsummer Night's Dream*, give some idea of the Prince's ecstatic and distraught state of mind. The procession finally disappears with the white-clad priests offering a prayer for the soul of the man who is to die. The music fades away to nothing as the piccolo, and four octaves lower, the bass clarinet and violoncellos, add their sad tones to the priests' solemn unison.

Timur, Liù and the Prince are left alone. The old King goes over to his son and tries to bring him back to reality. All he gets in reply is a dreamy version of Ex 211 and his son's rhapsodic "Don't you feel it? Her perfume is in the air and in the soul!" In desperation Timur begs Liù to talk to the Prince, to persuade him to come away with them where life is. "Life is here!" replies the Prince and cries "Turandot! Turandot!" Once more the tune of Ex 211 is heard *ff*, but it is cut short by a distant bloodcurdling cry of "Turandot!" from behind the scenes, the last invocation of her name by the condemned Prince of Persia. It is followed by a shriek of horror from the crowd which we can only imagine coincides with the stroke of the executioner's sword.

Timur turns pleadingly to the Prince: "Do you want to die like that?" The Prince replies firmly that Turandot's beauty makes him certain of victory and he hurls himself towards the giant gong to strike it and so proclaim his intention of trying to win the hand of the Princess. But the way is barred by the sudden appearance of three grotesque figures: Ping Pang and Pong.

These three Ministers of the Imperial Court are described in the score and in the libretto as "the Masks" and they are translations into Chinese, as it were, of the familiar "masks" of the commedia dell'arte which Gozzi incorporated in his play of *Turandot*. In the old Italian comedy, of course, the masks improvised their lines, taking no part in the main action, and retaining their individuality whatever the rest of the play was about: they were always Harlequin, Brighella, Truffaldino, Pulcinella, Tartaglia and Pantaleone whether the play was set in China or fairyland.

In Puccini's opera the original Gozzi *maschere* are reduced to three in number and—opera being what it is—not encouraged to improvise. But while musically Ping, Pang and Pong are sharply characterized to stand apart from the other characters in the story, they do not altogether stand apart from the action. From time to time we find them commenting on it, or just laughing cynically at it; but on their first appearance, at any rate, they intervene effectively enough in the drama to delay, without actually altering, the final course of events in any way. The fact that they are allowed to try to affect the issue at all in itself raises their dramatic status above that of the traditional *maschere* of the Italian theatre. On the other hand, as characters among themselves Ping, Pang and Pong are scarcely defined at all. They have none of the marked characteristics of personality and temperament which distinguish the Italian masks so clearly from each other, for they act and think more or less in concert throughout.

Nowhere in his operas does Puccini so abruptly and successfully change the whole character of his music as in the split second between the Prince's words as he goes to the gong and the appearance of the three masks. It is a transition from the sacred to the profane, from the tension and idealism of Love and Romance to the matter-of-factness of:

213

To the accompaniment of much characteristically cheerful and colourful "Chinese" scoring (triangle, celeste, glockenspiel and xylophone make frequent interjections) Ping, Pang and Pong warn the Prince against the door he so foolishly wants to enter. Beyond it lies nothing but torture and death. Each time the Prince tries to pass they hold him back. "Go home!" they tell him. "All the cemeteries are full up here! We have enough native madmen without you foreigners! Go back!" And to one of those entrancing tunes which seem to well up whenever they are singing, the Masks deride the Prince's infatuation for a mere princess:

214

What is a princess? they ask. A woman with a crown on her head and a robe with a fringe! But stripped—she's just flesh, raw meat that you can't even eat. Ping ("calmly and with comic dignity") returning to the perkiness of Ex 213, elaborates the theme. He tells the Prince to leave women alone, or take a hundred wives, because when it comes to it the sublime Turandot has only one face, one pair of arms and one pair of legs. Yes, very beautiful, but always the same. But with a hundred wives there would be legs to spare—two hundred arms, a hundred bosoms ("a hundred bosoms!" echo Pang and Pong) lying in a hundred beds.

The Masks laugh uproariously at their own joke and restraining the Prince once more, repeat loudly their admonition that he should return home. They are interrupted by the sound of voices coming from the balustrade of the loggia; looking up they see Turandot's maids who tell them to be quiet: the Princess is asleep. Two solo voices, supported at intervals by the rest of Turandot's maids, continue to call for silence in one of the most remarkable passages in the opera. The passage consists of this tune played three times:

215

It is only the third time that this phrase settles undisturbed in the key of F sharp minor suggested by the cadence of the fourth and fifth bars. Otherwise the accompaniment to it hovers harmonically between F sharp minor and G minor, and F sharp minor and F major simultaneously. It is not so much an experiment by Puccini in bitonality as in what one might call "tonal ambiguity". This passage of intriguing dissonance depends for its full subtle effect on the original orchestration of the whole sequence, on details like the celeste in unison with three flutes in their low register, the use of three muted trombones, the rapid off-beat *non-arpeggiate* chords of F major by the harp clashing with the F sharp minor of pizzicato violas and violoncellos, the *ppp* use of timpani, gong and side drum.

At the end of what might be called the second verse of the servants' number, Ping, Pang and Pong tell them roughly to stop chattering and go away. The servants withdraw and the third statement of the tune is rounded off by the Prince rapturously echoing the last words—"The darkness is filled with her perfume."

The Masks look at the Prince and shrug their shoulders. Very well, they decide, they must speak to him as a threesome. They group themselves round the Prince "in grotesque attitudes" and address him in a childish sing-song, warning him yet again against the folly of trying to solve Turandot's riddles:

216

The telescoped 5/8 version of the tune occurs as an instrumental postlude of a very "Chinese" character—oboe, xylophone and pizzicato violins giving naïve emphasis to a naïve tune.

Still the Prince is deaf to their words; all he hears is "not voices but the shadows of voices" that float through the darkness as the pale apparitions of Turandot's dead suitors appear on the ramparts. An off-stage chorus of four contraltos and four tenors call mournfully on the Prince to summon Turandot. They are instructed in the score to sing "mysteriously, as though from a distance, 'dragging' the sound, making a screen over the mouth with cupped hands." This short sequence is the only supernatural incident in the whole of *Turandot*, for what is often a little misleadingly described as a "fairy story" is otherwise made up of quite possible if rather improbable incidents. The magic of the music of this first act is such, however, that I doubt if one in a thousand who hear the opera does anything but accept the altogether dispensable introduction of ghosts into the action as the most natural happening in the world. It is, in fact, the music which makes this episode convincing; the melancholy voices of the dead are accompanied by what one can best describe as a "weird" chord for divided and muted strings repeated at a funereal three-in-a-bar pace, while the piccolo chirrups mournfully like some lost, unhappy night bird.

The ghostly voices cry "I love her! I love her! I love her!" and fade away into the darkness again. "No!" cries the Unknown Prince. "I alone love her!" This causes considerable cynical laughter among the Masks and to the lilting tune of Ex 214 (now accompanied by some busy part-writing for the strings) they tell the Prince that Turandot does not exist —nothing exists except Nothing, and the Tao. The Prince wrenches himself free, and rushes towards the gong, but he is held back for a moment by the sight of the executioner placing the head of the Prince of Persia on a stake. "That's love!" observe the Masks. "That's how the moon will kiss *your* face!", and the piccolo chirrups mournfully again.

Timur adds his plea once more, begging his son not to desert him and leave him to wander over the earth in his tortured old age.

"Is there no human voice," asks the old King in despair, "that will move your wild heart?"

There is a moment's quiet and Liù comes forward to plead tearfully with the Prince—"Signore, ascolta":

217

Signore, a-scolta! Ah, Signore, a-scolta! Liù non regge più! si spezza il cuor! Ahimè, ahimè

In this exquisite little aria Liù begs the Prince to heed their pleas and have pity. His name has been in her heart and on her lips in all their wanderings; if he fails in his wooing of Turandot she and Timur will perish in exile, the King will lose his son and she "the shadow of a smile."

Although "Signore, ascolta" sounds to us most typical of all that we associate with the sentimental Puccini, it is, in fact, another of the genuine Chinese folksongs which the composer incorporated so skilfully in the score of *Turandot*. It is a purely pentatonic melody (sung in the very key which conveniently enables it to be played on the black notes of the piano) originally called "Sian Chok", but unlike the Chinese tune in Ex 211, Puccini has harmonized it in his own western fashion and in a remarkable way transformed it into one of his most personal and touching musical utterances.

The extreme simplicity of the aria, so typical of the composer's loving characterization of the figure of Liù, is emphasized by the remarkable restraint of the orchestral accompaniment—a restraint which, needless to say, reveals some original and instantly recognizable Puccini touches, like the little ascending scales on the harp during Liù's last long phrase.

The Prince is deeply moved by Liù's appeal and begs her not to weep —"Non piangere, Liù":

218

In this gentle lyrical vein the Prince asks Liù, in return for the smile he gave her, to look after his father in exile. There is a touching and, after his display of obsessed determination, rather unexpected tenderness in the Prince's music which matches the affecting simplicity of Liù's appeal.

The smoothness of the transition from "Signore, ascolta" to "Non piangere, Liù" is repeated as we come to the third and last section of the finale which may be said to have begun with Liù's aria. From a simple phrase—

219

—a stirring ensemble of almost Verdian vigour, if not proportions, builds up. Timur and Liù beg the Prince to have pity on them; the three Masks return to the centre of things and try, unsuccessfully, to remove the Prince from the scene by force. With every moment the Prince's resolution increases until with three ecstatic cries of "Turandot!" accompanied by piercing off-stage trumpets he strides up to the gong and strikes it three times. The tune of Ex 211 rings out in a *fff* orchestral tutti in D major; Ping, Pang and Pong, their efforts unrewarded, rush away laughing derisively; Timur and Liù cling together in despair. There is an abrupt return to E flat minor and a clamorous unison repetition of Ex 219. As the curtain falls the Prince is still standing motionless and in ecstasy at the foot of the gong.

The first act of *Turandot* is perhaps the most exciting, original and impressive act Puccini ever wrote. Dramatically it is dominated by the figure of Turandot herself, who does not sing a note, but whose presence and personality we are aware of right from the start. She is established and characterized musically with such force and rare skill that one needs no visual evidence of her appearance on the loggia, for instance; a blind man, or a listener making his first acquaintance with the opera by gramophone records would know it from the music.

Although Puccini is not quite so extravagant with his musical ideas as he was in *Manon Lescaut,* the quality and profusion of his invention in this act of *Turandot* are unequalled anywhere else in his work. Ideas pour out incessantly, and though the dramatic and musical scheme may be seen to be episodic the act as a whole is distinguished by a remarkable sense of form and almost symphonic continuity. In one important technical respect the score of *Turandot* differs from the rest of Puccini: there is an entire absence of "conversation" music. Even the Masks, who sing prose, as it were, compared with the poetry of the other characters, do so on a lyrical plane. We no longer hear those typical sequences in which fragmentary themes are ingeniously developed or used as figures in the orchestral accompaniment; instead, the long sonorous phrase is the common means of communication, for the world of *Turandot* is the world of poetry.

ACT II

Scene 1: The front of a pavilion formed by a huge curtain curiously decorated with strange and fantastic Chinese devices. The curtain has three openings—one in the centre, and one at either side.

At the first notes from the orchestra—a vigorous reiteration of a descending sequence of three *"Turandot* chords" (Ex 206)—the curtain rises on a complete change of atmosphere and an episode of superb dramatic irrelevance which occupies the whole of this opening scene of the second act. For ten and a half minutes nothing "happens" on the stage; as in Gozzi's original play there were interludes for improvised comedy, gags and slapstick, so in Puccini's opera the Masks come forward to divert us in a "spot" of their own. In *Turandot*, understandably, the interlude is not for comic relief, but it is nevertheless filled with music providing a powerful contrast with what we have heard so far—a sequence of great lyrical beauty and originality unlike anything else Puccini ever wrote.

Ping is the first of the three Masks to appear, poking his head through the centre opening of the curtain and calling his companions, who emerge from the other two entrances to join him. Ping, who seems to be the senior and most serious partner of the trio, has called the others to discuss the general situation now that the gong has been struck. They agree that if the young stranger wins or loses they are prepared for either eventuality. Pang will prepare the wedding, Pong the funeral; there will be rose-coloured lanterns for a *festa*, white lanterns for mourning. They recite their catalogue of alternative duties to a typically charming and cheerful little Chinese tune, which Puccini repeats unconcernedly in the same key and with little harmonic variety or embellishment without a moment's hint of monotony:

220

The deliberate *chinoiserie* of both melody and orchestra which characterizes so much of the Masks' music throughout the opera is handled with consummate skill by the composer; it is never for a moment oppressive, exaggerated, or artificial. In a miraculous way it is always dead right and one cannot imagine Ping, Pang and Pong speaking in the accents of any other musical language. *Turandot* is the peak of Puccini's achievement in musical characterization, where the principal characters are defined with unprecedented clarity—Liù, the Prince, Timur, Turandot, the chorus and the Masks (who are treated as a more or less indivisible trinity, not as individuals), all are distinguished by immediately recognizable musical peculiarities.

In the same busy 2/4 Ping reflects sadly on the state of China, now rudely awakened after seventy thousand centuries of contented and peaceful sleep. "Everything went according to the oldest established order in the world," they all agree, "and then—Turandot was born." Now for years life has been a monotonous succession of three strokes on the gong three unsolved riddles and another head falls. The time changes for a brief passage and in the same tempo we hear Ex 214 again with a warmly-scored contrapuntal accompaniment. There is no apparent association between the tune this time and its earlier use in Act I; on this occasion the Masks are busy counting up the total of victims so far. In the year of the Mouse there were six; in the year of the Dog there were eight; while in the current, terrible year of the Tiger the total has reached 13, including the new stranger who is going to die shortly. "What a job! What a bore!" Very quietly the music of the great choral scene in Act I is recalled, and to a delicate and wonderfully scored *pp* version of Ex 209, Ping, Pang and Pong ask "What have we been reduced to? To Ministers of the Executioner," they declare "with comic wretchedness".

The cynical mood of disillusion that has prevailed in the scene so far is now dispelled by a lyrical sequence of quite remarkable and unexpected loveliness. The Masks one by one give way to the homesickness that suddenly afflicts them. Ping sings first—sighing for his house in Honan, set beside its little blue lake and surrounded by bamboo:

221

The peculiar enchantment of this scene is something without parallel in Puccini's music, perhaps because it is an intense expression of the composer's own most intimate personal feelings. Nostalgia was an emotion that was deeply embedded in Puccini's nature. Whenever they were written away from his home his letters were filled with longing to be back in his own house by the lake at Torre del Lago. In the summer of 1921, shortly after he had begun the composition of *Turandot*, he left Torre del Lago (now called Torre del Lago-Puccini) for good and moved to Viareggio. A factory had encroached on the peace and seclusion of the little lakeside village he had lived in for thirty years and life became intolerable; the move to the new villa he had built at Viareggio involved a journey of barely three miles, but it was clear that Puccini felt himself irreparably uprooted, a feeling that was probably aggravated rather than alleviated by his frequent return to the lake to shoot waterfowl.

The orchestral accompaniment contributes its own quota of magic to Ping's touching reflection—a gentle undulating figure like the water lapping at a lake's edge is created by flutes, clarinets, celeste and single note harmonics from the harp in its low register, all instructed to play *più piano possibile*. It is a superbly evocative sound made by the most ludicrously simple means.

"And here I am," comments Ping sadly, "wasting my life poring over sacred books——" Pong and Pang concur, adding their own nostalgic yearnings—Pong for his forests near Tsiang, Pang for his garden at Kiu that he will never see again. There is an exquisite and affecting sadness in the tune they sing, its touching melancholy rendered doubly effective, as so often happens, by the predominantly major-key character of the theme:

The three Masks sit motionless, "in ecstasy", as the final nostalgic comment comes from the orchestra—a touching, ravishing postlude of strings divided into 8 parts playing the tune of Ex 222 with a sudden breath-taking *pp* on the last four notes of the fourth bar.

There is a momentary pause and in a prosaic, matter-of-fact cadence the Masks make a gesture of despair as they return to the reality of a world filled with mad *innamorati*.

In most performances there occurs at this point the first of three cuts customarily made in the music of this scene, only one of which, the second marked C-D in the score (and which I will come to later), seems to me to be quite unjustifiable. The first cut, A-B, is of not very interesting music; the third, E-F, is of a repeated phrase which I am not convinced is entirely necessary, but which causes no structural damage to the music.

The observance of the cut A-B brings us a little sooner than the composer intended to a return of the sociable *chinoiserie* of the earlier part of the scene. The Masks revert to their pessimistic discussion of the unhappy state of China, with its endless, senseless slaughter of young men from Burma and Tartary, India and Samarkand, who come to lose their heads for love of Turandot. The Masks' recital is punctuated by the sound behind the scenes of trumpets and trombones, and the voices of the crowd repeating the blood-thirsty refrain of the executioners' assistants in Act I (Ex 209). Another warmly lyrical pentatonic tune emerges unexpectedly at this point, a tune to which the Masks sing their sad farewell to a dying China, and which bears a very close resemblance in its second and third bars to the melody sung by Liù in Ex 208:

At the end of this engaging sequence the second cut—C-D—is usually made, which involves the loss of a passage of ten bars, a quiet, solemn invocation to the Tiger, the Marshal of Heaven, to hasten the long-awaited night of Turandot's surrender. This brief, restful interlude, marked "molto calmo", and echoing the tune of Ex 214, was restored by Constant Lambert at the performances of the opera he conducted at Covent Garden in 1939. The singers concerned had never sung the passage before and so had to learn this unexpected addition to their evening's work from scratch; it was a traditional cut which had been faithfully observed for so many years that nobody could any longer remember why it had ever been made in the first place. Its reinstatement was a welcome supplement to one's experience of an opera already robbed by Puccini's death of so much that was vital that it can ill afford to be deprived of music the composer *did* live to write.

The omission of the passage C-D necessitates a slight alteration of the text and brings us quickly to the point when the Masks start looking forward to the night when they will be able to prepare the nuptial bed for Turandot and her husband, and spend the rest of the night until dawn singing a serenade beneath the lovers' balcony. In another long passage of effective unison singing, which is so characteristic of their music, Ping, Pang and Pong look up to an imaginary balcony and sing in praise of the Princess who has at last surrendered to love:

The accompaniment to this "serenade" is one of the most intriguing passages of orchestration in the opera, rich in original touches which are apparent to the ear in their total effect, but difficult to describe in detail without giving a note-by-note account of the activities of the individual instruments. One intriguing feature may be noted, however, and that is Puccini's use of a harp (he uses two in *Turandot*) which is played with paper placed between the strings to give a quaint muffled effect—a sound peculiar to the instrument played in this fashion and not in the least resembling the sound of a lute, which luteless orchestras hope to reproduce by employing the same method in *Die Meistersinger*, or the "banjo" in *The Girl of the Golden West*.

The final cut in the music, marked E-F in the score, is made in the course of this movement and for no other reason I can see than that the words of the libretto are slightly indelicate. Even though the music of this 14-bar passage is repeated immediately afterwards (so that we are not denied something we otherwise never hear at all, as we are in the case of the cuts A-B, C-D) there is no real musical justification for the omission of something which will stand repetition, and when the cut is made, also deprives us of an interesting sequence of orchestration.

The Masks end their long trio scene on a slow unison *glissando* to express their "comic fear" at the sound of drums, trumpets and trombones coming from behind the scenes—a sound that brings them back to reality with a jerk as they realize they are hearing the preliminary flourishes of another ceremony of riddles and yet another inevitable execution. As the Masks hurry off the curtain of the pavilion rises on

Scene 2: A vast square in front of the Imperial Palace. In the centre, a long and broad marble staircase ending in the arches of the wide royal terraces. There are three broad landings on the staircase.

The rhythmic beating of drums and clamour of trumpets which closed the first scene develop now into a march to accompany the ceremonial preparations for the ritual of Turandot's riddles, and the general assembling of the crowd, officials and the rest. The Mandarins, dressed in coats of blue and gold, arrive to the strains of a brass tune which, when it is played sloppily and *legato* without proper respect for the composer's marked accents, can sound perilously like an American college football song. The tempo of the march slackens for the arrival of the Eight Wise Men whose grave and imposing appearance with the sealed scrolls containing the answers to Turandot's enigmas is remarked upon in hushed tones by the crowd. The first tempo is resumed as the Masks enter, dressed in yellow ceremonial robes, and clouds of incense rise from tripods on either side at the summit of the staircase.

As the Emperor's standards are borne on to the scene the march begins working to a climax with the building up of the phrase:

225

The incense slowly disperses and the mood of the music becomes one of great and impressive solemnity as the Emperor Altoum becomes visible on his ivory throne, "like a god who appears through the clouds". He is completely white, very old and frail. The crowd hails him with a cry of "May the Emperor live ten thousand years!" and prostrates itself with its face to the ground. The square is bathed in a warm red light. The Unknown Prince stands upright at the foot of the staircase. Timur and Liù are on the left of the stage, among the crowd but plainly visible to the audience.

There is a moment's pause as the ceremonial mood of the music subsides into a sustained diminuendo chord which fades into nothing. The silence is broken by a clear and forceful phrase for trumpets and trombones in unison on the stage which I remember finding strangely familiar when I first heard *Turandot* at its first performance in Venice in the summer of 1926:

226

The first eight notes of that phrase immediately and inevitably arrested the attention of the English listener, for the notes are identical with those of the song "I am Chu Chin Chow of China", from the musical play, *Chu Chin Chow* which ran for 2,238 performances at His Majesty's Theatre, London, between 1916 and 1921. Puccini in fact saw and enjoyed *Chu Chin Chow* when he visited London in 1919, and while it is possible that he unconsciously lifted the tune from Frederick Norton's score, it seems more probable that the tune in *Turandot* and that in *Chu Chin Chow* had the same common traditional Chinese origin.

At the end of the fanfare there is another silence and there begins a scene of astonishing simplicity and dramatic power created by Puccini's inspired characterization of the old Emperor. In the tired and thin voice of a *decrepito* and very old man, the Emperor addresses the Unknown Prince. His words are entirely unaccompanied but punctuated by the orchestra—a unison C held by bass clarinet, bassoons, double bassoon, trombones, timpani, violoncellos and basses, assisted by bass drum and two gongs, alternating with a *pp* tremolo A by the strings with triangle, Chinese gong and bass xylophone adding their exotic overtones.

The austerity and restraint of these orchestral interjections create an atmosphere of solemn tension and suspense, focussing the attention firmly on what is being said. The Emperor tells of the fearful oath which binds him to his daughter and has made his sceptre drip with blood. "Enough of blood!" he says to the Prince. "Go on your way, young man!"

Firmly the Prince replies: "Son of Heaven, I ask to be put to the trial!" His phrase, like the Emperor's, is also unaccompanied, but it is echoed by an orchestral unison.

"Let me die," the Emperor beseeches the Prince, "without having to carry the burden of your young life."

The Prince answers in the same words and to the same tune as before, but with increased resolution in his voice which is reflected in the volume of the orchestral echo. The Emperor appeals once more, and once again the Prince replies "Son of Heaven, I ask to be put to the trial!", his words sung to the same tune as before but with the rhythm of the phrase subtly changed to express his growing determination and the orchestral echo quickened to suggest a growing impatience as well. Angrily, but majestically, the Emperor gives in to the stranger "drunk with death". So be it; let destiny take its course.

The crowd rises. A procession of women scatters flowers on the big staircase and the tune of Ex 225 is played slowly and softly by strings in unison.* The crowd, singing *pp* and then *ppp*, renews its wishes for the Emperor's long life. The Mandarin comes forward and repeats the edict he read at the beginning of Act I in a slightly more compact form with an almost exact replica of the orchestral accompaniment. Though it is rounded off, as before, with a shrill orchestral reference to Ex 205 there is no hysterical reaction by the crowd this time. Instead, we hear the voices of children behind the scenes singing their little hymn of praise to Turandot (Ex 211). The chorus, instructed to turn their backs on the audience, hum the tune in unison with the children, while the melody is doubled by two flutes in their low register and two alto saxophones which, for obvious aesthetic and historical reasons, are to be "on the stage, but hidden". During these twelve bars (to which an added orchestral richness is contributed by the violins divided into 8 parts) the Princess Turandot takes her place at the foot of the throne, looking as beautiful, cold and impassive as we have come to expect.

Perhaps no first words in all opera are set to such exacting music as the aria with which Turandot introduces herself. "In questa reggia" not only tells us in words the reason for Turandot's riddles and her hatred of men, but in the course of a few notes gives us, in purely musical terms, a clear picture of her character. It is tense, almost aggressively unrelaxed music with a strong undercurrent of melancholy to it which must surely be characteristic of the sense of frustration felt by any woman suffering from the psychopathic chastity Turandot has imposed upon herself. Just as the Princess is unlike any other Puccini heroine, so the melodic line of the opening phrase she sings is typical of the world that separates this music from the gentle lyricism of Mimi and Manon and Butterfly:

227

Molto lento

Many thousands of years ago, in this same palace, Turandot tells the Prince, an anguished cry rang out—the death cry of her ancestor, the pure and lovely Princess Lu-o-Ling who reigned in peace and happiness until China was invaded and conquered by the barbarian King of Tartary, and in a night of terror and atrocity she was murdered: "by a man, like you—like you, Stranger." That is the reason, Turandot continues, why

---

* The harp part in this passage is clearly intended by the composer to be played "non arpeggiata". Nine out of ten conductors, however, allow the harpist to spread the chords. I do not know why this is encouraged; it affects the whole character of the music. Neither Gino Marinuzzi nor Constant Lambert when they were at Covent Garden ever played it except as written, and so spared us a peculiarly sloppy effect.

she avenges herself on all those Princes who come from every part of the world to win her hand—to avenge that cry and that death.

Slowly and deliberately this part of the aria builds up in a series of short, tense phrases, sometimes two bars, sometimes only one bar long, with a surprisingly simple and effective orchestral accompaniment culminating at the words "O Principi, che a lunghe carovane . . ." ("You Princes, who come in long caravans from every part of the world . . .") in an exquisite passage of orchestration in which Puccini makes characteristic use (as he does throughout *Turandot*) of the piccolo played *pianissimo* and colouring the texture with the celeste in its lowest register.* The climax of the first part of the aria overlaps into the second with a theme of great lyrical warmth and beauty:

228

As so often happens with Puccini's "big" tunes when they first occur, it is the orchestra which plays this theme in full, and the singer who joins it at a later stage in its progress. In this case, Turandot's first words to the tune are not until the end of the second bar: "Mai nessun m'avrà!" ("No man shall ever possess me!"). The orchestra plays the theme again, a major third higher. Turandot, still singing only part of the tune, proclaims that hatred of the man who killed her royal ancestor lives on in her heart. It is only the third time the theme is heard (now in the key of D major, yet another major third higher), that Turandot sings the whole phrase—all but three of the last four notes in the second bar of Ex 228. As this is a tune which does not end at all tidily, the only way to stop it going on indefinitely and logically in the sequence already heard—G flat, B flat, D major—is to change the subject altogether. Turandot turns menacingly on the Prince and warns him not to try his fortune. In a fierce phrase she tells him "The enigmas are three, death is one!" The Prince retorts, defiantly taking the Princess's own phrase into a higher key, "No, no! The enigmas are three, life is one!" In yet a third and higher key Turandot and the Prince repeat their own maxims simultaneously, a glorious climax to yet another key-progression that could go on for ever:

229
Più sostenuto

The chorus brings the scene to an end urging Turandot, to the tune of Ex 228, to let the Prince stand his trial. The music dies down, the trumpets

---

* As a matter of fact, the celeste is asked to play a note a semi-tone lower than the lowest note usually found on this instrument, which does not normally produce a note sounding lower than middle C. Once or twice elsewhere in the score Puccini also takes the celeste down to the B natural below this.

on the stage play a piercing interval of a rising fifth to grip the attention in a most dramatic, compelling fashion and Turandot prepares to propound the first riddle.

"In questa reggia", which I have discussed in some detail, is unique in Puccini's work: a solo aria which depends for its ultimate dramatic and musical fulfilment on its transformation into a duet at its climax, and which is primarily concerned with the portrayal of character, rather than with an expression of emotion or situation. It is clear, now that we hear Turandot's music, that the nature of her personality has not been based on hearsay. She is all that the chorus, events and her general reputation led us to believe in Act I, and more. As an essay in musical characterization she is on an entirely different plane from any of Puccini's other women, no less human for being inhuman, no less mortal for being drawn on an heroic scale. That she is not immediately attractive to us is scarcely surprising, but there is no doubt, I think, that Puccini has succeeded in suggesting that her beauty and her fascination are things which it is worth trying to break down the hard, ice-cold exterior to reach.

In the same way that there was a deliberate symmetry in the form of the dialogue between the Emperor and the Prince, a formal design is also followed in the scene of the riddles which now begins. Turandot turns to the Prince and bids him listen; and the orchestra plays the theme—

It is to the tune of this that Turandot begins to ask her first enigma: "In the dark night there hovers a phantom, soaring upwards and spreading its wings over the infinite blackness of humanity. Everybody invokes it and everybody longs for it. It vanishes at dawn, but every night it is born again, and every day it dies!" Turandot's recital of her enigma is punctuated at intervals by an abrupt thumping sound from bassoon, double bassoon, timpani (on two notes simultaneously), bass drum and double bass; and we hear, too, for the first time, a poignant fragment played at this point by two solo violoncellos and marked by Puccini to be played, in a favourite phrase of Verdi's, "come un lamento":

It is a phrase that creates a sense of suspense and tension and adds a melodramatic touch to Turandot's delivery of the enigma. There is a moment's pause and using the same tune as the riddle was asked in (Ex 230) the Prince answers: Hope. The Eight Wise Men consult their scrolls and confirm that the answer is correct. Angrily, Turandot cries: "Yes! Hope which always deceives!"

Turandot comes nervously half-way down the staircase. She asks her second enigma: "It burns like a flame, but it is not a flame. If you are dying it grows cold, but when you dream of conquest it burns. It has a voice that you listen to with fear, and it is the colour of a dazzling sunset."

The musical pattern of the second riddle follows closely that of the first, though the voice part covers a slightly wider range as Turandot's discomfiture increases and the orchestral accompaniment is varied. This time the Prince hesitates before answering, and to the ominous echo of the speeded-up version of Ex 205 with its associations with death and torture, the Emperor and the crowd encourage him—"Speak! It is for your life!" From somewhere in the crowd there comes the plaintive voice of Liù, heard for the first and only time in this act: "It is for love!"

The Prince speaks, this time in a more vigorous and confident tone of voice, to the same tune as before (Ex 230): "Yes, Princess! When you look at me it burns and languishes in my veins. It is Blood!" The Eight Wise Men consult their scrolls. The answer is again correct. The crowd, unable to control its excitement, cheers the Prince and is set upon for its pains by Turandot's guards—at the Princess's savage command.

Turandot comes lower down the steps for the third and final riddle; the Prince falls on his knees. Again the musical pattern is much the same as before, but this time, adding urgency, intensity and a certain bad temper to the voice, the sequence is sung a semitone higher. "Ice that gives you fire, and from your fire takes more ice. Clear as day, yet inscrutable. The force that wills you free will make you a slave, yet, accepting you as a slave, will make you King!"

The Prince is silent. The *lamento* of Ex 231 becomes even more poignant in an altered form played by divided violas:

This, and the thumping of timpani, bass drum and double basses, are the only sounds to be heard. Turandot comes lower down the staircase and stands over the Prince, like some terrible bird of prey. She gloats over his silence and sneers at him: "Get up, Stranger! You are white with fear! And you know you are lost!" Again there is no reply. The sighing viola sequence creates a characteristic Puccini "audible silence".

"Get up, Stranger!" cries the Princess again. "The ice that makes fire —what is it?"

The suspense becomes almost intolerable as two solo violoncellos take over the descending sequence of Ex 232, and the phrase falls away in the low register of the instruments, like a last despairing gesture of hope-lessness and defeat.

Suddenly the Prince leaps to his feet, and still to the same tune (Ex 230) that has played its part in both questions and answers, he cries that Turandot herself has given him victory: "My fire will melt your ice—

Turandot!" For the last time the Eight Wise Men unroll their scrolls: the answer is "Turandot".

The crowd breaks into a jubilant Gloria to the victor, sung to the tune we have so far associated with Turandot herself (Ex 211), which merges into renewed, but *pp*, praises of the Emperor.

Turandot, filled with anguish, has climbed the staircase and standing beside the throne, now makes an impassioned appeal to her father not to cast his daughter into the arms of the stranger. The Emperor replies solemnly that the oath is sacred. "Rebelliously" the Princess cries that his daughter is sacred; he cannot give her away like a slave to die of shame. This short passage between father and daughter revives, a little unexpectedly, the theme of Ex 207 from the beginning of Act I, modified now to consist of the first seven notes of the phrase only, played twice—

before being repeated in another key. In practice the resemblance between this and the earlier theme is not so apparent as there is now no suggestion of the urgency and clamour of the original. The scoring of this passage also helps to disguise the relationship; the theme is played first by violins in octaves, with the violoncellos an octave lower; next, flutes and piccolo support the strings, and finally the violas and bass clarinet join in on another octave—an octave below the violoncellos and three octaves below the first violins. It is an orchestral passage of remarkable translucence and simplicity.

Turandot grows angrier and the music more animated as she turns on the Prince to swear that she will never be his. The Emperor repeats that the oath is sacred, and the crowd reminds her that the stranger risked his life for her.

The music of this sequence, which Puccini marks "Animando", is the only really sub-standard passage in the whole of *Turandot*. Its upward-surging chromatic approach to the climax is commonplace and cannot honestly be regarded as anything but—in that admirable American phrase—thoroughly "corny"; it has a curiously synthetic, pseudo-Richard-Straussian quality which is quite out of character. It is redeemed by the excitement of the climax itself, however, which finds Turandot unmoved. With a high C soaring each time over the crowd's repeated cry of "The oath is sacred" (to the tune of Ex 211), she asks the Prince "Do you want me in your arms by force, reluctant and trembling?"

The Prince completes the phrase with the reply: "No, no, almighty Princess! I want you afire with love!"—

At least, according to the composer's first thoughts the Prince completes the phrase as I have shown it here. Second thoughts—either the composer's or somebody else's—have added an optional variant of the third and fourth bars:

235

Vo - glio ar- den -te d'a - mor!

This has always seemed to me a most unfortunate error of judgment. It deprives the Prince's vocal line of its logical musical conclusion; it is inartistic; it is characterless. And it is asking for trouble. Very few tenors, once they have had the idea of this alternative put into their susceptible heads, will ever admit that they are incapable of hitting that top C, and none of them will ever see that it is the last three G's of the phrase which kill it stone dead. There was never a weaker cadence even in the crooner's repertoire. The temptation to have an undisturbed top C to himself, instead of merely sharing one with the soprano who sings Turandot, is one that should never have been put in any tenor's way, and I was glad to note that Mario Del Monaco, in the Decca recording of the opera, preferred to keep to the original musical conception of the cadence. The tenor in Mme Callas' recording was not so well advised.

The crowd applauds the Prince's determination and hails him as "Coraggioso! Audace! O forte!" Suddenly the shrill notes of Ex 230 are heard again, and the Prince, putting the unscrupulous and unsportsman-like behaviour of the Princess to shame, makes a bargain with her. "You asked me three riddles," he says, "and I solved all three. I am going to ask you only one. You do not know my name. Tell me my name before dawn and at daybreak I am willing to die." Turandot nods her acceptance of the deal.

The Prince's words are sung to a characteristic anticipation of a tune heard in full glory later in the opera. At this first hint of it the theme emerges quietly and unexpectedly, seemingly out of nowhere, an ascending violoncello phrase leading to its statement by violins accompanied only by divided violas and violoncellos. It is in this passage that the Prince sings the words "il mio nome non sai" ("you do not know my name") to the phrase so clearly anticipated in *The Girl of the Golden West* (Ex 151):

236

Moderato sostenuto

PRINCE: Il mio nome non sai —

To music of unusually piquant *chinoiserie*—saxophones, muted trumpets and trombones on the stage, while the pit orchestra contributes xylophone, side drum, a solo violoncello playing pizzicato in the treble clef and doubling notes on the celeste which, once again, include one not usually found on that instrument—the Emperor declares in his frail monotone that it is Heaven's wish that the Prince should be his son-in-law at dawn. The scene ends with a tremendous reprise of the Imperial Hymn (Ex 225), to which Puccini optimistically—or perhaps pessimistically—adds an organ to reinforce the *fff* of chorus and orchestra.

Perhaps more than in any opera Puccini wrote, with the possible exception of *Tosca*, the dramatic tension and interest of *Turandot* increases as the story progresses. Act I ended on a note of suspense, and Act II again leaves us eagerly wanting to know what happens next. The action, like that of *Tosca*, is concentrated into the space of a few hours. It was dusk at the beginning of the first act; at the end of the second it is later in the same evening, with the promise of further action to come to affect the outcome of the drama, one way or the other, not later than dawn.

Owing to the very nature of its dramatic form the musical continuity of the second act does not seem so unbroken and inevitable as that of the first. The deliberate formality of the scene between the Emperor and the Prince, the ritualistic symmetry of the asking and answering of the riddles, inevitably lead to a certain amount of musical repetition without much opportunity or need for variation.

But in place of the astonishing flow of sheer musical invention which floods the first act, more attention is paid to the building up and consolidation of character. Dramatically, as well as musically, the second act takes us a stage further in the development of the story. We know now what kind of person Turandot is, and we know more of the character of the Prince, who is by no means "an ordinary Puccini tenor" as many would have us believe.

Even the white-hot inspiration of the first act, however, has little, I think, to compare with the sustained originality and lyrical invention of the opening scene of the three Masks. Nowhere else in Puccini's operas is so much fine music so powerfully concentrated into such a short space of time, and only in *Manon Lescaut* was he ever quite so prodigal with his ideas, so uninhibited in his obvious enjoyment of the music he was writing, or so clearly stimulated by the novelty of his own new-found musical strength.

ACT III

Scene 1: The garden of the Palace. On the right, five steps lead to a pavilion which forms an ante-chamber to one of the wings of the Palace where Turandot's apartments are situated. It is night.

The curtain rises at once on a convincing demonstration of the power of dramatic context to transform the whole character of music. The characteristic *"Turandot* chord" that punctuated the Mandarin's proclamation and then added a colourful grotesqueness to the beginning of the trio of Masks, is now the unchanging harmonic basis of the superbly evocative and *misterioso* (Puccini's word) orchestral passage with the theme:

Three more strongly contrasted end-products of the same highly distinctive harmonic raw material can scarcely be imagined, and the final transformation into this nocturne with its richly scented atmosphere of suspense and romance is a superb example of Puccini's invention and orchestral skill. The orchestration, in particular, is extraordinarily effective and individual, and the student unwise enough to believe that he can learn as much as he wants of "this sort of thing" from the scores of Debussy should be reminded that while Puccini learned a great deal from some of the orchestral ideas of his great French contemporary, he contributed so much that was peculiarly his own that only those to whom all "impressionistic" scoring sounds alike and automatically "Debussy-ish", fail to see how strongly and unmistakably personal Puccini's scoring really was—even in those passages which are such easy prey for the influence-hunter like the opening of *Il Tabarro*, parts of *The Girl of the Golden West*, and this beginning of the third act of *Turandot*. If any detail may be singled out for attention in this orchestral passage it is Puccini's ingenious and characteristic combination of the top octave of the piccolo (played *pp*) in unison with the glockenspiel, celeste and high notes of the violin, which produces an unusual sound with something of the clear, silvery quality of a string harmonic. But this is only one of the numberless touches used by the composer in the creation of his last and one of the most immediately effective examples of musical scene-painting.

At the start of the scene the Prince is discovered seated on the steps, listening to the distant voices of the Heralds proclaiming Turandot's edict: "Tonight none shall sleep in Peking." Like a sad refrain in the distance the Herald's last phrase is echoed "come un lamento" by the people: "None shall sleep"—"Nessun dorma!"—and rounded off by violins on their G string in unison with a solo horn:

238
Molto sostenuto

Nes-sun dor-ma!   Nes-sun dor-ma!

With that sense of symmetry so noticeable in *Turandot* the formula of the orchestral opening (Ex 237), followed by the voices of the Heralds, the crowd's echo, and the orchestral cadence, is played three times altogether. The second time the Heralds, a little further in the distance, continue the proclamation: "On pain of death the Stranger's name must be discovered." The third time, echoed still more distantly by the people of Peking, they repeat the first part of the proclamation: "Tonight none shall sleep in Peking."

The voices die away in the distance as the crowd sadly echoes the words "Nessun dorma!" The mood of the music changes with a characteristic change of key. The *misterioso* melancholy of the opening nocturne is dispersed by the clear matter-of-factness of the key of G major. It is still night; the strings are still muted; but there is a determination and confidence in the Prince's voice as he echoes the words, but not the tune, of the chorus: "Nessun dorma!"

The Prince addresses his reflections to Turandot who, like the people of Peking, also does not sleep but stands in her cold room gazing at the stars that shine with love and with hope. "But my mystery is enclosed within me", sings the Prince—"il mio mistero è chiuso in me"—and none shall know his name until he himself reveals it to the Princess at sunrise. "Let the night be ended! Let the stars set! At dawn I shall be victorious!"

The Prince's "Nessun dorma!", the nearest approach to a conventionally "typical" Puccini aria in *Turandot*, is a sequence of extraordinary simplicity and economy of musical means employed in the creation of some of the loveliest music in the opera. The formal construction of the aria is a fascinating subject worth studying for a moment. It is composed of two briefly stated ideas: "A" is harmonic, the alternation of two chords rooted in the key of G major with an almost austere vocal line. The second idea, "B", is melodic, a full version in D major (the key in which the aria ends) of the string tune heard in Ex 236, which the Prince now sings to the words "Ma il mio mistero è chiuso in me". Section "B" ends on a half-close and a truncated version of Section "A" is repeated. From behind the scenes the tune of Ex 236 is now taken up by a chorus of women's voices lamenting that no one knows the stranger's name and so all must die. The melody is taken over by the Prince, who ends with a triumphant coda, followed by a *ff* orchestral reprise of Ex 236.

"Nessun dorma!" is understandably the most popular and frequently heard of the individual numbers in *Turandot* for it does bear some superficial resemblance to the manner of Puccini's other famous tenor arias; but like them its fullest effect is made only in its dramatic context, where its firm lines form a striking contrast of mood and colour to the evocative chiaroscuro of the music which precedes it. It differs from the others in one important respect, however, and that is in the intense concentration of Puccini's ideas into a small space and that extraordinary economy of means I have already referred to, which enables the composer to make his point when he cuts down the repetition of Section "A" by telescoping the passage into half its original length and yet convincing us subconsciously that we have heard the entire passage twice. As a demonstration of original formal construction this aria of the Prince's is one of the most individual in all Puccini's music.

A rapid and skilful transition leads from the ecstatic clamour of the orchestral postlude of the Prince's aria to the entrance of the three Masks who emerge from the bushes in the garden, followed by a small group of figures, dim in the darkness of the night and gradually increasing in number. Ping, Pang and Pong, as they did in the first act, are now playing a part in the drama once more. In their unmistakably individual musical accent they beg the Prince to stop star-gazing and realize what is happening. Death is knocking at every door in Peking, shouting: The name! The name!

"Well, what do you want of me?" asks the Prince.

"You say what *you* want," they reply. "Is it love? Very well, here you are." Ping pushes a group of alluringly beautiful and semi-nude girls towards the Prince, a gesture which usually justifies the inclusion of a choreographer's name among the programme credits at performances of *Turandot* (for the girls go through some dancelike motions to seduce the Prince), and is accompanied by a few bars of slow and intriguingly exotic music to which Pang and Pong contribute flowery testimonials to the young ladies' charms.

The tempo changes once more to a vigorous pentatonic sequence of *chinoiserie*. The Prince rejects the dancing girls and the offer of another group of young women who surround him and attempt to distract him by singing.

"Is it riches you want?" ask the Masks in despair. "You shall have all the treasures you desire!", and at a sign from Ping baskets, chests and bags filled with gold and precious stones are brought in to a horn tune which has developed out of the pentatonic figures of the preceding passages:

This theme is the *ostinato* worked up instrumentally and chorally as the

Masks urge the Prince to accept riches, power—anything so long as he will leave the city and so spare everybody's life. The Prince raises his arms in an invocation to heaven, calling on the dawn to break and put an end to this nightmare.

Ping tries a new approach and the music grows suddenly melancholy as he warns the stranger that he does not know what things the cruel Princess is capable of:

Pang and Pong take the theme into another key, adding their grim predictions of what will happen to them all, what unheard-of tortures and lingering death they will suffer if the Prince's name is not revealed; and a brief ensemble develops as the crowd joins in to plead fervently with the Masks. The Prince stands firm, rejecting their pleas and their threats. "Let the world crumble, I want Turandot!"

There is a sudden fierce return to the tempo and mood of Ex 239 as the crowd draw their daggers and threaten the Prince, crying that he shall not have Turandot, he will die before they do; and they demand to know his name.

Suddenly there are shouts of "Here is the name!" and through the garden a group of guards drag in Timur and Liù, bruised, exhausted and covered with blood. "They don't know my name," cries the Prince.

"This is the old man and the girl who were talking to you yesterday evening. They know your name," replies Ping, and with Pang and Pong he turns towards the Palace calling to the Princess.

The solemn sound of Ex 211 is heard, *ff*, reinforced by trumpets and trombones behind the scenes, and Turandot appears. Everyone, except Ping, falls prostrate and for the first time Turandot's theme is played quietly, the violas and bass clarinet playing the tune against harmony supplied by second violins and violoncellos (in three parts)—a rich, warm sound that is entirely unexpected after our experience of the way the theme has been treated so far.

Ping advances humbly towards the Princess and informs her that the silent Timur and Liù know the stranger's name. "We have instruments to prise open their teeth and irons to drag out the name", he adds in a rapid conversational tone. As expressed by their regular spokesman, Ping, the character of the Masks has undergone an important change. In Act I their attitude to the Prince was cynical but friendly; they did their best to dissuade him, and regretted that he should be so obstinate as to ignore their advice. In their big scene in the second act we learned how warm and human were the hearts that beat behind the cynical exterior, and how genuinely sad they were that China should have declined so far from its days of peace and dignity. Now, in this scene of the third act they have turned as bloodthirsty and ruthless as the very Princess whose régime they deplored in their nostalgia for their lakes and bamboo forests.

Turandot ignores Ping and turns haughtily to the Prince with the ironic observation that he looks pale. She addresses her words to the rather unexpected return of the theme of Ex 207 played at length but in an increasingly distorted form as the dialogue continues. The Prince replies that it is her own fear that sees the pallor of the dawn reflected on his face. "These two do not know me," he says.

"We shall see!" snaps Turandot. Timur is brought before her. "The name!" she demands. Before Timur can do more than look helpless, Liù runs forward to say that she alone knows the name.

"You know nothing, slave!" exclaims the Prince.

"I know his name," Liù continues, "and my greatest joy is to keep the secret, to be its sole possessor." The mood of Ex 207 is dispelled violently by the crowd who demand that Liù shall be bound and beaten and forced to speak. The Prince stands in front of Liù to protect her but is seized and bound by the guards at Turandot's command. Liù, pinned to the ground on her knees, promises the Prince that she will not speak.

"The name! The name!" Ping insists. Liù answers gently: "Your servant begs forgiveness, but is unable to obey", and she screams as one of the soldiers twists her wrists, "Let her go!" cries the Prince in despair.

"No . . . no . . ." says Liù quietly. "I shall not scream any more; they're not hurting me, no one has touched me." Then turning to the soldiers: "Torture me, but gag me so that he doesn't hear." Liù weakens for a moment and cries that she cannot resist any more. Turandot orders her to be released and tells her to speak. "I would rather die!" says Liù.

There is a moment's pause and Turandot, bewildered and touched for an instant, asks Liù what it is that gives her heart such strength to suffer. Liù replies *dolcissimo*: "Princess, it is love." "Love!" the Princess echoes in an astonished whisper, impressed by the sound of a word she has never heard uttered before.

Perhaps the most astonishing feature of this whole episode of Liù's torture is the understatement of the music compared with the torture scene in *Tosca*. There is no underlining of Liù's agony by sudden loud orchestral exclamations, nor any musical building up of excitement or tension. The scene makes its effect with a simplicity and almost unbearable pathos created by the repetition of a single seven-note phrase—

241

—played without variation, first by a solo violin in the register shown above, then a solo violoncello an octave lower, followed by an oboe in the violin register, a solo horn an octave lower, and finally the bassoon an octave lower than that. Throughout the scene double basses, violoncellos and timpani sustain a tremolo pedal E.

Liù answers Turandot's half-amazed, half-incredulous exclamation of

"Amore!" with a confession of love she has never made before: the love she has for the Prince. She glories in the tortures and torments she suffers, she explains, for they are her last sacrifice for the man she loves, for the man who, by her silence, will win Turandot and Turandot's love. Liù's confession is expressed in music of such outstanding lyrical beauty and sadness, that it is only the impracticable brevity of the episode which prevents it ranking as an aria like "Signore, ascolta!" Again the secret of its effect is in the fantastic simplicity of the conception which consists of little more than the repetition of a theme first played by a solo violin and which the voice part joins from time to time in this manner:

The solo violin, indeed, has the tune throughout which it plays un-muted, joined in due course by the rest of the violins, muted and *divisi*, sometimes an octave higher, sometimes in the same register. It is an accompaniment which develops into one of Puccini's most moving and typically effective passages of scoring where the strings play the tune in unison across two or three octaves with a minimum of harmonic filling to concentrate the attention on the pathos and emotional intensity of the melody.

With a sudden violence Turandot orders the secret to be torn from the girl; Ping calls for Pu-Tin-Pao and the crowd supports him in clamouring for Liù to be put to the torture as Ex 209 is heard in a harsher, more sinister form than ever. The giant form of the executioner appears with his assistants in the background, and Liù tries in vain to break through the throng which surrounds her. Then, at last, her resistance breaks down; she asks the Princess to listen to her.

"You who are clothed in ice, you also will love him," she tells her. "Before dawn breaks I shall close my eyes, and he will be victorious—I shall close my eyes, so that I do not see him again."

What is in effect Liù's farewell is developed from a theme of heart-rending pathos, which scarcely has need of the composer's instruction that it should be played *con dolorosa espressione*:

243

The student-composer could find few finer instances among modern composers of the art of constructing a tune than this. Liù's aria builds sadly, simply and inevitably to its tragic climax: she snatches a dagger from a soldier and stabs herself, falling dead at the feet of the Prince.

The death of the last of Puccini's "Little Girls" has many musical characteristics in common with the death of his first, his second and his third. The familiar reiterated elegiac rhythm associated with the final moments of Manon, Mimi and Butterfly plays an important part once more in one of the most exquisitely conceived passages of orchestration in all *Turandot,* and is largely remarkable for the important part played by the oboe which, with the exception of one silent bar, doubles the vocal line in the same register as the singer throughout, thus confounding all one's well-grounded notions that the instrument used in this way is death to the voice part.

At the moment of Liù's suicide the orchestra embarks *fortissimo* on an almost note-for-note reprise of the tune which remains the musical accompaniment to the action which follows. When Liù stabs herself the crowd shouts in desperation to her to tell them the name; but the slave girl dies without uttering another word. The Prince sees that she is dead calling her "O mia piccola Liù" to a phrase which (I imagine by coincidence) resembles very closely the opening phrase of "Non piangere, Liù!" (Ex 218). A "great silence full of terror" comes over the crowd. Turandot looks at Liù lying on the ground, then with an angry gesture seizes a whip from the executioner's assistant and strikes the soldier who allowed Liù to snatch his dagger. Timur staggers through the crowd to where Liù is lying, and kneeling beside the body beseeches her to open her eyes: it is dawn and she should awake. "An intense feeling of pity, of confusion and remorse pervades", the stage directions state. "An expression of torment passes over Turandot's face. Ping notices it and goes over to the old man to order him away roughly. As he approaches him, however, his natural cruelty and harshness give way to tenderness." Ping tells the old man to rise up: Liù is dead. With an agonized cry Timur warns that the spirit of the innocent victim will avenge itself upon them. At Timur's words the crowd is seized with terror that the dead girl will become a malignant spirit, because she was the victim of injustice, and will be transformed, according to popular superstition, into a vampire.

This time the tune of Ex 243 comes to an end with Timur's cry of "si vendicherà!", its *fortissimo* climax followed by a hushed, repeated sequence of great harmonic beauty for the chorus, who beg the sad shade of Liù for forgiveness and mercy. Gently the little slave's body is lifted up and slowly borne away by the crowd. As the procession moves off, the tune of Ex 243 returns once more, its first eight bars played *pp* but unmuted and *molto dolcemente* by the violins in octaves, punctuated by chords by oboes, celeste and tubular bells. Timur tenderly takes hold of Liù's hand as he walks slowly beside her. "Sweet Liù," he sings. "let us take the road together again. Like this, with your hand in mine. I know where you are going, and I shall follow you to be near you in the night that has no morning."

Timur's moving epilogue brings the tune of Ex 243 near to its coda. Ping, Pang and Pong are deeply affected as a feeling of human compassion comes over them for the first time in the many long years of terror that have now come to an end. Ping has seen death without laughing at

it; Pong's heart has begun to beat again; and to Pang the death of Liù
weighs on his heart like a stone. The three Masks follow the procession
which has now moved out of sight. From the distance comes the sound of
sopranos singing the first three bars of Ex 243 in unison with a flute and a
solo violin; then, more distant still, the final cadence of the chorus's
supplication to Liù, accompanied by the last bars Puccini lived to write
for the orchestra, six bars which include the affecting and extraordinarily
imaginative *ppp* instrumental punctuation by piccolo, oboe and celeste at
one end of the register, and bass clarinet and double bass at the other:

As the voices fade the thin, pathetic sound of the piccolo dies away on
its high E flat, a touching, ethereal sound. Turandot, whose head has been
covered in a white veil by her servants, and the Prince are alone on the
scene.

At this point in the first performance of *Turandot* at La Scala Toscanini
laid down his baton and turning to the audience said: "Qui finisce
l'opera lasciata incompiuta dal Maestro, perché a questo punto il Maestro
è morto"—"Here ends the opera left unfinished by the Master, for at this
point the Master died." It was not until the second performance that the
opera was played with the last duet and finale of the opera which had
been completed by Franco Alfano from sketches left by Puccini.

I will confess that since first hearing Alfano's appendix to *Turandot* at
the first performance in Venice in 1926 (an experience which by coincidence followed immediately on my seeing Reinhardt's production of
Gozzi's play in Salzburg) I have always succeeded in being able to leave
the theatre at the end of the scene of Liù's death. After that first dutiful
experience I have seen little point in staying to hear music which to my
mind is completely irrelevant and redundant, no matter how sincere and
loyally devoted, or even skilful a labour of love it was to compile.
Musicians, for some reason, have always had a mania for "finishing"
unfinished works. If they are not finishing Schubert's Unfinished
Symphony for him, they are busy finishing Mozart's *Zaïde* or Weber's
Drei Pintos. But whereas it would involve a great deal of work to restore,
for instance, Michelangelo's Entombment in the National Gallery to its
original unfinished state once somebody had decided to "complete" it,
it is an easy matter to detach, and even easier to discard and forget
altogether the "completion" of an unfinished piece of music. What is
surprising is not that this merciful loophole exists, but that nobody has

seen fit to take advantage of it in the case of *Turandot* since 25th April, 1926.

We know from Puccini's correspondence and conversation during the last months of his life that the duet and finale were to be the key to the whole problem of the last scene of *Turandot*. And there is no doubt that there was a problem: the problem of giving musical and dramatic conviction to the rest of the story, with its happy ending—at least, for two of its protagonists.

As the libretto stood at Puccini's death, when Turandot and the Prince are left alone on the stage, the stranger tears the veil from the Princess's face and kisses her passionately. Turandot confesses that she has loved him from the beginning, but begs him to go, taking his secret with him. The Prince defiantly tells her his name: he is Calaf, son of King Timur of Tartary. For a moment, Turandot realizes that she has him in her power, though she makes no sign that she recognizes he must be a direct descendant of the King of Tartary whose conquest of China had led to the murder of her ancestor, Lo-u-ling, and so started the whole business of Turandot's riddles. The Prince does not weaken, however. Trumpets sound as the dawn breaks and the scene changes to the exterior of the Imperial Palace.

The Emperor, surrounded by his court, and watched by a vast crowd, is seated at the top of a long marble staircase. Turandot enters and walks up the stairs. She addresses the Emperor. "I know the name of the stranger," she declares. Then, "looking straight at Calaf who is at the foot of the staircase, vanquished, she murmurs sweetly, almost with a sigh: 'His name is Love.' " The opera ends with a choral hymn in praise of love.

Puccini's epitaph might well have been taken from the Prince's own words: "Il mio mistero è chiuso in me", for although he left thirty-six sheets of manuscript sketches of the music he intended for the end of the opera, there seems to have been very little indication in them of the climax he envisaged. There has inevitably been a great deal of speculation not only on what Puccini might have written had he lived, but on whether his death was not in its way something of a merciful release for him, because he could never have done justice to the ending he had planned.

Except that such speculation can have no positive critical value either way, I have never subscribed to the view that the final scenes of *Turandot* would have been beyond Puccini's powers, that the subject was too big for him, an unrealizable dream and so on. The whole course that his development was taking in the creation of the opera points towards a climax likely to have been entirely different from anything he had written before, and I do not see why he should have failed in his object. I do not doubt that if Puccini had died after finishing only the first act of *Turando* there would have been some ready to regard his death as a merciful release from the problem of composing the trio of the Masks, on the evidence o the libretto which, as it does in the case of the final passages of the opera demands a very different kind of music from that which we commonl associate with the composer.

The end of *Turandot* might have been anti-climax; it might have been magnificent. How can one possibly tell? One thing is certain, however: Alfano's "completion" tells us nothing that could not have been better left unsaid. The final duet and closing scene of *Turandot* were something Puccini dreamed of; and no man, we have been told, can continue another's dream. It should surely be possible at this stage in the opera's history for an adult audience to be able to take the happy ending for granted and leave the opera where Puccini left it. For the incorrigibly inquisitive there is always the printed libretto if they must learn the details leading up to the traditional fairy tale coda, "they all lived happily ever after".

Puccini's half-joking, half-serious and, as it turned out, tragically accurate prophecy that *Turandot* would never be finished and that at the first performance somebody would come forward and say "at this point the Master died", is well known. But it may be noticed that he made no reference to the possibility of another composer finishing the opera for him. Alfano's "completion" is generally tolerated as innocuous and undistracting; nobody, so far as I know, has condemned it for what is surely its greatest fault: its entire unnecessity. As an essay in orchestration it shows Alfano to have been a strangely unreceptive pupil of the master. There are hacks in Hollywood and even in the wilds of Sussex who could have made the orchestra in these final unfortunate pages a greater credit to the *Scuola di Puccini*. There are few composers in either place, however, who would have permitted themselves such a monstrously banal, amateurishly inept sequence as the passage which begins at Fig 47 in the score and ends with the words: "Io son Calaf, figlio di Timur!" Legend attributes this unbelievably "corny" musical sequence to Arturo Toscanini—an allegation which could explain its survival in the score. Those who have commended this supplement for Alfano's restraint in not attempting to imitate Puccini must have had this grotesque passage in mind. Nothing was ever less like Puccini.

As nobody has put forward any artistic justification for the continued retention of Alfano's appendix to an opera which is no longer the largely unfamiliar and semi-popular work it was even 20 years ago, and which therefore no longer needs any apology or explanation, it seems a pity that the occasion of Puccini's centenary should not have been used as an opportunity to perform *Turandot* as its composer left it and as it was first performed.

There was a moment in the summer of 1958 when it seemed that at last the "completion" was going to be jettisoned. At the opening performance of the season at the Verona Arena, the conductor laid down his baton at the point where 32 years previously Toscanini had laid down his. The orchestra, followed by the audience of 25,000, rose from their seats and stood in silence. But after a minute's silent commemoration the performance was resumed. What might have been an epoch-making break with an unnecessary tradition that has been tolerated too long proved to be no more than a sentimental interlude. It was an opportunity which, I fear, has now been lost.

With the gramophone, however, one is fortunately able to choose exactly when and where to bring down the final curtain, and my own feeling of satisfaction this independence gives me could be further increased only by the publication by Messrs Ricordi of some form of facsimile of Puccini's manuscript sketches. We know what Alfano made of them; it is high time we were allowed to know what it was Alfano based his completion on. It would be a more fitting tribute to Puccini's memory.

Ending as it does with the death of Liù, Puccini's music inevitably leaves us with a strong and lasting impression of the little slave girl's character, almost indeed at the expense of the others. Liù, of all the characters in his operas, was perhaps Puccini's most personal creation. Unlike Manon and Mimi, Butterfly and Minnie, she had no previous existence in a novel or a play. She is entirely absent from Gozzi's tale, though the idea of a slave who also loves the Prince but loses him to Turandot is certainly found in the original play. But the influence of Gozzi's Adelma (who is a captive princess, and not slave-class at all) on the course of the story is infinitely greater and more dramatic than that of Liù in Puccini's opera. In the opera Liù could be dispensed with altogether without affecting the outcome of the drama in any way; the nearest she comes to playing an active part is in the brief moment in the last act when she impresses Turandot with her declaration that it is love which gives her strength to suffer and resist. It was Puccini's intention originally to make Liù's death affect Turandot so deeply as to soften the Princess's heart, but this idea never materialized. But if, as she stands, she is not essential to the plot, Liù was absolutely essential to Puccini, and since she did not exist she had to be invented—the last and most pathetic of the composer's "Little Girls", who died without knowing any happiness but the treasured memory of the Prince's smile, and whose death was mourned apart from a momentary reaction by the Prince, only by the unhappy old Timur.

Liù is an inspired piece of musical portraiture painted with quite remarkably few strokes of the brush. In terms of simple statistics her entire part consists of no more than 164 bars, and in a great many of those she does not sing more than a single note. But as a musical character, commanding attention and sympathy from the first note she sings to the last, Puccini never surpassed the picture, drawn with such a masterly simplicity and sureness of touch (and perhaps more than a little from life, when we remember the tragedy of Doria), of the tragically devoted Liù.

The brilliant characterization of Turandot, on the other hand, often passes unnoticed largely, one suspects, because it is forgotten that the Princess is an intentionally cold and unsympathetic study. Turandot is unique among the women in Puccini's operas in being hard to get. Butterfly, Tosca, and Sister Angelica have been wooed and won—and in the case of Angelica, ruined as well—before the action begins, while Manon and Mimi are in their lovers' arms by the end of the first act. Even Minnie, with the exception of Turandot the most reluctant of Puccini's heroines, has succumbed to Dick Johnson before the curtain falls on Act II. But Turandot is still unconquered at the point where Puccini died—

unconquered, and her portrait incomplete, for the composer's tragic death deprived us of the most important opportunity for characterization of all: the characterization of the transformed personality of the Princess in love. We cannot begin to guess what this would have meant in terms of music, except that the final duet must inevitably have allowed Turandot to make her first contribution of lyric poetry to Puccini's most poetic score.

The better I come to know *Turandot* the less do I find myself agreeing with the view of some that Calaf is "just another Puccini tenor", and Timur just another "tenor's father". The character of the Prince develops steadily and impressively; he has moments of tenderness which contrast vividly with a fearlessness and obsessive resolution convincingly expressed in musical terms. As for Timur, one cannot allow that he is merely a "tenor's father" or, as Mr George Marek describes him in his book on Puccini, "as big a bore as the aged and infirm always are on the operatic stage".*

Timur is as carefully drawn a character as any of them. He has no more than 84 bars to sing in the whole opera and among them not only the moving appeals to his son in the first act, but the intensely pathetic epilogue to Liù's death. I may have been lucky to hear Ezio Pinza sing the the part in the 1930's but even that uncommon performance was merely a confirmation of what had long been visible in Puccini's score.

I have called *Turandot* Puccini's most poetic score. It is this rare quality of poetry, I believe, that distinguishes *Turandot* from all Puccini's other music and makes it his most stimulating and fascinating work. It is the element of poetry which, although it is spoken with the unmistakable accent of the composer of *La Bohème* and *Madam Butterfly*, raises Puccini's music for the first time on to a plane of nobility. When at the end of his life he entered a legendary world of Emperors and Princesses, Kings and Princes, his music seemed to acquire a genuine dignity which went deeper than the theatrical dignity of the "mood music" suitable for ceremonial stage action. There is something regal in the musical bearing of Turandot, Calaf and Timur which is quite new, and, by providing a contrasting element, emphasizes the humble origin of Liù and intensifies the pathos of her death. This unfamiliar quality of nobility in Puccini's music is one of the most interesting aspects of *Turandot*, for it is a quality which had always been absent from the composer's emotional range, and one which it seemed unlikely would ever enter into it. Its presence in this opera, like so much else in it, is one more subject for endless, frustratingly fruitless speculation on the path Puccini would have taken had he lived a normal span.

"Il mio mistero è chiuso in me. . . ." Few composers have ever taken so enthralling and insoluble a mystery to the grave with them as the composer of *Turandot*.

By the time this study appeared in print a great many words had

---

* Mr Marek is a good factual reporter but I fear an uncertain critic. He goes so far on one occasion as to proclaim that "certain of Schönberg's principles were absorbed by him [Puccini] and can be found in the music of *Turandot*". Alas, Mr Marek offers no chapter and verse in support of this quaint discovery.

been written and broadcast in assessment and re-assessment of Puccini's position in music at the time of his centenary. Few composers whose music has undergone the ordeal by centenary, however, have ever had less need of this type of benefit than Puccini. Where the Beethoven and Mozart bicentenaries inevitably led to the revival of many unfamiliar, but not necessarily unworthy works by these composers which the public repertoire is normally just not big enough to hold, Puccini's centenary brought to light very little that was not already universally familiar and firmly established in the public's affections. Festival performances of *Le Villi*, *Edgar* and *La Rondine* may have come as a new experience for some, but for others even these have not rated as altogether neglected works in recent years. Both *Le Villi* and *La Rondine* have been broadcast and performed on the stage as spontaneous, non-commemorative items since the war.

Puccini's centenary, in fact, came at a time in history when his audience had grown to proportions undreamed of during the composer's unprecedentedly successful lifetime. As I have already suggested, radio, television, films and the long-playing record have brought his music to millions who have never been inside an opera house. But although they are denied the physical experience and excitement of the living theatre, these millions are nevertheless affected by Puccini's sense of drama and consummate theatrical craftsmanship because they are affected by the *music* which alone can bring these elements to life.

In spite of this—or perhaps because of it—no doubt young composers will continue to find Puccini's music "cheap" and "empty"; for some reason it is usually composers, not critics or the public, who still feel like this about Puccini. In a curious way they seem to resent him because he belongs to our own times; his works are still in copyright and make a maddeningly profitable appeal to the ordinary listener. In consequence he is a constant source of subconscious envy whom they regard as a little more than a rather better-class Italian Gershwin whose early death alone prevented him going to Hollywood and settling in his true artistic environment. If we had been celebrating the centenary of Puccini's death instead of his birth doubtless it would have been a different story; at present, Puccini is still too damn' close for some people's comfort.

Puccini is a unique figure in the history of opera. He is not a composer of great operas: he is a great opera composer—a distinction which will be understood by those who love *The Magic Flute* and *Otello*, but have room in their hearts for the gentle appeal of *La Bohème* and *Madam Butterfly*. Puccini does not hold his position, as some would have us believe, by virtue of some freak "gimmick" which appeals to the public; "gimmicks" do not last over seventy years as *Manon Lescaut* and *La Bohème* have lasted. It is a position that has been established and maintained by those uniquely personal gifts of melody and drama and warmth of heart which have formed the subject of this book.

"Contro tutti e contro tutto fare opera di melodia." Puccini once scribbled this admonition on one of his manuscripts and he observed its principle rigidly throughout his career: in face of everybody and everything he made his operas of melody, that highly individual, easily remembered and immediately endearing melody which is the most personal and powerful element of operas which have inspired the respect of the discerning musician, the enthusiasm of the man in the street, and the undying affection of both.

APPENDIX

An "Index of Contexts" by which the reader may refer to the dramatic situation in which the more familiar individual items occur in Puccini's operas.

MANON LESCAUT

	Page
Donna non vidi mai	25
Guardate, pazzo son	45
In quelle trine morbide	32
Intermezzo	40
L'ora, o Tirsi	36
Sola, perduta	47
Tra voi, belle	23
Tu, tu, amore	37

LA BOHÈME

Che gelida manina	60
Donde lieta uscì (Mimi's Farewell)	72
Mimì è civetta	71
O Mimì, tu più non torni	74
O soave fanciulla	62
Quando me'n vo' (Musetta's Waltz Song)	66
Sì, mi chiamano Mimì	60
Sono andati?	77
Vecchia zimarra	77

TOSCA

E lucevan le stelle	105
Mario! Mario! (Love Duet)	90
O dolci mani	106
Recondita armonia	89
Tre sbirri, una carrozza (Finale Act I)	94
Vissi d'arte	100

MADAM BUTTERFLY

Addio fiorito asil   134
Ancora un passo (Entrance of Butterfly)   118
Dovunque al mondo   116
Nello shosi (Humming Chorus)   131
Tu, tu, piccolo Iddio (Death of Butterfly)   137
Un bel dì, vedremo   125
Viene la sera (Love Duet)   122

THE GIRL OF THE GOLDEN WEST

Ch'ella mi creda libero   166
Io non son che una povera fanciulla   153
Laggiù nel Soledad   150
Minnie, dalla mia casa   150
Or son sei mesi   160
Se sapeste come il vivere   158
Una parola sola   160

IL TABARRO

Hai ben ragione   178
Nulla! Silenzio!   182
Perchè non m'ami più?   181

SUOR ANGELICA

Senza mamma   191

GIANNI SCHICCHI

Firenze è come un albero fiorito   201
O mio babbino caro   203

TURANDOT

Gira la cote! (Chorus)   216
In questa reggia   231
Nessun dorma!   239
Non piangere, Liù   223
Perchè tarda la luna? (Invocation to the Moon—Chorus) 217
Signore, ascolta   222
Tanto amore segreto   243
Trio of the Masks   225
Tu che di gel sei cinta (Death of Liù)   243

GENERAL INDEX

Adami, Giuseppe, 174, 183n, 211
Aida, 10, 168
Alexandra, Queen, 139
Alfano, Franco, 245, 247, 248
Après-midi d'un faune, L', 12
Arlecchino (Busoni), 212
Arnolfo, 202

Barber of Seville, The (Paisiello), 111
Barber of Seville, The (Rossini), 111, 146
Bazzini, Antonio, 211
Beethoven, 26, 250
Belasco, David, 111, 113, 139, 140, 148
Bernard, Tristan, 173
Bernhardt, Sarah, 83, 110, 113
Birraio di Preston, Il, 145
Bishop, Sir Henry, 37
Bizet, 10, 12, 21, 68, 97
Boccaccio, 196
Bohème, La (Leoncavallo), see *Vita di Bohème, La*
Bohème, La (Puccini), 9, 11, 12, 13, 19, 29, 43, 47, 49, 51-81, 83, 84, 87, 88, 91, 92, 93n, 104, 107n, 111, 112, 113, 118, 122, 135, 146, 154, 164, 175, 177, 196, 198, 202, 203, 209, 214, 249, 250
Boris Godunov, 212
Brahms, 38
Busoni, Ferruccio, 212

Callas, Maria Meneghini, 236
"Camptown Races", 145
Capriccio sinfonico (Puccini), 55
Carmen, 10, 21, 63, 67, 68, 170
Caruso, Enrico, 62
Catalani, Alfredo, 19
Cavalleria rusticana, 10, 17, 56
Chu Chin Chow, 230
Civinini, Guelfo, 139
Complete Opera Book (Kobbé), 116
Covent Garden, 17, 23, 83, 111, 113, 139, 174, 186, 196, 211, 228, 231
Crisantemi (Puccini), 43, 44, 46, 48, 55

D'Annunzio, Gabriele, 173
Dante, 11, 48, 196, 197, 209
Dearly Beloved (Kern), 122
Debussy, Claude, 12, 143, 178, 238
Delibes, Léo, 118
Disney, Walt, 36
Divina Commedia, La, 11
Don Giovanni, 146
Doria, see Manfredi, Doria
Drei Pintos, Die, 245
Duke of York's Theatre, London, 113
Dumas (fils), Alexandre, 113, 212

East Lynne, 192n
Edgar, 18, 21, 83, 106, 107n, 250
Elisabetta in Derbyshire, 145
Emilia di Liverpool, 145
Entführung aus dem Serail, Die, 170
Entombment, The (Michelangelo), 245

Falstaff, 17, 60, 185, 198
Famous Mozart Operas (Hughes), 9, 12
Fanciulla del West, La (see *Girl of the Golden West, The*)
Fantasia (Disney), 36
Faust (Gounod), 22
Femme et le Pantin, La, 140
Fiorentino, Father Dante Del, 118, 140
First Symphony (Sibelius), 118
Forzano, Giovacchino, 173, 186, 196, 197, 211
Foster, Stephen, 145
Franchetti, Alberto, 83, 110

Gershwin, George, 250
Giacosa, Giuseppe, 19, 51, 80, 83, 84, 111, 140, 211
Gianni Schicchi, 9, 173, 194, 196-210, 211
Giotto, 202
Girl of the Golden West, The, 100, 139-171, 173, 175, 183, 185, 194, 196, 214, 215, 217, 228, 236, 238
Gold, Didier, 173, 174
Gollywog's Cakewalk, 143
Götterdämmerung, 52
Gounod, 22
Gozzi, Carlo, 211, 212, 219, 225, 245, 248
Great Opera Houses (Hughes), 52n, 85n

Henry, O., 80
His Majesty's Theatre, London, 230
Houppelande, La, 173, 174

Illica, Luigi, 19, 51, 80, 83, 84, 111, 140
Immortal Bohemian, The, 118, 140
Inferno (Dante), 196
Iris, 155

Jeritza, Maria, 101

Kern, Jerome, 122
King Lear, 139
Kobbé, Gustave, 116

Lakmé, 118

Lambert, Constant, 228, 231
Leoncavallo, Ruggiero, 10, 18, 51, 52, 56
Liszt, 12
Long, John Luther, 111, 113, 129, 136
Louÿs, Pierre, 140
Lucia di Lammermoor, 170
Lupa, La, 56, 107n

Madam Butterfly (Puccini), 9, 11, 12, 19,
    47, 111-138, 140, 146, 155, 169, 175,
    194, 196, 203, 212, 217, 249, 250
Madame Butterfly (John Luther Long), 113
Magic Baton, The, 112n
Magic Flute, The, 250
Manfredi, Doria, 140, 248
Manon (Massenet), 18
Manon Lescaut, 9, 10, 17-50, 51, 52, 55, 56,
    57, 63, 71, 75, 83, 89, 107n, 113, 122,
    132, 146, 154, 175, 188, 196, 198, 214,
    224, 237, 250
Marek, George, R., 170, 249, 249n
Marie Antoinette, 140
Marinuzzi, Gino, 231
Mascagni, Pietro, 10, 26, 81, 155
Massenet, Jules, 18, 25
Medici family, 202
Meistersinger von Nürnberg, Die, 146n, 228
Metropolitan Opera House, New York,
    139, 140, 145, 173, 174, 186, 196, 211
Michelangelo, 245
Midsummer Night's Dream, A, 219
Monaco, Mario Del, 236
Mozart, 9, 12, 33, 37, 120, 135, 146, 245,
    250
Mugnone, Leopoldo, 84
Murger, Henri, 51, 52, 53, 79, 80, 81

Nabucco, 10
National Gallery, London, 245
Norton, Frederick, 230

Oberto, Conte di Bonifacio, 11
"Old Dog Tray, The", 146
Otello, 139, 250

Pagliacci, I, 10, 17
Paisiello, Giovanni, 111
Pearl Fishers, The, 170
Petrouchka, 176
Piave, Francesco Maria, 113
Pinza, Ezio, 249
Prévost, Abbé, 18, 25, 46, 49
Puccini, Elvira (wife), 140
Puccini, Iginia (sister), 186

Ravel, Maurice, 163
Reinhardt, Max, 245
Requiem Mass (Puccini), 88n, 187
Ricordi, Giulio, 18, 19, 80, 83, 106
Rigoletto, 117

Rimsky-Korsakov, 12
Ronde, La, 173
Rondine, La, 173, 250
Rossini, 111, 146

Sacchi, Filippo, 112n
Sacre du Printemps, Le, 36
Sadler's Wells Theatre, London, 173
Sardou, Victorien, 83, 102, 103, 110
Scala, La, Milan, 111, 112, 118, 123, 132,
    211, 245
Scala Museum, La, 88n, 187
Scènes de la vie de Bohème, 51, 52, 79
Schanne, Alexandre, 79, 80
Schönberg, Arnold, 249n
Schubert, 245, 250
Shakespeare, 81, 139
Shaw, Bernard, 23
Sheridan, Margaret, 126
Sibelius, 118
Siegfried, 194
Simoni, Renato, 211
Sole e amore, 72n
Specht, Richard, 114n
Storchio, Rosina, 112, 112n
Story of Manon Lescaut and of the Chevalier
    des Grieux, The (Prévost), 18, 40
Strauss, Richard, 132, 235
Stravinsky, Igor, 36, 176
Suor Angelica, 10, 173, 174, 186-195, 196,
    209, 210, 211

Tabar, 79
Tabarro, Il, 9, 43, 100, 163, 173, 174-185,
    194, 196, 197n, 205, 209, 210, 211, 238
Teatro Costanzi, Rome, 83
Teatro dell'Opera, Rome, 85n
Teatro Grande, Brescia, 111, 112
Teatro Politeama, Viareggio, 159n
Teatro Regio, Turin, 17, 51
Theatre Royal, Manchester, 51
Third Symphony (Brahms), 38
Tosca (Puccini), 9, 11, 19, 38, 75, 83-110,
    113, 140, 146, 162, 169, 175, 187, 196,
    203, 204, 214, 216, 218n, 237, 242
Tosca, La (Sardou), 83, 110
Toscanini, Arturo, 51, 52, 71n, 75, 112n,
    114n, 139, 211, 212, 245, 247
Traviata, La, 78, 104, 111, 113, 212
Trilby, 11
Trionfo d'amore, Il, 211
Tristan und Isolde, 37, 213
Trittico, Il, 171, 173-210, 211
Turanda (Antonio Bazzini), 211
Turandot (Busoni), 212
Turandot (Gozzi), 212, 219
Turandot (Puccini), 9, 10, 11, 30, 42, 47,
    98, 107, 114, 137, 138, 140, 144, 146,
    154, 165, 166, 167, 170, 171, 174, 185,
    211-251

Unfinished Symphony (Schubert), 245

Verdi, 9, 10, 11, 12, 17, 26, 30, 60, 81, 83,
    84, 88n, 89, 104, 113, 132, 139, 162,
    185, 195, 212, 217, 223, 233
Verga, Giovanni, 56
Verona Arena, 247
Vienna Opera, 101
Villi, Le, 10, 11, 17, 18, 21, 39, 173, 192,
    250
Vita di Bohème, La (Leoncavallo), 51, 52
Voltaire, 93n

Wally, La, 19
Wagner, 12, 18, 37, 52, 194, 213
Weber, 245
Williams, Stephen, 52
Wodehouse, P. G., 80

Zaïde, 245
Zangarini, Carlo, 139

INDEX OF PUCCINI'S ORCHESTRATION

Alto saxophone, 217, 231, 236

Bass clarinet, 25, 28, 42, 43, 45, 47, 74, 87, 94, 101, 123, 124, 125, 128, 129, 135, 143, 149, 157, 161, 166, 176, 200, 215, 219, 230, 235, 241, 245

Bass drum, 103, 137, 161, 167, 168, 230, 233, 234

Bass xylophone, 230

Bassoon, 33, 34, 39, 44, 45, 47, 92, 103, 115, 120n, 127, 128, 129, 135, 143, 144, 149, 157, 161, 162, 164, 166, 200, 207, 215, 230, 233, 242

Bells, 95, 143, 159, 187, 193, 194, 206, 244

Brass, 143, 162, 229

Celeste, 92, 107, 148, 154, 168, 193, 216, 217, 220, 221, 227, 232, 232n, 237, 238, 244, 245

Chinese gong, 214, 217, 230

Clarinet, 32, 33, 39, 43, 44, 47, 48, 59, 62, 101, 103, 105, 124, 125, 128, 135, 151, 154, 161, 166, 176, 181, 202, 209, 216, 217, 227

Cor anglais, 28, 34, 35, 39, 47, 103, 127, 137, 143, 149, 161, 200, 207, 216

Cornet, 23, 182

Cymbals, 187, 193

Double bass, 26, 45, 92, 94, 101, 103, 123, 125, 131, 136, 137, 150, 163, 164, 166, 175, 184, 200, 204, 214, 215, 216, 218, 230, 233, 234, 242, 245

Double bassoon, 150, 161, 230, 233

Flute, 25, 28, 31, 32, 33, 39, 41, 43, 47, 48, 62, 69, 70, 76, 78, 88, 90, 92, 96, 97, 101, 103, 117, 123, 124, 125, 129, 130, 131, 133, 144, 151, 152, 154, 157, 166, 175, 176, 181, 190, 214, 216, 217, 221, 227, 231, 235, 245

Fonica, 143, 155

Glockenspiel, 57, 120, 148, 193, 217, 220, 238

Gong, 12, 103, 121, 137, 221, 230

Harp, 26, 39, 43, 62, 69, 70, 73, 74, 76, 78, 88, 92, 96, 103, 107, 120n, 122, 123, 124, 125, 128, 129, 131, 137, 143, 145, 146, 154, 157, 162, 192, 193, 204, 217, 221, 223, 227, 228, 231n

Horn, 26, 42, 66, 67, 103, 104, 107, 121, 124, 125, 128, 130, 131, 144, 154, 161, 162, 164, 166, 167, 179, 192, 200, 205, 216, 239, 242

Japanese bells, 155

Oboe, 33, 34, 35, 41, 47, 48, 73, 92, 94, 103, 125, 129, 133, 149, 152, 153, 162,
178, 179, 207, 216, 221, 242, 244, 245

Organ, 95, 187, 193, 237

Percussion (see under separate instruments)

Piano, 187, 193, 194, 195

Piccolo, 32, 34, 41, 47, 57, 62, 67, 70, 76, 94, 101, 122, 123, 133, 148, 153, 187, 191, 193, 214, 216, 218, 219, 222, 232, 235, 238, 245

Side drum, 87, 100, 103, 109, 167, 204, 205, 208, 215, 221, 229, 236

Strings, 24, 25, 26, 27, 33, 34, 35, 36, 41, 43, 47, 48, 58, 59, 60, 62, 70, 73, 76, 88, 92, 118, 121, 122, 129, 131, 133, 144, 149, 150, 151, 154, 155, 161, 162, 163, 166, 168, 178, 179, 182, 183, 188, 189, 190, 207, 218, 222, 227, 230, 231, 235, 239

Timpani, 39, 92, 136, 137, 157, 161, 163, 167, 221, 230, 233, 234, 242

Triangle, 69, 70, 107, 193, 220, 230

Trombone, 95, 135, 137, 161, 166, 167, 214, 215, 216, 218, 221, 227, 229, 230, 236, 241

Trumpet, 39, 41, 56, 57, 63, 64, 67, 95, 121, 125, 137, 153, 157, 161, 167, 168, 178, 187, 189, 193, 201, 207, 214, 215, 216, 218, 223, 227, 229, 230, 232, 236, 241, 246

Tubular bells (see Bells)

Viola, 25, 26, 39, 40, 41, 42, 43, 60, 96, 101, 102, 103, 106, 118, 123, 124, 128, 130, 137, 146, 153, 154, 155, 157, 162, 166, 177, 181, 189, 190, 214, 215, 216, 218, 221, 234, 235, 236, 241

Viola d'amore, 131

Violin, 25, 26, 41, 58, 59, 73, 74, 78, 101, 102, 107, 118, 121, 122, 123, 124, 125, 128, 130, 131, 133, 146, 150, 153, 154, 155, 157, 158, 166, 167, 175, 177, 190, 192, 202, 214, 216, 221, 231, 235, 236, 238, 239, 241, 242, 243, 244, 245

Violoncello, 25, 26, 28, 39, 40, 41, 43, 45, 60, 70, 73, 74, 90, 94, 101, 103, 105, 106, 110, 118, 135, 136, 137, 146, 153, 155, 157, 163, 175, 177, 178, 181, 184, 200, 204, 215, 216, 219, 221, 230, 233, 234, 235, 236, 241, 242

Wood-wind, 26, 32, 33, 34, 35, 47, 58, 66, 74, 87, 101, 107, 120, 121, 125, 133, 143, 149, 150, 163, 167, 181, 188, 200, 201, 206, 215, 217

Xylophone, 214, 220, 221, 236

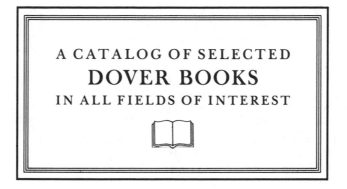

A CATALOG OF SELECTED
DOVER BOOKS
IN ALL FIELDS OF INTEREST

A CATALOG OF SELECTED DOVER BOOKS IN ALL FIELDS OF INTEREST

DRAWINGS OF REMBRANDT, edited by Seymour Slive. Updated Lippmann, Hofstede de Groot edition, with definitive scholarly apparatus. All portraits, biblical sketches, landscapes, nudes. Oriental figures, classical studies, together with selection of work by followers. 550 illustrations. Total of 630pp. 9⅛ × 12¼.
21485-0, 21486-9 Pa., Two-vol. set $29.90

GHOST AND HORROR STORIES OF AMBROSE BIERCE, Ambrose Bierce. 24 tales vividly imagined, strangely prophetic, and decades ahead of their time in technical skill: "The Damned Thing," "An Inhabitant of Carcosa," "The Eyes of the Panther," "Moxon's Master," and 20 more. 199pp. 5⅜ × 8½. 20767-6 Pa. $3.95

ETHICAL WRITINGS OF MAIMONIDES, Maimonides. Most significant ethical works of great medieval sage, newly translated for utmost precision, readability. Laws Concerning Character Traits, Eight Chapters, more. 192pp. 5⅜ × 8½.
24522-5 Pa. $4.50

THE EXPLORATION OF THE COLORADO RIVER AND ITS CANYONS, J. W. Powell. Full text of Powell's 1,000-mile expedition down the fabled Colorado in 1869. Superb account of terrain, geology, vegetation, Indians, famine, mutiny, treacherous rapids, mighty canyons, during exploration of last unknown part of continental U.S. 400pp. 5⅜ × 8½. 20094-9 Pa. $7.95

HISTORY OF PHILOSOPHY, Julián Marías. Clearest one-volume history on the market. Every major philosopher and dozens of others, to Existentialism and later. 505pp. 5⅜ × 8½. 21739-6 Pa. $9.95

ALL ABOUT LIGHTNING, Martin A. Uman. Highly readable non-technical survey of nature and causes of lightning, thunderstorms, ball lightning, St. Elmo's Fire, much more. Illustrated. 192pp. 5⅜ × 8½. 25237-X Pa. $5.95

SAILING ALONE AROUND THE WORLD, Captain Joshua Slocum. First man to sail around the world, alone, in small boat. One of great feats of seamanship told in delightful manner. 67 illustrations. 294pp. 5⅜ × 8½. 20326-3 Pa. $4.95

LETTERS AND NOTES ON THE MANNERS, CUSTOMS AND CONDITIONS OF THE NORTH AMERICAN INDIANS, George Catlin. Classic account of life among Plains Indians: ceremonies, hunt, warfare, etc. 312 plates. 572pp. of text. 6⅛ × 9¼. 22118-0, 22119-9, Pa. Two-vol. set $17.90

ALASKA: The Harriman Expedition, 1899, John Burroughs, John Muir, et al. Informative, engrossing accounts of two-month, 9,000-mile expedition. Native peoples, wildlife, forests, geography, salmon industry, glaciers, more. Profusely illustrated. 240 black-and-white line drawings. 124 black-and-white photographs. 3 maps. Index. 576pp. 5⅜ × 8½. 25109-8 Pa. $11.95

THE BOOK OF BEASTS: Being a Translation from a Latin Bestiary of the Twelfth Century, T. H. White. Wonderful catalog real and fanciful beasts: manticore, griffin, phoenix, amphivius, jaculus, many more. White's witty erudite commentary on scientific, historical aspects. Fascinating glimpse of medieval mind. Illustrated. 296pp. 5⅜ × 8¼. (Available in U.S. only)   24609-4 Pa. $6.95

FRANK LLOYD WRIGHT: ARCHITECTURE AND NATURE With 160 Illustrations, Donald Hoffmann. Profusely illustrated study of influence of nature—especially prairie—on Wright's designs for Fallingwater, Robie House, Guggenheim Museum, other masterpieces. 96pp. 9¼ × 10¾.   25098-9 Pa. $7.95

FRANK LLOYD WRIGHT'S FALLINGWATER, Donald Hoffmann. Wright's famous waterfall house: planning and construction of organic idea. History of site, owners, Wright's personal involvement. Photographs of various stages of building. Preface by Edgar Kaufmann, Jr. 100 illustrations. 112pp. 9¼ × 10.
23671-4 Pa. $8.95

YEARS WITH FRANK LLOYD WRIGHT: Apprentice to Genius, Edgar Tafel. Insightful memoir by a former apprentice presents a revealing portrait of Wright the man, the inspired teacher, the greatest American architect. 372 black-and-white illustrations. Preface. Index. vi + 228pp. 8¼ × 11.   24801-1 Pa. $10.95

THE STORY OF KING ARTHUR AND HIS KNIGHTS, Howard Pyle. Enchanting version of King Arthur fable has delighted generations with imaginative narratives of exciting adventures and unforgettable illustrations by the author. 41 illustrations. xviii + 313pp. 6⅛ × 9¼.   21445-1 Pa. $6.95

THE GODS OF THE EGYPTIANS, E. A. Wallis Budge. Thorough coverage of numerous gods of ancient Egypt by foremost Egyptologist. Information on evolution of cults, rites and gods; the cult of Osiris; the Book of the Dead and its rites; the sacred animals and birds; Heaven and Hell; and more. 956pp. 6⅛ × 9¼.
22055-9, 22056-7 Pa., Two-vol. set $21.90

A THEOLOGICO-POLITICAL TREATISE, Benedict Spinoza. Also contains unfinished *Political Treatise*. Great classic on religious liberty, theory of government on common consent. R. Elwes translation. Total of 421pp. 5⅜ × 8½.
20249-6 Pa. $6.95

INCIDENTS OF TRAVEL IN CENTRAL AMERICA, CHIAPAS, AND YUCATAN, John L. Stephens. Almost single-handed discovery of Maya culture; exploration of ruined cities, monuments, temples; customs of Indians. 115 drawings. 892pp. 5⅜ × 8½.   22404-X, 22405-8 Pa., Two-vol. set $15.90

LOS CAPRICHOS, Francisco Goya. 80 plates of wild, grotesque monsters and caricatures. Prado manuscript included. 183pp. 6⅞ × 9⅞.   22384-1 Pa. $5.95

AUTOBIOGRAPHY: The Story of My Experiments with Truth, Mohandas K. Gandhi. Not hagiography, but Gandhi in his own words. Boyhood, legal studies, purification, the growth of the Satyagraha (nonviolent protest) movement. Critical, inspiring work of the man who freed India. 480pp. 5⅜ × 8½. (Available in U.S. only)
24593-4 Pa. $6.95

ILLUSTRATED DICTIONARY OF HISTORIC ARCHITECTURE, edited by Cyril M. Harris. Extraordinary compendium of clear, concise definitions for over 5,000 important architectural terms complemented by over 2,000 line drawings. Covers full spectrum of architecture from ancient ruins to 20th-century Modernism. Preface. 592pp. 7½ × 9⅝. 24444-X Pa. $15.95

THE NIGHT BEFORE CHRISTMAS, Clement Moore. Full text, and woodcuts from original 1848 book. Also critical, historical material. 19 illustrations. 40pp. 4⅝ × 6. 22797-9 Pa. $2.50

THE LESSON OF JAPANESE ARCHITECTURE: 165 Photographs, Jiro Harada. Memorable gallery of 165 photographs taken in the 1930's of exquisite Japanese homes of the well-to-do and historic buildings. 13 line diagrams. 192pp. 8⅜ × 11¼. 24778-3 Pa. $10.95

THE AUTOBIOGRAPHY OF CHARLES DARWIN AND SELECTED LETTERS, edited by Francis Darwin. The fascinating life of eccentric genius composed of an intimate memoir by Darwin (intended for his children); commentary by his son, Francis; hundreds of fragments from notebooks, journals, papers; and letters to and from Lyell, Hooker, Huxley, Wallace and Henslow. xi + 365pp. 5⅜ × 8. 20479-0 Pa. $6.95

WONDERS OF THE SKY: Observing Rainbows, Comets, Eclipses, the Stars and Other Phenomena, Fred Schaaf. Charming, easy-to-read poetic guide to all manner of celestial events visible to the naked eye. Mock suns, glories, Belt of Venus, more. Illustrated. 299pp. 5¼ × 8¼. 24402-4 Pa. $7.95

BURNHAM'S CELESTIAL HANDBOOK, Robert Burnham, Jr. Thorough guide to the stars beyond our solar system. Exhaustive treatment. Alphabetical by constellation: Andromeda to Cetus in Vol. 1; Chamaeleon to Orion in Vol. 2; and Pavo to Vulpecula in Vol. 3. Hundreds of illustrations. Index in Vol. 3. 2,000pp. 6⅛ × 9¼. 23567-X, 23568-8, 23673-0 Pa., Three-vol. set $38.85

STAR NAMES: Their Lore and Meaning, Richard Hinckley Allen. Fascinating history of names various cultures have given to constellations and literary and folkloristic uses that have been made of stars. Indexes to subjects. Arabic and Greek names. Biblical references. Bibliography. 563pp. 5⅜ × 8½. 21079-0 Pa. $8.95

THIRTY YEARS THAT SHOOK PHYSICS: The Story of Quantum Theory, George Gamow. Lucid, accessible introduction to influential theory of energy and matter. Careful explanations of Dirac's anti-particles, Bohr's model of the atom, much more. 12 plates. Numerous drawings. 240pp. 5⅜ × 8½. 24895-X Pa. $5.95

CHINESE DOMESTIC FURNITURE IN PHOTOGRAPHS AND MEASURED DRAWINGS, Gustav Ecke. A rare volume, now affordably priced for antique collectors, furniture buffs and art historians. Detailed review of styles ranging from early Shang to late Ming. Unabridged republication. 161 black-and-white drawings, photos. Total of 224pp. 8⅜ × 11¼. (Available in U.S. only) 25171-3 Pa. $13.95

VINCENT VAN GOGH: A Biography, Julius Meier-Graefe. Dynamic, penetrating study of artist's life, relationship with brother, Theo, painting techniques, travels, more. Readable, engrossing. 160pp. 5⅜ × 8½. (Available in U.S. only) 25253-1 Pa. $4.95

HOW TO WRITE, Gertrude Stein. Gertrude Stein claimed anyone could understand her unconventional writing—here are clues to help. Fascinating improvisations, language experiments, explanations illuminate Stein's craft and the art of writing. Total of 414pp. 4⅜ × 6⅜. 23144-5 Pa. $6.95

ADVENTURES AT SEA IN THE GREAT AGE OF SAIL: Five Firsthand Narratives, edited by Elliot Snow. Rare true accounts of exploration, whaling, shipwreck, fierce natives, trade, shipboard life, more. 33 illustrations. Introduction. 353pp. 5⅜ × 8½. 25177-2 Pa. $8.95

THE HERBAL OR GENERAL HISTORY OF PLANTS, John Gerard. Classic descriptions of about 2,850 plants—with over 2,700 illustrations—includes Latin and English names, physical descriptions, varieties, time and place of growth, more. 2,706 illustrations. xlv + 1,678pp. 8½ × 12¼. 23147-X Cloth. $75.00

DOROTHY AND THE WIZARD IN OZ, L. Frank Baum. Dorothy and the Wizard visit the center of the Earth, where people are vegetables, glass houses grow and Oz characters reappear. Classic sequel to *Wizard of Oz*. 256pp. 5⅜ × 8. 24714-7 Pa. $4.95

SONGS OF EXPERIENCE: Facsimile Reproduction with 26 Plates in Full Color, William Blake. This facsimile of Blake's original "Illuminated Book" reproduces 26 full-color plates from a rare 1826 edition. Includes "The Tyger," "London," "Holy Thursday," and other immortal poems. 26 color plates. Printed text of poems. 48pp. 5¼ × 7. 24636-1 Pa. $3.50

SONGS OF INNOCENCE, William Blake. The first and most popular of Blake's famous "Illuminated Books," in a facsimile edition reproducing all 31 brightly colored plates. Additional printed text of each poem. 64pp. 5¼ × 7. 22764-2 Pa. $3.50

PRECIOUS STONES, Max Bauer. Classic, thorough study of diamonds, rubies, emeralds, garnets, etc.: physical character, occurrence, properties, use, similar topics. 20 plates, 8 in color. 94 figures. 659pp. 6⅛ × 9¼. 21910-0, 21911-9 Pa., Two-vol. set $15.90

ENCYCLOPEDIA OF VICTORIAN NEEDLEWORK, S. F. A. Caulfeild and Blanche Saward. Full, precise descriptions of stitches, techniques for dozens of needlecrafts—most exhaustive reference of its kind. Over 800 figures. Total of 679pp. 8⅛ × 11. Two volumes. Vol. 1 22800-2 Pa. $11.95
Vol. 2 22801-0 Pa. $11.95

THE MARVELOUS LAND OF OZ, L. Frank Baum. Second Oz book, the Scarecrow and Tin Woodman are back with hero named Tip, Oz magic. 136 illustrations. 287pp. 5⅜ × 8½. 20692-0 Pa. $5.95

WILD FOWL DECOYS, Joel Barber. Basic book on the subject, by foremost authority and collector. Reveals history of decoy making and rigging, place in American culture, different kinds of decoys, how to make them, and how to use them. 140 plates. 156pp. 7⅞ × 10¾. 20011-6 Pa. $8.95

HISTORY OF LACE, Mrs. Bury Palliser. Definitive, profusely illustrated chronicle of lace from earliest times to late 19th century. Laces of Italy, Greece, England, France, Belgium, etc. Landmark of needlework scholarship. 266 illustrations. 672pp. 6⅛ × 9¼. 24742-2 Pa. $14.95

ILLUSTRATED GUIDE TO SHAKER FURNITURE, Robert Meader. All furniture and appurtenances, with much on unknown local styles. 235 photos. 146pp. 9 × 12. 22819-3 Pa. $8.95

WHALE SHIPS AND WHALING: A Pictorial Survey, George Francis Dow. Over 200 vintage engravings, drawings, photographs of barks, brigs, cutters, other vessels. Also harpoons, lances, whaling guns, many other artifacts. Comprehensive text by foremost authority. 207 black-and-white illustrations. 288pp. 6 × 9. 24808-9 Pa. $8.95

THE BERTRAMS, Anthony Trollope. Powerful portrayal of blind self-will and thwarted ambition includes one of Trollope's most heartrending love stories. 497pp. 5⅜ × 8½. 25119-5 Pa. $9.95

ADVENTURES WITH A HAND LENS, Richard Headstrom. Clearly written guide to observing and studying flowers and grasses, fish scales, moth and insect wings, egg cases, buds, feathers, seeds, leaf scars, moss, molds, ferns, common crystals, etc.—all with an ordinary, inexpensive magnifying glass. 209 exact line drawings aid in your discoveries. 220pp. 5⅜ × 8½. 23330-8 Pa. $4.95

RODIN ON ART AND ARTISTS, Auguste Rodin. Great sculptor's candid, wide-ranging comments on meaning of art; great artists; relation of sculpture to poetry, painting, music; philosophy of life, more. 76 superb black-and-white illustrations of Rodin's sculpture, drawings and prints. 119pp. 8⅜ × 11¼. 24487-3 Pa. $7.95

FIFTY CLASSIC FRENCH FILMS, 1912–1982: A Pictorial Record, Anthony Slide. Memorable stills from Grand Illusion, Beauty and the Beast, Hiroshima, Mon Amour, many more. Credits, plot synopses, reviews, etc. 160pp. 8¼ × 11. 25256-6 Pa. $11.95

THE PRINCIPLES OF PSYCHOLOGY, William James. Famous long course complete, unabridged. Stream of thought, time perception, memory, experimental methods; great work decades ahead of its time. 94 figures. 1,391pp. 5⅜ × 8½. 20381-6, 20382-4 Pa., Two-vol. set $23.90

BODIES IN A BOOKSHOP, R. T. Campbell. Challenging mystery of blackmail and murder with ingenious plot and superbly drawn characters. In the best tradition of British suspense fiction. 192pp. 5⅜ × 8½. 24720-1 Pa. $3.95

CALLAS: PORTRAIT OF A PRIMA DONNA, George Jellinek. Renowned commentator on the musical scene chronicles incredible career and life of the most controversial, fascinating, influential operatic personality of our time. 64 black-and-white photographs. 416pp. 5⅜ × 8¼. 25047-4 Pa. $8.95

GEOMETRY, RELATIVITY AND THE FOURTH DIMENSION, Rudolph Rucker. Exposition of fourth dimension, concepts of relativity as Flatland characters continue adventures. Popular, easily followed yet accurate, profound. 141 illustrations. 133pp. 5⅜ × 8½. 23400-2 Pa. $3.95

HOUSEHOLD STORIES BY THE BROTHERS GRIMM, with pictures by Walter Crane. 53 classic stories—Rumpelstiltskin, Rapunzel, Hansel and Gretel, the Fisherman and his Wife, Snow White, Tom Thumb, Sleeping Beauty, Cinderella, and so much more—lavishly illustrated with original 19th century drawings. 114 illustrations. x + 269pp. 5⅜ × 8½. 21080-4 Pa. $4.95

SUNDIALS, Albert Waugh. Far and away the best, most thorough coverage of ideas, mathematics concerned, types, construction, adjusting anywhere. Over 100 illustrations. 230pp. 5⅜ × 8½. 22947-5 Pa. $4.95

PICTURE HISTORY OF THE NORMANDIE: With 190 Illustrations, Frank O. Braynard. Full story of legendary French ocean liner: Art Deco interiors, design innovations, furnishings, celebrities, maiden voyage, tragic fire, much more. Extensive text. 144pp. 8⅞ × 11¾. 25257-4 Pa. $10.95

THE FIRST AMERICAN COOKBOOK: A Facsimile of "American Cookery," 1796, Amelia Simmons. Facsimile of the first American-written cookbook published in the United States contains authentic recipes for colonial favorites—pumpkin pudding, winter squash pudding, spruce beer, Indian slapjacks, and more. Introductory Essay and Glossary of colonial cooking terms. 80pp. 5⅜ × 8½. 24710-4 Pa. $3.50

101 PUZZLES IN THOUGHT AND LOGIC, C. R. Wylie, Jr. Solve murders and robberies, find out which fishermen are liars, how a blind man could possibly identify a color—purely by your own reasoning! 107pp. 5⅜ × 8½. 20367-0 Pa. $2.50

THE BOOK OF WORLD-FAMOUS MUSIC—CLASSICAL, POPULAR AND FOLK, James J. Fuld. Revised and enlarged republication of landmark work in musico-bibliography. Full information about nearly 1,000 songs and compositions including first lines of music and lyrics. New supplement. Index. 800pp. 5⅜ × 8¼. 24857-7 Pa. $15.95

ANTHROPOLOGY AND MODERN LIFE, Franz Boas. Great anthropologist's classic treatise on race and culture. Introduction by Ruth Bunzel. Only inexpensive paperback edition. 255pp. 5⅜ × 8½. 25245-0 Pa. $6.95

THE TALE OF PETER RABBIT, Beatrix Potter. The inimitable Peter's terrifying adventure in Mr. McGregor's garden, with all 27 wonderful, full-color Potter illustrations. 55pp. 4¼ × 5½. (Available in U.S. only) 22827-4 Pa. $1.75

THREE PROPHETIC SCIENCE FICTION NOVELS, H. G. Wells. *When the Sleeper Wakes, A Story of the Days to Come* and *The Time Machine* (full version). 335pp. 5⅜ × 8½. (Available in U.S. only) 20605-X Pa. $6.95

APICIUS COOKERY AND DINING IN IMPERIAL ROME, edited and translated by Joseph Dommers Vehling. Oldest known cookbook in existence offers readers a clear picture of what foods Romans ate, how they prepared them, etc. 49 illustrations. 301pp. 6⅛ × 9¼. 23563-7 Pa. $7.95

SHAKESPEARE LEXICON AND QUOTATION DICTIONARY, Alexander Schmidt. Full definitions, locations, shades of meaning of every word in plays and poems. More than 50,000 exact quotations. 1,485pp. 6½ × 9¼. 22726-X, 22727-8 Pa., Two-vol. set $29.90

THE WORLD'S GREAT SPEECHES, edited by Lewis Copeland and Lawrence W. Lamm. Vast collection of 278 speeches from Greeks to 1970. Powerful and effective models; unique look at history. 842pp. 5⅜ × 8½. 20468-5 Pa. $11.95

THE BLUE FAIRY BOOK, Andrew Lang. The first, most famous collection, with many familiar tales: Little Red Riding Hood, Aladdin and the Wonderful Lamp, Puss in Boots, Sleeping Beauty, Hansel and Gretel, Rumpelstiltskin; 37 in all. 138 illustrations. 390pp. 5⅜ × 8½. 21437-0 Pa. $6.95

THE STORY OF THE CHAMPIONS OF THE ROUND TABLE, Howard Pyle. Sir Launcelot, Sir Tristram and Sir Percival in spirited adventures of love and triumph retold in Pyle's inimitable style. 50 drawings, 31 full-page. xviii + 329pp. 6½ × 9¼. 21883-X Pa. $7.95

AUDUBON AND HIS JOURNALS, Maria Audubon. Unmatched two-volume portrait of the great artist, naturalist and author contains his journals, an excellent biography by his granddaughter, expert annotations by the noted ornithologist, Dr. Elliott Coues, and 37 superb illustrations. Total of 1,200pp. 5⅜ × 8.
Vol. I 25143-8 Pa. $8.95
Vol. II 25144-6 Pa. $8.95

GREAT DINOSAUR HUNTERS AND THEIR DISCOVERIES, Edwin H. Colbert. Fascinating, lavishly illustrated chronicle of dinosaur research, 1820's to 1960. Achievements of Cope, Marsh, Brown, Buckland, Mantell, Huxley, many others. 384pp. 5¼ × 8¼. 24701-5 Pa. $7.95

THE TASTEMAKERS, Russell Lynes. Informal, illustrated social history of American taste 1850's–1950's. First popularized categories Highbrow, Lowbrow, Middlebrow. 129 illustrations. New (1979) afterword. 384pp. 6 × 9.
23993-4 Pa. $8.95

DOUBLE CROSS PURPOSES, Ronald A. Knox. A treasure hunt in the Scottish Highlands, an old map, unidentified corpse, surprise discoveries keep reader guessing in this cleverly intricate tale of financial skullduggery. 2 black-and-white maps. 320pp. 5⅜ × 8½. (Available in U.S. only) 25032-6 Pa. $6.95

AUTHENTIC VICTORIAN DECORATION AND ORNAMENTATION IN FULL COLOR: 46 Plates from "Studies in Design," Christopher Dresser. Superb full-color lithographs reproduced from rare original portfolio of a major Victorian designer. 48pp. 9¼ × 12¼. 25083-0 Pa. $7.95

PRIMITIVE ART, Franz Boas. Remains the best text ever prepared on subject, thoroughly discussing Indian, African, Asian, Australian, and, especially, Northern American primitive art. Over 950 illustrations show ceramics, masks, totem poles, weapons, textiles, paintings, much more. 376pp. 5⅜ × 8. 20025-6 Pa. $6.95

SIDELIGHTS ON RELATIVITY, Albert Einstein. Unabridged republication of two lectures delivered by the great physicist in 1920–21. *Ether and Relativity* and *Geometry and Experience*. Elegant ideas in non-mathematical form, accessible to intelligent layman. vi + 56pp. 5⅜ × 8½. 24511-X Pa. $2.95

THE WIT AND HUMOR OF OSCAR WILDE, edited by Alvin Redman. More than 1,000 ripostes, paradoxes, wisecracks: Work is the curse of the drinking classes, I can resist everything except temptation, etc. 258pp. 5⅜ × 8½. 20602-5 Pa. $4.95

ADVENTURES WITH A MICROSCOPE, Richard Headstrom. 59 adventures with clothing fibers, protozoa, ferns and lichens, roots and leaves, much more. 142 illustrations. 232pp. 5⅜ × 8½. 23471-1 Pa. $3.95

PLANTS OF THE BIBLE, Harold N. Moldenke and Alma L. Moldenke. Standard reference to all 230 plants mentioned in Scriptures. Latin name, biblical reference, uses, modern identity, much more. Unsurpassed encyclopedic resource for scholars, botanists, nature lovers, students of Bible. Bibliography. Indexes. 123 black-and-white illustrations. 384pp. 6 × 9. 25069-5 Pa. $8.95

FAMOUS AMERICAN WOMEN: A Biographical Dictionary from Colonial Times to the Present, Robert McHenry, ed. From Pocahontas to Rosa Parks, 1,035 distinguished American women documented in separate biographical entries. Accurate, up-to-date data, numerous categories, spans 400 years. Indices. 493pp. 6½ × 9¼. 24523-3 Pa. $10.95

THE FABULOUS INTERIORS OF THE GREAT OCEAN LINERS IN HISTORIC PHOTOGRAPHS, William H. Miller, Jr. Some 200 superb photographs capture exquisite interiors of world's great "floating palaces"—1890's to 1980's: *Titanic, Ile de France, Queen Elizabeth, United States, Europa,* more. Approx. 200 black-and-white photographs. Captions. Text. Introduction. 160pp. 8⅜ × 11¾. 24756-2 Pa. $9.95

THE GREAT LUXURY LINERS, 1927-1954: A Photographic Record, William H. Miller, Jr. Nostalgic tribute to heyday of ocean liners. 186 photos of Ile de France, Normandie, Leviathan, Queen Elizabeth, United States, many others. Interior and exterior views. Introduction. Captions. 160pp. 9 × 12. 24056-8 Pa. $10.95

A NATURAL HISTORY OF THE DUCKS, John Charles Phillips. Great landmark of ornithology offers complete detailed coverage of nearly 200 species and subspecies of ducks: gadwall, sheldrake, merganser, pintail, many more. 74 full-color plates, 102 black-and-white. Bibliography. Total of 1,920pp. 8⅜ × 11¼. 25141-1, 25142-X Cloth. Two-vol. set $100.00

THE SEAWEED HANDBOOK: An Illustrated Guide to Seaweeds from North Carolina to Canada, Thomas F. Lee. Concise reference covers 78 species. Scientific and common names, habitat, distribution, more. Finding keys for easy identification. 224pp. 5⅜ × 8½. 25215-9 Pa. $6.95

THE TEN BOOKS OF ARCHITECTURE: The 1755 Leoni Edition, Leon Battista Alberti. Rare classic helped introduce the glories of ancient architecture to the Renaissance. 68 black-and-white plates. 336pp. 8⅜ × 11¼. 25239-6 Pa. $14.95

MISS MACKENZIE, Anthony Trollope. Minor masterpieces by Victorian master unmasks many truths about life in 19th-century England. First inexpensive edition in years. 392pp. 5⅜ × 8½. 25201-9 Pa. $8.95

THE RIME OF THE ANCIENT MARINER, Gustave Doré, Samuel Taylor Coleridge. Dramatic engravings considered by many to be his greatest work. The terrifying space of the open sea, the storms and whirlpools of an unknown ocean, the ice of Antarctica, more—all rendered in a powerful, chilling manner. Full text. 38 plates. 77pp. 9¼ × 12. 22305-1 Pa. $4.95

THE EXPEDITIONS OF ZEBULON MONTGOMERY PIKE, Zebulon Montgomery Pike. Fascinating first-hand accounts (1805-6) of exploration of Mississippi River, Indian wars, capture by Spanish dragoons, much more. 1,088pp. 5⅜ × 8½. 25254-X, 25255-8 Pa. Two-vol. set $25.90

A CONCISE HISTORY OF PHOTOGRAPHY: Third Revised Edition, Helmut Gernsheim. Best one-volume history—camera obscura, photochemistry, daguerreotypes, evolution of cameras, film, more. Also artistic aspects—landscape, portraits, fine art, etc. 281 black-and-white photographs. 26 in color. 176pp. 8⅜ × 11¼. 25128-4 Pa. $13.95

THE DORÉ BIBLE ILLUSTRATIONS, Gustave Doré. 241 detailed plates from the Bible: the Creation scenes, Adam and Eve, Flood, Babylon, battle sequences, life of Jesus, etc. Each plate is accompanied by the verses from the King James version of the Bible. 241pp. 9 × 12. 23004-X Pa. $9.95

HUGGER-MUGGER IN THE LOUVRE, Elliot Paul. Second Homer Evans mystery-comedy. Theft at the Louvre involves sleuth in hilarious, madcap caper. "A knockout."—Books. 336pp. 5⅜ × 8½. 25185-3 Pa. $5.95

FLATLAND, E. A. Abbott. Intriguing and enormously popular science-fiction classic explores the complexities of trying to survive as a two-dimensional being in a three-dimensional world. Amusingly illustrated by the author. 16 illustrations. 103pp. 5⅜ × 8½. 20001-9 Pa. $2.50

THE HISTORY OF THE LEWIS AND CLARK EXPEDITION, Meriwether Lewis and William Clark, edited by Elliott Coues. Classic edition of Lewis and Clark's day-by-day journals that later became the basis for U.S. claims to Oregon and the West. Accurate and invaluable geographical, botanical, biological, meteorological and anthropological material. Total of 1,508pp. 5⅜ × 8½.
21268-8, 21269-6, 21270-X Pa. Three-vol. set $26.85

LANGUAGE, TRUTH AND LOGIC, Alfred J. Ayer. Famous, clear introduction to Vienna, Cambridge schools of Logical Positivism. Role of philosophy, elimination of metaphysics, nature of analysis, etc. 160pp. 5⅜ × 8½. (Available in U.S. and Canada only) 20010-8 Pa. $3.95

MATHEMATICS FOR THE NONMATHEMATICIAN, Morris Kline. Detailed, college-level treatment of mathematics in cultural and historical context, with numerous exercises. For liberal arts students. Preface. Recommended Reading Lists. Tables. Index. Numerous black-and-white figures. xvi + 641pp. 5⅜ × 8½.
24823-2 Pa. $11.95

HANDBOOK OF PICTORIAL SYMBOLS, Rudolph Modley. 3,250 signs and symbols, many systems in full; official or heavy commercial use. Arranged by subject. Most in Pictorial Archive series. 143pp. 8⅛ × 11. 23357-X Pa. $6.95

INCIDENTS OF TRAVEL IN YUCATAN, John L. Stephens. Classic (1843) exploration of jungles of Yucatan, looking for evidences of Maya civilization. Travel adventures, Mexican and Indian culture, etc. Total of 669pp. 5⅜ × 8½.
20926-1, 20927-X Pa., Two-vol. set $11.90

CATALOG OF DOVER BOOKS

DEGAS: An Intimate Portrait, Ambroise Vollard. Charming, anecdotal memoir by famous art dealer of one of the greatest 19th-century French painters. 14 black-and-white illustrations. Introduction by Harold L. Van Doren. 96pp. 5⅜ × 8½.
25131-4 Pa. $4.95

PERSONAL NARRATIVE OF A PILGRIMAGE TO ALMANDINAH AND MECCAH, Richard Burton. Great travel classic by remarkably colorful personality. Burton, disguised as a Moroccan, visited sacred shrines of Islam, narrowly escaping death. 47 illustrations. 959pp. 5⅜ × 8½. 21217-3, 21218-1 Pa., Two-vol. set $19.90

PHRASE AND WORD ORIGINS, A. H. Holt. Entertaining, reliable, modern study of more than 1,200 colorful words, phrases, origins and histories. Much unexpected information. 254pp. 5⅜ × 8½. 20758-7 Pa. $5.95

THE RED THUMB MARK, R. Austin Freeman. In this first Dr. Thorndyke case, the great scientific detective draws fascinating conclusions from the nature of a single fingerprint. Exciting story, authentic science. 320pp. 5⅜ × 8½. (Available in U.S. only) 25210-8 Pa. $6.95

AN EGYPTIAN HIEROGLYPHIC DICTIONARY, E. A. Wallis Budge. Monumental work containing about 25,000 words or terms that occur in texts ranging from 3000 B.C. to 600 A.D. Each entry consists of a transliteration of the word, the word in hieroglyphs, and the meaning in English. 1,314pp. 6⅜ × 10.
23615-3, 23616-1 Pa., Two-vol. set $31.90

THE COMPLEAT STRATEGYST: Being a Primer on the Theory of Games of Strategy, J. D. Williams. Highly entertaining classic describes, with many illustrated examples, how to select best strategies in conflict situations. Prefaces. Appendices. xvi + 268pp. 5⅜ × 8½. 25101-2 Pa. $5.95

THE ROAD TO OZ, L. Frank Baum. Dorothy meets the Shaggy Man, little Button-Bright and the Rainbow's beautiful daughter in this delightful trip to the magical Land of Oz. 272pp. 5⅜ × 8. 25208-6 Pa. $5.95

POINT AND LINE TO PLANE, Wassily Kandinsky. Seminal exposition of role of point, line, other elements in non-objective painting. Essential to understanding 20th-century art. 127 illustrations. 192pp. 6½ × 9¼. 23808-3 Pa. $4.95

LADY ANNA, Anthony Trollope. Moving chronicle of Countess Lovel's bitter struggle to win for herself and daughter Anna their rightful rank and fortune—perhaps at cost of sanity itself. 384pp. 5⅜ × 8½. 24669-8 Pa. $8.95

EGYPTIAN MAGIC, E. A. Wallis Budge. Sums up all that is known about magic in Ancient Egypt: the role of magic in controlling the gods, powerful amulets that warded off evil spirits, scarabs of immortality, use of wax images, formulas and spells, the secret name, much more. 253pp. 5⅜ × 8½. 22681-6 Pa. $4.50

THE DANCE OF SIVA, Ananda Coomaraswamy. Preeminent authority unfolds the vast metaphysic of India: the revelation of her art, conception of the universe, social organization, etc. 27 reproductions of art masterpieces. 192pp. 5⅜ × 8½.
24817-8 Pa. $5.95

CHRISTMAS CUSTOMS AND TRADITIONS, Clement A. Miles. Origin, evolution, significance of religious, secular practices. Caroling, gifts, yule logs, much more. Full, scholarly yet fascinating; non-sectarian. 400pp. 5⅜ × 8½.
23354-5 Pa. $6.95

THE HUMAN FIGURE IN MOTION, Eadweard Muybridge. More than 4,500 stopped-action photos, in action series, showing undraped men, women, children jumping, lying down, throwing, sitting, wrestling, carrying, etc. 390pp. 7⅞ × 10⅝.
20204-6 Cloth. $21.95

THE MAN WHO WAS THURSDAY, Gilbert Keith Chesterton. Witty, fast-paced novel about a club of anarchists in turn-of-the-century London. Brilliant social, religious, philosophical speculations. 128pp. 5⅜ × 8½.
25121-7 Pa. $3.95

A CEZANNE SKETCHBOOK: Figures, Portraits, Landscapes and Still Lifes, Paul Cezanne. Great artist experiments with tonal effects, light, mass, other qualities in over 100 drawings. A revealing view of developing master painter, precursor of Cubism. 102 black-and-white illustrations. 144pp. 8¾ × 6⅝.
24790-2 Pa. $5.95

AN ENCYCLOPEDIA OF BATTLES: Accounts of Over 1,560 Battles from 1479 B.C. to the Present, David Eggenberger. Presents essential details of every major battle in recorded history, from the first battle of Megiddo in 1479 B.C. to Grenada in 1984. List of Battle Maps. New Appendix covering the years 1967–1984. Index. 99 illustrations. 544pp. 6½ × 9¼.
24913-1 Pa. $14.95

AN ETYMOLOGICAL DICTIONARY OF MODERN ENGLISH, Ernest Weekley. Richest, fullest work, by foremost British lexicographer. Detailed word histories. Inexhaustible. Total of 856pp. 6½ × 9¼.
21873-2, 21874-0 Pa., Two-vol. set $17.00

WEBSTER'S AMERICAN MILITARY BIOGRAPHIES, edited by Robert McHenry. Over 1,000 figures who shaped 3 centuries of American military history. Detailed biographies of Nathan Hale, Douglas MacArthur, Mary Hallaren, others. Chronologies of engagements, more. Introduction. Addenda. 1,033 entries in alphabetical order. xi + 548pp. 6½ × 9¼. (Available in U.S. only)
24758-9 Pa. $13.95

LIFE IN ANCIENT EGYPT, Adolf Erman. Detailed older account, with much not in more recent books: domestic life, religion, magic, medicine, commerce, and whatever else needed for complete picture. Many illustrations. 597pp. 5⅜ × 8½.
22632-8 Pa. $8.95

HISTORIC COSTUME IN PICTURES, Braun & Schneider. Over 1,450 costumed figures shown, covering a wide variety of peoples: kings, emperors, nobles, priests, servants, soldiers, scholars, townsfolk, peasants, merchants, courtiers, cavaliers, and more. 256pp. 8⅜ × 11¼.
23150-X Pa. $9.95

THE NOTEBOOKS OF LEONARDO DA VINCI, edited by J. P. Richter. Extracts from manuscripts reveal great genius; on painting, sculpture, anatomy, sciences, geography, etc. Both Italian and English. 186 ms. pages reproduced, plus 500 additional drawings, including studies for *Last Supper*, *Sforza* monument, etc. 860pp. 7⅞ × 10¾. (Available in U.S. only) 22572-0, 22573-9 Pa., Two-vol. set $31.90

THE ART NOUVEAU STYLE BOOK OF ALPHONSE MUCHA: All 72 Plates from "Documents Decoratifs" in Original Color, Alphonse Mucha. Rare copyright-free design portfolio by high priest of Art Nouveau. Jewelry, wallpaper, stained glass, furniture, figure studies, plant and animal motifs, etc. Only complete one-volume edition. 80pp. 9⅜ × 12¼. 24044-4 Pa. $9.95

ANIMALS: 1,419 COPYRIGHT-FREE ILLUSTRATIONS OF MAMMALS, BIRDS, FISH, INSECTS, ETC., edited by Jim Harter. Clear wood engravings present, in extremely lifelike poses, over 1,000 species of animals. One of the most extensive pictorial sourcebooks of its kind. Captions. Index. 284pp. 9 × 12.
23766-4 Pa. $9.95

OBELISTS FLY HIGH, C. Daly King. Masterpiece of American detective fiction, long out of print, involves murder on a 1935 transcontinental flight—"a very thrilling story"—NY Times. Unabridged and unaltered republication of the edition published by William Collins Sons & Co. Ltd., London, 1935. 288pp. 5⅜ × 8½. (Available in U.S. only) 25036-9 Pa. $5.95

VICTORIAN AND EDWARDIAN FASHION: A Photographic Survey, Alison Gernsheim. First fashion history completely illustrated by contemporary photographs. Full text plus 235 photos, 1840–1914, in which many celebrities appear. 240pp. 6½ × 9¼. 24205-6 Pa. $6.95

THE ART OF THE FRENCH ILLUSTRATED BOOK, 1700–1914, Gordon N. Ray. Over 630 superb book illustrations by Fragonard, Delacroix, Daumier, Doré, Grandville, Manet, Mucha, Steinlen, Toulouse-Lautrec and many others. Preface. Introduction. 633 halftones. Indices of artists, authors & titles, binders and provenances. Appendices. Bibliography. 608pp. 8⅜ × 11¼. 25086-5 Pa. $24.95

THE WONDERFUL WIZARD OF OZ, L. Frank Baum. Facsimile in full color of America's finest children's classic. 143 illustrations by W. W. Denslow. 267pp. 5⅜ × 8½. 20691-2 Pa. $7.95

FRONTIERS OF MODERN PHYSICS: New Perspectives on Cosmology, Relativity, Black Holes and Extraterrestrial Intelligence, Tony Rothman, et al. For the intelligent layman. Subjects include: cosmological models of the universe; black holes; the neutrino; the search for extraterrestrial intelligence. Introduction. 46 black-and-white illustrations. 192pp. 5⅜ × 8½. 24587-X Pa. $7.95

THE FRIENDLY STARS, Martha Evans Martin & Donald Howard Menzel. Classic text marshalls the stars together in an engaging, non-technical survey, presenting them as sources of beauty in night sky. 23 illustrations. Foreword. 2 star charts. Index. 147pp. 5⅜ × 8½. 21099-5 Pa. $3.95

FADS AND FALLACIES IN THE NAME OF SCIENCE, Martin Gardner. Fair, witty appraisal of cranks, quacks, and quackeries of science and pseudoscience: hollow earth, Velikovsky, orgone energy, Dianetics, flying saucers, Bridey Murphy, food and medical fads, etc. Revised, expanded In the Name of Science. "A very able and even-tempered presentation."—The New Yorker. 363pp. 5⅜ × 8.

20394-8 Pa. $6.95

ANCIENT EGYPT: ITS CULTURE AND HISTORY, J. E Manchip White. From pre-dynastics through Ptolemies: society, history, political structure, religion, daily life, literature, cultural heritage. 48 plates. 217pp. 5⅜ × 8½. 22548-8 Pa. $5.95

SIR HARRY HOTSPUR OF HUMBLETHWAITE, Anthony Trollope. Incisive, unconventional psychological study of a conflict between a wealthy baronet, his idealistic daughter, and their scapegrace cousin. The 1870 novel in its first inexpensive edition in years. 250pp. 5⅜ × 8½. 24953-0 Pa. $5.95

LASERS AND HOLOGRAPHY, Winston E. Kock. Sound introduction to burgeoning field, expanded (1981) for second edition. Wave patterns, coherence, lasers, diffraction, zone plates, properties of holograms, recent advances. 84 illustrations. 160pp. 5⅜ × 8¼. (Except in United Kingdom) 24041-X Pa. $3.95

INTRODUCTION TO ARTIFICIAL INTELLIGENCE: SECOND, EN-LARGED EDITION, Philip C. Jackson, Jr. Comprehensive survey of artificial intelligence—the study of how machines (computers) can be made to act intelligently. Includes introductory and advanced material. Extensive notes updating the main text. 132 black-and-white illustrations. 512pp. 5⅜ × 8½. 24864-X Pa. $8.95

HISTORY OF INDIAN AND INDONESIAN ART, Ananda K. Coomaraswamy. Over 400 illustrations illuminate classic study of Indian art from earliest Harappa finds to early 20th century. Provides philosophical, religious and social insights. 304pp. 6⅜ × 9⅜. 25005-9 Pa. $9.95

THE GOLEM, Gustav Meyrink. Most famous supernatural novel in modern European literature, set in Ghetto of Old Prague around 1890. Compelling story of mystical experiences, strange transformations, profound terror. 13 black-and-white illustrations. 224pp. 5⅜ × 8½. (Available in U.S. only) 25025-3 Pa. $6.95

ARMADALE, Wilkie Collins. Third great mystery novel by the author of *The Woman in White* and *The Moonstone*. Original magazine version with 40 illustrations. 597pp. 5⅜ × 8½. 23429-0 Pa. $9.95

PICTORIAL ENCYCLOPEDIA OF HISTORIC ARCHITECTURAL PLANS, DETAILS AND ELEMENTS: With 1,880 Line Drawings of Arches, Domes, Doorways, Facades, Gables, Windows, etc., John Theodore Haneman. Sourcebook of inspiration for architects, designers, others. Bibliography. Captions. 141pp. 9 × 12. 24605-1 Pa. $7.95

BENCHLEY LOST AND FOUND, Robert Benchley. Finest humor from early 30's, about pet peeves, child psychologists, post office and others. Mostly unavailable elsewhere. 73 illustrations by Peter Arno and others. 183pp. 5⅜ × 8½. 22410-4 Pa. $4.95

ERTÉ GRAPHICS, Erté. Collection of striking color graphics: *Seasons, Alphabet, Numerals, Aces* and *Precious Stones*. 50 plates, including 4 on covers. 48pp. 9⅜ × 12¼. 23580-7 Pa. $6.95

THE JOURNAL OF HENRY D. THOREAU, edited by Bradford Torrey, F. H. Allen. Complete reprinting of 14 volumes, 1837–61, over two million words; the sourcebooks for *Walden*, etc. Definitive. All original sketches, plus 75 photographs. 1,804pp. 8½ × 12¼. 20312-3, 20313-1 Cloth., Two-vol. set $120.00

CASTLES: THEIR CONSTRUCTION AND HISTORY, Sidney Toy. Traces castle development from ancient roots. Nearly 200 photographs and drawings illustrate moats, keeps, baileys, many other features. Caernarvon, Dover Castles, Hadrian's Wall, Tower of London, dozens more. 256pp. 5⅜ × 8¼. 24898-4 Pa. $6.95

AMERICAN CLIPPER SHIPS: 1833–1858, Octavius T. Howe & Frederick C. Matthews. Fully-illustrated, encyclopedic review of 352 clipper ships from the period of America's greatest maritime supremacy. Introduction. 109 halftones. 5 black-and-white line illustrations. Index. Total of 928pp. 5⅜ × 8½.
25115-2, 25116-0 Pa., Two-vol. set $17.90

TOWARDS A NEW ARCHITECTURE, Le Corbusier. Pioneering manifesto by great architect, near legendary founder of "International School." Technical and aesthetic theories, views on industry, economics, relation of form to function, "mass-production spirit," much more. Profusely illustrated. Unabridged translation of 13th French edition. Introduction by Frederick Etchells. 320pp. 6⅛ × 9¼. (Available in U.S. only)
25023-7 Pa. $8.95

THE BOOK OF KELLS, edited by Blanche Cirker. Inexpensive collection of 32 full-color, full-page plates from the greatest illuminated manuscript of the Middle Ages, painstakingly reproduced from rare facsimile edition. Publisher's Note. Captions. 32pp. 9⅜ × 12¼.
24345-1 Pa. $4.95

BEST SCIENCE FICTION STORIES OF H. G. WELLS, H. G. Wells. Full novel *The Invisible Man*, plus 17 short stories: "The Crystal Egg," "Aepyornis Island," "The Strange Orchid," etc. 303pp. 5⅜ × 8½. (Available in U.S. only)
21531-8 Pa. $6.95

AMERICAN SAILING SHIPS: Their Plans and History, Charles G. Davis. Photos, construction details of schooners, frigates, clippers, other sailcraft of 18th to early 20th centuries—plus entertaining discourse on design, rigging, nautical lore, much more. 137 black-and-white illustrations. 240pp. 6⅛ × 9¼.
24658-2 Pa. $6.95

ENTERTAINING MATHEMATICAL PUZZLES, Martin Gardner. Selection of author's favorite conundrums involving arithmetic, money, speed, etc., with lively commentary. Complete solutions. 112pp. 5⅜ × 8½.
25211-6 Pa. $2.95

THE WILL TO BELIEVE, HUMAN IMMORTALITY, William James. Two books bound together. Effect of irrational on logical, and arguments for human immortality. 402pp. 5⅜ × 8½.
20291-7 Pa. $7.95

THE HAUNTED MONASTERY and THE CHINESE MAZE MURDERS, Robert Van Gulik. 2 full novels by Van Gulik continue adventures of Judge Dee and his companions. An evil Taoist monastery, seemingly supernatural events; overgrown topiary maze that hides strange crimes. Set in 7th-century China. 27 illustrations. 328pp. 5⅜ × 8½.
23502-5 Pa. $6.95

CELEBRATED CASES OF JUDGE DEE (DEE GOONG AN), translated by Robert Van Gulik. Authentic 18th-century Chinese detective novel; Dee and associates solve three interlocked cases. Led to Van Gulik's own stories with same characters. Extensive introduction. 9 illustrations. 237pp. 5⅜ × 8½.
23337-5 Pa. $4.95

Prices subject to change without notice.

Available at your book dealer or write for free catalog to Dept. GI, Dover Publications, Inc., 31 East 2nd St., Mineola, N.Y. 11501. Dover publishes more than 175 books each year on science, elementary and advanced mathematics, biology, music, art, literary history, social sciences and other areas.